UNIX
Working with Unix and Xenix

PRISMA Computer Courses are structured, practical guides to mastering the most popular computer programs. PRISMA books are course books, giving step-by-step instructions, which take the user through basic skills to advanced functions in easy to follow, manageable stages.

Now available:

Excel 4.0 for Windows
Lotus 1-2-3 2.4
MS-DOS 3.3 to 5.0
UNIX
Windows 3.0 and 3.1
WordPerfect 5.1
WordPerfect for Windows

Hans-Josef Heck

UNIX

Working with Unix and Xenix

PRISMA COMPUTER COURSE

Prisma Computer Courses first published in Great Britain 1992 by

McCarta Ltd
P.O. Box 2996
London N5 2TA London

Translation: George Hall
Production: LINE UP text productions

© Rowohlt Taschenbuch Verlag GmbH, Reinbek bei Hamburg
For the English translation
© 1993 Uitgeverij Het Spectrum B.V. Utrecht

ISBN 1 85365 380 2

British Library Cataloguing-in-Publication Data.
A catalogue record for this book is available from the British Library.

Contents

Foreword

If you want to get the most out of your computer, you need a powerful operating system. In addition, if you do not wish to be tied to one hardware supplier or software company, you need a standard operating system. UNIX is the only system which fulfils both requirements. However, UNIX can also offer much more:

■ UNIX supports more than one user.
■ Each user can run more than one program at the same time and thus work on several tasks in parallel.
■ UNIX is a mature operating system, which means that it will run in a predictable way if you install it correctly.
■ It is a modular system and thus adaptable.
■ Hardware manufacturers, software companies and users have accepted UNIX as a standard, which means that its future is guaranteed.
■ User communication is integrated into the system.
■ Several users are able to make simultaneous use of programs and data under UNIX, without problems arising. PC networks with these capabilities are expensive and certainly not standardized.
■ UNIX has an independent printer spooler which can be programmed.
■ The UNIX user network (USENET/EUnet) provides world-wide mail, news and archives services.
■ The UNIX basic package contains more than 250 utility programs.
■ A sophisticated user interface, the shell, when used as a programming language, makes it possible to write programs which execute programs. In this way, you can combine the many utilities to perform complete tasks.
■ UNIX is developing as the basis for both smaller and larger networks.

The increasing significance of UNIX is indicated by the growing number of publications concerning this operating system. The objective of this book is to fill a void: it is a value-for-money book which illustrates how to handle the operating system by working at the computer itself, at the same time outlining the fundamental concepts of data processing and the structure of this operating system. Because of clear step-by-step instructions, it is also suitable for beginners.

Finally, some explanation of the notation used in this book. New, relevant terminology is printed in **bold** when introduced. Commands, options, parameters and error messages are also printed in **bold** letters. The names of files, directories and programs are printed in *italics*. If you have to combine two keystrokes, they are written with a hyphen, <Ctrl-D>, for example. Other operational keys are written with a capital letter, for example, <Shift> or <Return>.

1 Introduction

1.1 The nature of this book

Depending on what you are used to, you will find UNIX either a clear and simple or a complicated operating sytem. Operating systems consist of programs which are responsible for the organization and the management of computer processes. The operating system also determines the way in which you communicate with the computer. An introduction to an operating system is also an introduction to data processing in general. Accordingly, this book is also suitable for those who are not yet familiar with data processing.

The easiest way to start is in an environment within which you are working with other users. One reason for this is that hardware problems are then of no concern to you. Moreover, in such a situation, there must be a system manager present who can give assistance with any queries.

If you possess the necessary know-how to operate a computer with an 80286*, 80386 or 80486 processor, you can acquire and install a version of UNIX. This book is divided into two sections. In the first part, chapters 2 to 10, we shall concentrate on the user. In the second part, we shall deal with the installation and UNIX system management.

1.2 UNIX versions

Many versions of UNIX have been brought on to the market in the last few years. UNIX is more than 20 years old and in this time the system has undergone

---

* However an 80286 (PC - AT) is not sufficiently powerful to run Unix at an acceptable speed.

many development stages. Versions 6 and 7 were the first versions which to be made available to universities, and were developed there further. The next stage was the so-called *System III*, and eventually, in 1983, *System V* emerged. Many firms had their own versions such as VENIX, Sinix, AIX, Vitrix (from DEC), HP-UX (from Hewlett Packard), UTX (from Armdahl), and AUX (from Apple), the name 'UNIX' only being applied to the original AT&T version. The most well-known and widespread version was *XENIX*, but has been replaced by UNIX System V/386 which merges XENIX and System V and will itself be replaced by System V Release 4.

The university which has contributed the most to the development of UNIX is Berkeley University in California. Its version is not as widespread as XENIX but has been foremost in the world of workstations, which are single user systems for engineers. Many utilities which nowadays belong to System V originated in the Berkeley school. This has its own production department, the Berkeley Software Distribution company, which manufactured its own UNIX version under the name BSD4.x, now part of System V Release 4.

In 1983 AT&T recognized the market position of UNIX and declared **System V a standard system**. However, despite this, several competing versions exist and there is no single standard UNIX.

In the latest version, UNIX System V.4, the three market leaders, XENIX, BSD4.x and UNIX System V are integrated.

Even if you are working with a system which is running a previous or later version of UNIX, you can also work with this book since we shall discuss elementary use of the operating system which has changed little in the last twenty years. Finally, we advise you to contact your system manager or dealer if you encounter problems arising from incompatibility.

1.3   The best way to use this book

All books in this series presume that you are working with the system which is being described. Many books concerning UNIX confine themselves to showing how to handle the programs. This book, in contrast, indicates the structural link between the various software and hardware components. This introduction to the operating system is a general introduction to data management at the same time. We shall present this in an exploratory way: not just present a range of examples but guide you, step by step, through the deeper levels of the operating system so that the logical links become obvious.

Hence this book is not really a manual. Although a different topic will be dealt with in each chapter, it will not be confined to that chapter. On the contrary - whatever is necessary to understand UNIX and handle the system will be introduced at the relevant place, even if the topic is also dealt with in a later chapter. This means that the later chapters depend on the previous ones. Even if you know something about UNIX, we advise you to read from the beginning.

Owing to the fact that we explain a great deal in a couple of hundred pages, it is not enough to practice examples. Making summaries, studying references and trying out the theory are preconditions of full comprehension.

All sections, including those in which apparently exceptional problems are outlined, explore details as well as basic know-how. In many cases, they indicate how to react to error messages. We advise you to try out all the examples on your computer.

Another factor which distinguishes this book from other common books about UNIX is that we presume that individual PC users who wish to work with UNIX should also be able to use the information supplied here. In addition to using the system, they should become familiar

with system administration, which is more elaborate
than under MS-DOS. If you are going to install UNIX
yourself, you should work through this book in the following order of sequence:

1 chapters 2 and 4.2
2 chapters 11 and 12
3 chapters 4.3 to 6
4 sections 13.1 to 13.8
5 chapters 7 to 9
6 sections 13.9 and 13.10
7 chapters 10 and 14.2

Caution   UNIX is not MS-DOS! Under MS-DOS you
                 can generally restart a 'hanging' or 'frozen'
                 computer without any damage by making
                 a reset. UNIX does not allow this! A reset
                 may cause serious problems. You should
                 always shut down properly using a specific
                 command.

Therefore: do not begin pressing random keys wildly if
you find yourself in a desperate situation with a hanging
terminal. First make a critical analysis of what you have
done and try to follow the procedures in this book.

It is not our intention to frighten you off. We are only
concerned with saving you the double misery of a faulty
solution for a problem which may occur.

PART 1
THE UNIX USER

2 Computers in general

2.1 Programs and data

Computers are devices which are able to store, transmit and process *information*. Information, often called *data*, can be text or diagrams, or, for instance, pictures or sheet music.

The *commands* or *instructions* determine what happens to these data. A number of instructions collectively form a *program*. Programs are the *subjects* which guide and process the data.

In principle, all modifications are executed by data transport commands. In this, *memory addresses* play a central part: that which is to be stored, transmitted or processed is located at an address in the memory.

Operation	Data 1 (Address 1)	Data 2 (Address 2)
Save	What	Where
Transmit	From where	To where
Process	What	with what

2.2 Levels in the system

Programs control the *hardware*. The hardware is the ultimate level in the hierarchy of the computer system. The hardware executes all instructions and modifies data (see the figure below).

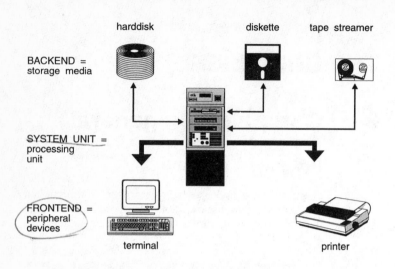

The data are processed in the **system unit**. The system unit consists of a number of *boards* or *cards*, contained in a box and supplied with power.

In a model computer, each board fulfils a certain function:

- The processor board is the heart of the computer. The CPU (Central Processing Unit) controls the operation of the electronic components of the computer, by means of which the data processing takes place.
- The memory card contains the internal memory in which programs and data are stored during working.
- The I/O cards (Input/Output) regulate the communication with the peripheral devices which are connected. The interfaces for the keyboard and the first printer are often located on the mother board.

The cards are linked by system buses. A *system bus* is a socket equipped with contacts into which the card is plugged. The data, addresses and operating codes are transported via these contacts.

The system stores programs and data on external devices, such as harddisks and diskettes (floppy disks). In order to manage programs and data, they are stored in units called **files**. On every disk (harddisk or diskette) there is at least one **directory** in which the name, the address on disk and other information concerning the file is stored.

Devices for input and output, for example keyboard, monitor and printer, facilitate communication between the external world and the computer system.

The second level of the computer system is formed by the *operating system*. The operating system organizes and manages all actions in the computer. It consists of a group of programs which collectively regulate the following:

■ They make decisions concerning how the system components, for instance, the processor, the internal memory or the printer, should be used.
■ They manage the files on the harddisk and diskettes and indicate what you may and may not do with these.
■ They take care of the transport of data within the computer itself and to and from the peripheral devices.

The third level consists of the user-oriented programs, or in short, the **user programs**. Applications and user interfaces belong to this category. Applications include word processing, book-keeping and graphic programs, but they may also be *utilities* which are programs which facilitate working with the computer. Utility programs are used for copying files, printing texts or disk management. A *user interface* is frequently placed between the operating system and the user. This is actually a kind of program which makes it easier to perform everyday tasks on the computer. A well-known example of a user interface is X Windows which is becoming very common on UNIX computers.

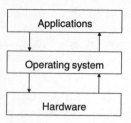

2.3   The PC starting procedure

When you switch a PC on, the following takes place:

- The hardware is tested,
- the operating system is loaded from disk and started up, and
- if required, a user interface is loaded and activated.

'Loading' means that a program is copied from a permanent storage medium to the internal memory or *working memory*. All data placed in working memory are lost as soon as the power supply is disconnected. The operating system and the user interface must then be reloaded.

The system has to receive the instructions from somewhere in order to test the hardware and load the operating system. For this purpose, a small amount of memory which cannot be deleted has been added on the mother board. This memory contains a small program which executes this task. The operating system, once activated, loads all other programs.

3 Working with UNIX

3.1 Modes

UNIX is a *multi-user system*, which means that more than one user can work with it simultaneously.

If all tasks which have to be implemented were to be neatly carried out in order of sequence, there would be long delays. This is avoided by dividing the processor calculation time into smaller units. These smaller units are subsequently assigned to all tasks which are waiting to be dealt with. Thus, they all share the processor calculation time; this process is also called *time sharing*. Because the processor works extremely quickly, the user hardly notices that the processor is being collectively used.

A second feature of UNIX is *multitasking*: you can activate a new program while the operating system is still busy processing previous commands. This means that not only is the processor calculation time being shared by all users, it is also divided over multiple tasks specified by users or by programs.

3.2 The system manager

In a system as complex as this, the system requires a system manager. The system manager is called *root*. Due to the fact that a system manager has more priviledges than a normal user, he is also sometimes referred to as the *superuser*. In the device directory, the system manager's station is called the *console*.

The connection for the console is always on the mother board, thus in the immediate neighbourhood of the processor. The connector for this purpose at the back of the computer is often indicated by Console. Many versions of UNIX only allow system management by way of this connector.

3.3   Single user or multi-user

Although UNIX is a multi-user system, it always first
"comes-up" single-user and checks the complete system. This operating mode is specifically meant for the
System Manager only, who - having all rights - is able to
alter everything in the system.

When the computer has been started up, the decision
must be made as to whether multi-user operation
should be brought into use or not. This decision can
either be incorporated in the system or be assigned to
the person who starts up the system.

If the system remains in single-user operation, access
to the computer should be safeguarded by the secret
password of the System Manager. Otherwise anyone
coming into contact with the device would be able to
manipulate or destroy the system. If this protection is
not available, only the System Manager should have
access to the room where the central unit is located.

It is obvious that users may not work in each other's directories and files, or read programs from other users.
Accordingly, there is a safeguard system in which right
of access is linked to the user name.

If you are your own system manager and a single user
at the same time, it would seem obvious that you would
wish to work in the single-user mode. However, you
should **never** execute management tasks while you are
busy with your normal work. We recommend that you
work in the multi-user mode if you wish to do this. Carry
out your normal work as a user without any special priviledges: you can then, for example, only delete user
files. If you work as system manager, you can delete *all*
files. If anything goes wrong while you are working as a
normal user, you can always log in as the system manager at another station in order to attempt to solve the
problem. In the single-user mode, this is not possible.

4 Beginning with UNIX

4.1 The initial situation

We shall presume that you are working at a terminal in an extensive system or on a PC.

If you are working on a PC, there are two possibilities:

1   UNIX has not yet been installed, perhaps because you wish to economize or because you wish to gain experience with the installation. Before proceeding with this chapter, you should first install the operating system and become acquainted with the most important management tasks. See chapters 11 and 12.

2   UNIX has been installed, for example by your dealer, and the password for *root*, the system manager, has been determined. In addition, you have been registered under a user name, for instance '*guest*' and a directory */usr/guest* has been created for you. (The slash differs from that in MS-DOS.) In this case, you should first activate the system before you can log in as the user. After each session, you may close down the system but many UNIX systems are left running continuously. Before shutting down, read chapter 12 in order to become familiar with the system requirements.

When you have started the system, your situation is comparable to that of a user at a terminal of a large UNIX computer. The system manager of a large multi-user system has the job of registering you as a new user in the password file, of creating a directory for you and specifying your work environment.

Before beginning work, you should read the following information concerning the keyboard.

4.2   The keyboard > characters > programs > devices

Each program and each device requires data and in-structions in order to be able to implement its tasks. One source of this information is the keyboard. The key-board generates characters. A group of characters together form a *string*. The significance of a character or string is determined by the program or device. A key-stroke does not always produce the same result in every program.

The command used to activate a function often differs from program to program or device to device. This means that you will have to become familiar with each new program and each new device.

Even when characters are interpreted as data, it may occur that the same character will appear differently on the screen than on the printer. Both devices, in fact, have different *character codes*. Unfortunately, there are a great many character sets and this means that data have to be converted for transmission to another device or to another computer system.

The keyboards of various types of PCs and terminals also differ from one another, although the differences tend to be small. (See overleaf.)

In principle, the keys are grouped in blocks. The largest block contains the keys from the traditional typewriter, supplemented by two typical computer keys, the <Ctrl> key and the <Alt> key (both left and right).

The numeric keypad is located at the right-hand side of the keyboard. The keys here fulfil two functions: in the numeric mode (with <NumLock> active), you are able to type numbers; if you switch off <NumLock>, you can move the *cursor* across the screen. The cursor is a flashing stripe or block which indicates, on your screen, the input insertion point. The form of the cursor may be chosen: block or underlining, flashing or not. In this book the cursor is represented by []. On some modern keyboards, there is a separate block of cursor keys between the main block and the numeric keypad.

On older PC keyboards, the *function* keys are located to the left of the main block. On more modern keyboards, they are located along the top.

Switches are keys which allow you to switch functions on or off. You will probably recognize these from the old-fashioned typewriter: <CapsLock>, when activated, ensures that all letters subsequently typed are displayed as capitals. The <Shift> key does the same if you hold it down while typing a letter. In addition, the <Shift> key produces the special characters shown on the main block keys above the normal letters. The <Ctrl> (Control) and <Alt> (Alternate) keys have functions which can be compared to that of the <Shift> key, in as much as a combination of one of these with a normal letter activates a new feature.

Not all characters which you can generate using a key-stroke or a key combination can be displayed on the screen. Firstly, this is purely because there are less fewer characters than key combinations and, secondly, because a great number of key combinations are interpreted as operating codes. For example, in UNIX, the <Return> key (often marked Enter and often called the Enter key) is used to move the cursor key to a new line: a *line feed* and *carriage return*. Using the <Backspace> key, the character to the left of the cursor is deleted and the cursor moves one position to the left, deleting the character there. The <Esc> key is used as a switch between two modes: if you press the <Esc> key, the first character subsequently specified is not interpreted as a piece of data but as a command.

Most programs and devices recognize two modes: the *input mode* or *text mode* and the *command mode*. In the input mode the characters which are typed are interpreted as data which are to be processed. In the com-

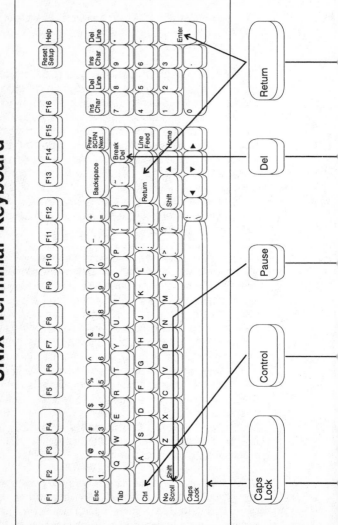

UNIX Terminal Keyboard

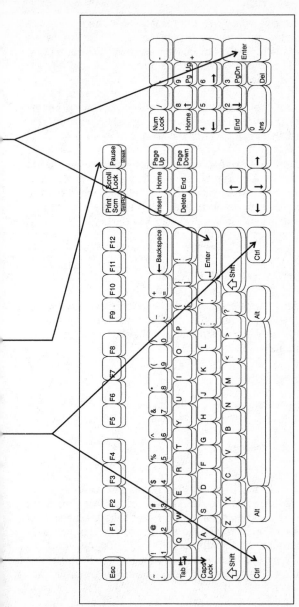

UNIX PC Keyboard

mand mode, they are interpreted as commands. The keys mentioned above (Return, Backspace, Esc) generate the characters <Ctrl-m>, <Ctrl-h> and <Ctrl-[>. These characters have the same significance for almost all programs and devices.

Because the character which you create by pressing the <Ctrl> key and the m simultaneously cannot be displayed, this is written as <Ctrl-m> or ^M.

The markings on the keys are thus only relevant to the letters and numbers which you can type, and not to all the special characters which are available in combination with the operating keys. Try out a key in combination with the <Shift> key, the <Alt> key and with <Shift> and <Alt> together.

4.3   Access to the system

In order to gain access to the system, the exchange of characters between the station and the central unit should take place smoothly. When started up, your screen may look like this:

```
xenix386!login:
```

Or this message may be displayed:

```
uxschool
Uniplus+ System V.2
login:
```

uxschool is the name of this computer, *xenix386* and *Uniplus+ System V.2* the version of UNIX being used and *login:* is the command to enter a user name. This must be done in small letters, unless the name contains one or more capital letters. UNIX distinguishes very precisely between small and capital letters: if you enter 'billy binkerhill' while UNIX expects 'Billy Binkerhill', access will be denied.

If you make a typing error, it is possible to delete the
input or a part of it. In many UNIX systems, for example
XENIX 2.3, the <Backspace> key (<Ctrl-h>) and <Ctrl-u> are
active from the outset: the <Backspace> key enables you
to delete one character to the left of the cursor; <Ctrl-u>
enables you to remove the entire input.
There are also UNIX systems in which the functions
only become active subsequent to the login procedure;
these systems require a number sign (#) in order to
delete a character, or an at sign (@) before the deletion
of the entire input. This has a historical background: the
<Ctrl> key is not used in the telex system which was
adopted during the development of UNIX. If you perform a deletion using the number sign, the character remains on your screen. This is rather confusing. It is advisable to use an @ sign to delete the entire input and to
begin again. In this case, the previous input does not
disappear from the screen, but the cursor moves to a
new line and this prevents confusion.

Type the user name, for example '*guest*' and conclude
the input by pressing <Return>:

```
login:guest<Return>
```

When the system asks you to specify data using the
keyboard, you should always conclude the input by
pressing <Return>. In subsequent explanations we shall
assume that this is self-evident and, accordingly, we do
not need to repeat this instruction.

If no password has been determined yet, you can begin
working with the system. We recommend that you deal
with this weak point in the system first. Using a password not only safeguards the data, it also allows access
to the system to only those who know the password.

4.4   Login problems

Beware of logging in at an active terminal. The login
procedure could be a trap by another user to discover

your password, using a program to emulate the login procedure. To protect against such a trick, answer each login instruction by typing <Ctrl-D>. In this way, the active login procedure is discontinued and a new login procedure is started up.

Below, we shall discuss a number of problems with login procedures:

1　You cannot log in because the command **login:** just does not appear on your screen. A possible cause of this might be that there is no link as yet between the station where you are working and the computer. The station has probably been switched on later, or the computer is not yet adjusted to the *baud rate* of the terminal. The baud rate is the speed with which the data exchange between the two devices takes place. In that case, press <Return> or <Return> and <Ctrl-D> and wait a moment. Perhaps you may have to repeat this manoeuvre a couple of times. It may also occur that there is absolutely no transport of data between the devices. In that case, check the connections. If this has no effect, consult the system manager.

2　The system requests a password, although you are sure that no password yet exists:

```
login:guest<Return>
password:
```

This problem may be caused by a typing error: perhaps you have typed *'gest'* instead of *'guest'*, and thus, you have specified the wrong user name. Or perhaps you have pressed a key which does not generate a character on the screen. You may have applied an incorrect deletion procedure (see section 4.3).

You will be requested to specify a password if a user name is given which is unknown to the system. In these cases, you cannot rectify the user name. You have no choice but to complete the procedure. First press <Return> to specify a blank password. The system now discontinues the login procedure with an error message and offers you a new chance to login in.

```
login:gest<Return>
password:<Return>
Login incorrect!
login:
```

3   The system requests the password but you do not know it. It may be that the system manager does not allow access to the system, under any circumstances, without a password and has therefore allocated you a password. You will have to request this. When you type a password, to ensure secrecy, it does not appear on the screen. If you make a mistake, the login procedure is discontinued with an error message and you must begin the login procedure again.

If you have forgotten your password, you must approach the system manager who can alter or delete the password in the password file.

4   The system requests the password but the command appears in capitals on your screen:

```
login:GEST<Return>
PASSWORD:
```

The cause of this problem is that you have specified an incorrect user name in capitals. You have, thus, made two errors in one go. Press <Return> to solve the problem. The error message **LOGIN INCORRECT** and the **LOGIN** command which follows both appear in capitals on your screen. Press <Ctrl-D> (without <Return>) and the **login** command will be given again, but this time correctly.

```
login:GEST<Return>
PASSWORD:<Return>
```

```
LOGIN INCORRECT!
LOGIN:<Ctrl-D>

login:
```

<Ctrl-D> is the command meaning **end of input**, or more precisely, **end of transmission** used to terminate the login procedure. This occurs, but a new login procedure is automatically activated. After pressing <Ctrl-D>, do not press <Return>: this would be interpreted as the conclusion of the new input for the new login procedure. Some UNIX systems do not recognize <Ctrl-D> in the function described here. Instead, they expect <Ctrl-z> as the EOT (End Of Transmission) sign. In addition, <Ctrl-z> is frequently used as the EOF sign (End Of File).

5   After logging in, one of the following error messages appears on the screen:

```
login:guest<Return>
No directory
login:
```

```
login:guest<Return>
Unable to change directory to "/usr/guest"
login:
```

UNIX cannot switch to your directory. It may be that the system manager has forgotten to create a directory for you, but it is also feasible that there is another reason why your directory is unreadable. In both cases, you will have to approach the system manager.

6   After logging in, one of the error messages mentioned in point 5 appears on the screen:

```
login:guest<Return>
Unable to change directory to "/usr/guest"
login:
```

The system manager has forgotten to specify the directory you will use when he registered you as a user. Thus, in this case too, you will have to approach the system manager.

7   You have gained access to the system but the system appears chaotic: only capitals appear on the screen. The reason for this is that you have typed your name in capitals. You must first *log out* and then log in again to solve the problem.

Caution   First read section 4.7 which explains logging out. You should certainly not try to start up the system again by means of the reset button or the on/off switch. UNIX cannot cope with this. Once you have logged in, you will also have to log out using the appropriate procedure.

4.5   Activating the user interface

When you have identified yourself as a user, the login procedure will activate your user interface. Which program this is depends on what the system manager has specified.

You are probably already familiar with a menu-operated user interface. A menu like this consists of a list of programs from which you can make a choice. There are no other options. You can also work with UNIX in this way. However, if you wish to make use of all the possibilities provided by UNIX, you should have a user interface which enables you to type commands yourself.

Under UNIX, there are several of this type of user interface. Experienced users call an interface like this a *shell*. The *Bourne shell* is the oldest version and is generally accepted as being the standard. Nowadays UNIX is also supplied with the *C shell*. In addition, the most recent versions are also supplied with the *Korn shell*. Neither of these versions are fully compatible with

the Bourne shell; in other words, instructions and procedures from the Bourne shell may not be understood by
the C shell or the Korn shell but the incompatibilities will
probably not affect the new user.

Besides these three shells, additional shells can be ob-
tained, either as *Public Domain Software, Shareware* or
from appropriate software houses. *P.D. Software* and
Shareware may be freely circulated. The *Shareware*
authors request some recompense if a user actually
uses the program. In the USA this system works well in
getting around the tedious copyright clauses. In the UK
the programs are well-used but the voluntary contribu-
tions are often forgotten.

Finally, when the shell has been activated, something
really happens on the screen. Exactly what that is depends on what the system manager - and later yourself
- has specified in the start-up procedure. Start-up
procedures are programs containing commands which
are run automatically after login. These are the equivalent of AUTOEXEC.BAT under MS-DOS.

The system appears with a *prompt*; every interactive
program, i.e. a program which requires input from the
user, uses a certain sign to indicate that the user can
enter data or commands. The prompt serves this purpose. Since almost every program has its own prompt,
you can recognize the program by its prompt. The
Bourne shell appears with a number sign when you
have logged in as the system manager:

#

Normal users see a dollar sign as prompt under the
Bourne shell:

$

Accordingly, you can recognize by the prompt whether
you are logged in as a normal user or as the system
manager.

4.6 Problems after logging in

1   The percentage sign % appears as prompt. In fact,
    nothing has gone wrong: you have logged in but
    the C shell has been activated. Since this is nearly
    compatible with the Bourne shell you can just con-
    tinue working. The C shell can interpret the com-
    mands directed at the Bourne shell. If the prompt
    disturbs you, ask the system manager for help or
    start the Bourne shell under the C shell. Type *sh*
    behind the percentage sign, thus:

```
%sh
$ []
```

The name of the Bourne shell is thus simply **sh**.
The C shell is called **csh**. If you have activated the
Bourne shell, you can quit it again by pressing <Ctrl-
D>. You then return to the C shell. The reverse
procedure can also take place: under the Bourne
shell, you can activate the C shell using the command:

```
csh
```

and quit it using <Ctrl-D>.

2   An arrow or a word or something similar appears as
    the prompt. Again nothing has gone wrong. The
    prompt display has altered in the start-up proce-
    dure. In fact, you do not need to do anything. You
    will find out later in which shell you are working.

3   The system asks which type of terminal you are
    working with. This question is based on the fact that
    different kinds of terminals are linked to the com-
    puter. Your system manager knows the type on
    which you are working.

4.7   Logging out is obligatory!

If you wish to finish a session under UNIX, you should not, under any circumstances, just switch off the computer. You should first neatly close UNIX using the *logging out* procedure. To do this, you only have to specify the known command <Ctrl-D>. In this way, you let the shell know that you are not planning to enter any more commands. This means that the program should end. The command should be given at the beginning of a new line, directly after the prompt:

```
$<Ctrl-D>
```

Nothing may be placed in front of <Ctrl-D>, not even invisible characters. If you try, for instance, to type <Ctrl-g> followed by <Ctrl-D>, an error message will be displayed.

```
$<Ctrl-g><Ctrl-D><Return>
<Ctrl-g>:not found
$<Ctrl-D>

login:[]
```

<Ctrl-D> is an operating code. Operating codes are processed directly, without you having to press <Return>. Input which does not consist of operating characters is only processed when you press <Return>.

You should not just switch off your terminal instead of logging out. In most systems, your station remains logged in on the computer and any unauthorized user can continue working in your directory by switching on your terminal again.

On large commercial systems, users and usage are recorded. If you do not log out, someone else can work under your name and you may be held responsible for problems and costs arising from this unauthorized usage. Therefore, keep your password a secret and always log out before quitting.

4.8   Specifying or altering the password

You have logged in as required and the prompt from the Bourne shell ($) is displayed on the screen. You can now specify a password using the command **passwd**. Type the command and confirm it using <Return>. The program acknowledges your request and asks you to type the new password:

```
$passwd<Return>
Changing password for guest
New password:
```

Subsequently enter a password. It does not appear on the screen, but in order to ascertain that you have not make a mistake, you will be asked to type it again. If the passwords do not match, you will have to begin again after an error message:

```
$passwd<Return>
Changing password for guest
New password:      <Return>
Re-enter new password:      <Return>
They don't match; try again.
New password:        <Return>
Re-enter new password:        <Return>
$[]
```

Altering a password takes place in the same way; for security reasons the system requests the previous password again.

```
$passwd<Return>
Changing password for guest
Old password:      <Return>
New password:      <Return>
Re-enter new password:      <Return>
$[]
```

Passwords should, depending on the installed version, consist of at least five or six characters, of which at least two should be letters along with at least one other character. If you specify a password of more than thirteen characters, the fourteenth and all subsequent characters will be ignored.

You should be able to remember the password, especially the superuser! Do not choose a password from your immediate surroundings. It is also not very clever to write it down on a piece of paper on your desk. All predictable passwords, for example the name of your partner, are also not suitable since they can easily be found out by malicious acquaintances. The best thing to do is to choose a new password regularly, and certainly when you know the passwords of your colleagues!

When specifying a password, you may receive the following error messages:

- Password is too short - must be at least 6 digits.
- Password must contain at least two alphabetic characters and at least one numeric or special character.
- Password must differ by at least 3 positions.
- Too many failures - try later.

Now that you have a password, try it out. Log out and then in again. Hopefully, you have not already forgotten the password.

```
$<Ctrl-D>

login:guest<Return>
password:      <Return>
$[]
```

If you have forgotten your password and you are your own system manager, you can log in as root and specify a new password for the user.

```
#passwd guest
New password:      <Return>
```

```
Re-enter new password:      <Return>
#[]
```

4.9 Peripheral devices and device drivers

Generally, the following devices are linked to a UNIX computer:

■ A terminal or a PC with a terminal emulator: the screen and the keyboard enable the communication between the user and UNIX. A terminal emulator is a special program which enables a PC to function as a terminal.
■ A printer to print the output.
■ A harddisk to store the data.
■ A tape streamer for making a backup of the harddisk, for archive purposes and for the transport of large programs and data files.
■ Additional hard or floppy disk drives for the storage and transport of data.

In order to use these devices, special programs called *driver programs* or *device drivers* are required. These are programs which are linked to the kernel of the UNIX system. If you wish to add new drivers, you need to have a UNIX system which can be reconfigured. Adding new drivers is called *linking*. If you do not have a UNIX version which can be reconfigured, approach your dealer.

If you wish to work with an application, you should load and execute the application. The command to do this usually begins with the name of the program. Behind this, you should specify where the program can find the data which is to be processed and, finally, you should specify to where the output should be sent. The command may look like this:

```
Program name <input data-from where >output
data-to where
```

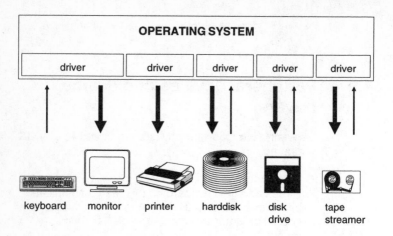

The data are normally located in files which are stored
on the harddisk, on diskettes or on magnetic tape. You
will regularly have to retrieve data from devices and directories or transport these using devices. You are required to specify the names of these as well. In order to
keep the structure of the commands uniform, UNIX regards not only programs and data but also directories
and devices as files. Thus, the command can assume
the following forms:

```
Program name <device >device
Program name <device >file
Program name <file >device
Program name <file >file
Program name <directory >file
Program name <directory >device
```

Under UNIX you may use a file or a device for the address of both input and output. It must be clearly specified whether it is input or output. The less-than and
greater-than signs are used here. The < sign indicates
input; the > sign indicates output. However, some programs may not require the > or < signs or may even
know where data are located without being told.

5 The terminal

5.1 The terminal as input and output device

Normally, the keyboard and the screen are only linked to each other via the central unit.
The character generated by the keyboard is processed by the driver, transmitted to the screen as 'echo' and then passed on to the application.

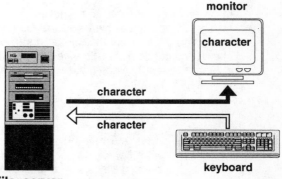

monitor

character

character

character

keyboard

file server

Under UNIX, all devices are registered in a separate directory, *dev* (device). This directory is immediately under the root directory. The root directory has no name. It is represented by a slash (/). The full name of the directory containing the devices is thus */dev*. The name of a device is then added to this, again separated by a slash, for example, */dev/tty01*.

You can request the names of the connected terminals using the command **who**. The system will then transmit a list of all current users to the screen including the number of their terminals and the time at which they logged in. If you only wish to request the name of your own terminal, type **who am i**.

```
$who am i
guest     tty01     Dec 25 07:38
$[]
```

Thus, you are working at terminal *tty01*. 'tty' is an abbreviation for telex (teletype). In the initial stages of data
processing, the telex was used as terminal.

The full name of your terminal is: **/dev/tty01**. If a program is to receive its input from the keyboard, type the
full name in the command: *</dev/tty01*. If you wish to
send the output of the program to your terminal screen,
type *>/dev/tty01*.

In order to ensure that the input from your keyboard
now appears on your own screen, you need a special
instruction which links the chosen input device to the
chosen output device. This is the command **cat** ('con-
catenate'= join). The complete command is as follows:

```
$cat </dev/tty01 >/dev/tty01
[]
```

Note :   That you should press the <Return> key
             after specifying commands will no longer
             be explicitly stated in this book. You have
             learned this by now. If nothing happens
             after giving a command ask yourself if you
             have remembered to press the <Return>
             key.

             Commands, names of programs and in-
             and output must always be separated by a
             space. If you do not do this, an error mess-
             age appears, such as **cat...:not found**,
             which means that the computer cannot
             find the program called cat....

However, you may also use the greater-than and smaller-than signs as separators. This is perhaps a little confusing - if you omit all the spaces in the above mentioned cat command, the command is nevertheless

correctly implemented. In order to avoid any problems, it is best to make a habit of always using spaces as separators.

The cursor is now located at the beginning of the next line. The *cat* program is now active and awaits input from the keyboard. Type a line. As you are typing, the text is sent to your screen as an echo. When you have pressed <Return> to conclude the input, cat will execute the entire line. The result is that the line is displayed twice on your screen.

```
$cat </dev/tty01 >/dev/tty01
Here is a news flash. Owing to lack of interest,
                        tomorrow has been cancelled.
Here is a news flash. Owing to lack of interest,
                        tomorrow has been cancelled.
```

Thus, your input is normally passed on line by line to the program. If you wish to end the program, you should inform it that it will not receive any more information. This is done using the command <Ctrl-D>, which must always be placed **at the start of a new line**.

```
$cat </dev/tty01 >/dev/tty01
Here is a news flash. Owing to lack of interest
                        tomorrow has been cancelled.
Here is a news flash. Owing to lack of interest
                        tomorrow has been cancelled.
<Ctrl-D>
$[]
```

The complete command **cat** demands considerable typing. The chance of errors, particularly when using special characters, is substantial. This can be reduced if you predefine the input and output devices which are mainly in use. For this reason, UNIX is equipped with a standard input and output routine. If you give a command without specifying the input and output channels, UNIX will choose the default routines.

You can determine these default routines yourself, although UNIX in principle makes it even easier by recog-
nizing the keyboard as the default input device and the
screen as the default output device.

In addition to these standard routines, *stdin* (input) and
stdout (output), UNIX has one more variable, *stderr*.
This is the default channel for error messages. Normally, this will also be your screen, but you may make
this the printer, another screen of a text file.

This means that instead of having to type the command
cat</dev/tty01>/dev/tty01, you can also just type **cat**.
Try this out.
The next topic deals with sending messages to another
user. The first thing you must do is to find out which
users have logged in. To do this, type the instruction
who.

```
$who
root      console     dec 25 07:00
guest     tty01       dec 25 07:38
$[]
```

The system manager has risen early and has logged in
on the /dev/console terminal. Many UNIX systems only
allow the system manager to log in at this terminal.

If you are working with a PC, you will probably be the
only user. You should change this. The XENIX *multi-
screen* function makes it possible to log in on the same
PC as a second user, for instance as *root*.
Press <Alt-F2>. The screen is cleared and the command
for a new login procedure appears on the top line. You
are now working at terminal *tty02*. Log in as **root**. If you
press <Alt-F1>, you will return to the previous terminal
tty01. If you request a list of users once more using
who, you will now see that you are not alone in the system.

```
$who
root      tty02       dec 25 07:45
```

```
guest    tty01      dec 25 07:38
$[]
```

Send a message to *root*. The input comes from your keyboard, the standard input device. Accordingly, you do not have to specify this in the command. You do have to send the output to the proper terminal. This is *tty02* or *console*, depending on the situation.

```
$cat >/dev/tty02
Working at night ruins family life!
<Ctrl-D>
$[]
```

For the superuser manager it is not clear who has sent this message. The system manager's screen will only display

```
#Working at night ruins family life!
```

5.2   The terminal interface

You can alter the way the terminal reacts to meet your own requirements. You have already become acquainted with a number of these possibilities:

■ The echo of the input to the screen can be suppressed. This occurs, for example, when typing the password.
■ The input is processed line by line, only after you have pressed <Return>.
■ Operating codes, for instance <Ctrl-D> and <Ctrl-s>, are used to instruct the *user process* how it should react when the processes are resumed. (We shall return to the term 'process' later.)
■ You can delete a character which has been entered before it is passed on to the program. The character is removed from the input using <Backspace> or <Ctrl-h>.

In order to understand the workings of the terminal and to adjust these to your own requirements, you should become familiar with these routines: all these processes are possible due to the fact that the terminal driver passes the input to the *terminal interface* of the operating system. This interface has two modes: the *raw mode* and the *canonical mode*.

In the **raw mode**, all input is passed directly to the program. It is not possible to process this raw material first. In addition, it is not possible to pass on operating codes. This implies, for example, that <Ctrl-D> does not function and therefore it is not possible to discontinue any processes. We advise you to avoid the raw mode wherever possible.

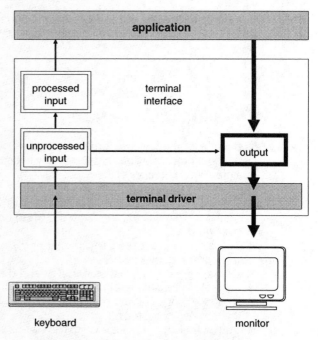

You can determine the way the terminal interface reacts in the **canonical mode** using the instruction **stty** (set tty).

In order to process the input properly, the following conditions should be fulfilled:

1   You should be able to correct the input before this is passed on to the program. Thus it should be possible to delete the previous characters or line.

2   You should be able to indicate that the input is complete and that the program can begin processing it.

3   You should be able to indicate to a program which is running that no more input will follow.

4   The output should be able to be interrupted and then continued.

5   You should be able to discontinue the program which is being run.

Below, we shall deal with the most important specifications which produce these effects.

UNIX calls the character which removes a previous character **ERASE**. Normally, **ERASE** has the value 9, in the ASCII table the value 8. Using the command **stty** you are able to select another computer character for **ERASE**.

You probably know that the *bit pattern* which implements a certain instruction is specified in a code table. The invisible characters are also represented by a bit pattern. There is a bit pattern for the letter 'a' and also one for the 'line feed, new line'. The bit patterns are numbered, and that number is the ASCII value.

ASCII stands for American Standard Code for Information Interchange. The character set described by this standard has been gradually extended in the course of time. Nowadays, there are diverse extended character sets, which does not always make it easy to generate the correct characters on a particular device.

ERASE has the ASCII value 8. This value is generated
by pressing <Backspace> or <Ctrl-h>. Some systems allow
you to define key functions yourself. If you are not sure
which character belongs to a specific key, you can easily discover the value by applying a small program.

Under UNIX, an entire line is removed using the instruction **KILL**, which has the ASCII value 21, the key combination <Ctrl-u>. In general, the cursor then moves to the
next line so that you are able to type new data. The
ASCII value of **KILL** can also be altered.

```
$blablabla<Ctrl-u>
[]
```

Under UNIX, moving to a new line has the effect of pas-
sing on the typed input to the program. Moving to a new
line is called **NL** (New Line) and has the unchangeable
ASCII value 10, corresponding to the key combination
<Ctrl-j>. This is described as 'Line Feed' in the ASCII
table.

Up until now, you have used the <Return> key for this
function. This corresponds to the key combination <Ctrl-
m>. However, the <Return> key has an ASCII value of 13.
As long as you are working in the canonical mode, this
value will be adjusted automatically by the user interface. In the raw mode, you will have to type <Ctrl-j> in
order to send the input on the line to the program. Of
course, you may also type <Ctrl-j> in the canonical mode
if you wish.

```
$cat<Ctrl-j>
Everything OK?<Ctrl-j>
Everything OK
<Ctrl-D>
$[]
```

You conclude the input using an **EOF** code (End Of
File), which has an ASCII value of 4. In the ASCII table,
this character is called **EOT** (End Of Transmission). The
corresponding key combination is <Ctrl-D>.

You may adjust the value of the EOF character yourself if you wish. Many UNIX systems use ASCII value 3, which represents **ETX** (End Of Text). The corresponding key combination is <Ctrl-c>.

If you type an EOF character, all the input which is currently located in the buffer is processed by the user interface and passed on to the program. The EOF character itself is ignored.

```
$cat
Yes or No<Ctrl-D>Yes or No<Ctrl-m>

<Ctrl-D>
$[]
```

In the example above, <Return> or <Ctrl-m> moves the user to the beginning of a new blank line. A new EOF character on that line leads to the processing of the blank line. The **cat** command which was initially activated cannot process this and presumes that no more input will follow. The process is discontinued, which is, in fact, the correct interpretation of the EOF character.

The **STOP** character indicates to the user process that it must be interrupted temporarily. This situation is known as **XOFF**: X refers to transmission and OFF means off. This character has the ASCII value 19 (DC3). The corresponding key combination is <Ctrl-s> and cannot be altered. In the case of two consecutive stop characters, the second is ignored.

The stop sign is particularly useful if the output to the screen does not fit on the screen, while the program is not geared to producing output per screen page.

The opposite of the stop character is the **START** character: the program resumes processing (**XON**). The ASCII value is 17 (DC1) and the corresponding key combination is <Ctrl-q>. However, you can also adapt the user interface in such a way that each keystroke, except the Stop sign <Ctrl-s>, can be used as a START character.

You can try out both commands using the **cal** instruction. This transports a calender for a whole year to the screen, without taking into consideration the amount of lines which fit on to the screen.

```
$cal 2002
```

The calender for the year 2002 now scrolls over your screen. As the month of December rolls over the screen, January is long gone. Give the command once more, but this time press <Ctrl-s> immediately. The output on your screen is now frozen. By pressing a random key (except <Ctrl-s>), you can now examine the way your user interface has been defined: if nothing happens, this means that you can only use <Ctrl-q> as the starting sign.

When working at the terminal, the command **INTR** is of considerable importance. This has the function of interrupting all processes which are currently taking place at the terminal. The shell prompt then appears on the screen. This command is particularly important if you lose control over what is going on, or if you notice that things are occurring unintentionally. The ASCII value of INTR is 127 (DEL); the corresponding key is <Del>

```
$cat
Yes or No<Del>
$
```

The instruction to transport the string 'Yes or No' to the screen is not completed. Only the echo from the keyboard is displayed. When you press the <Del> key, the shell prompt appears once more.

Note   The <Del> key does not always work. If the raw mode is active (because a program requires that for instance), you cannot discontinue the process in this way. The same happens when a program neutralizes the <Del> key because it does not wish to be interrupted. In such cases, programs will sometimes provide other possibilities to discontinue the process.

On some UNIX systems <Ctrl-C> acts as the interrupt key.

Just to be complete, we shall also mention the **QUIT** sign, which works just as the interrupt signal, the only difference being that the command first saves a copy of the current process in memory. The contents of the working memory are saved under the name **core** on the harddisk. The ASCII value of **QUIT** is 28 (FS), the key combination is <Ctrl-\>.

You will find a table containing bit patterns, ASCII values and keystrokes in the appendix.

5.3 Problems with the terminal

If your screen behaves strangely, perhaps displaying nothing or only illegible symbols, read this section carefully. If this does not help solve your problems, you will have to approach the system manager.

You may have pressed the <Pause> key which may also be called No Scroll or Hold Screen. The <Pause> key only works locally and instructs your terminal to discontinue the output to your screen. Not all terminals recognize the <Pause> key. If you press the <Pause> key again, the output will be resumed once more, but all the characters which have been dammed up will be sent to your screen in one go, since the central unit has kept on working in the meantime.

Or perhaps you have accidentally generated a **STOP** sign by pressing <Ctrl-s>. Try to get the process going again by pressing <Ctrl-q>.

If only capitals are displayed on your screen, you have pressed <CapsLock>. This key is located just above the left-hand <Shift> key on modern PC keyboards, so that a mistake is easily made. The <CapsLock> key is a switch which only alters the function of the alphanumeric keys

in the main block of the keyboard, unless you are working with an exceptional type of keyboard.

The cause of a problem may also be a typing error
caused by the similarity between the number '1' and the
letter 'l'. If you give the command

```
$1s
```

with the intention of gaining an oversight on your screen
of the directory in which you are working, the system will
reply

```
1s:not found
```

You meant to give the command

```
$ls
```

using the l for 'list'. A similar problem may occur with the
number '0' and a capital O. Both characters have their
own bit pattern - you must not confuse them. To help
prevent this, the zero often has a slash or a dot.

Perhaps the greater-than sign (>) suddenly appears on
your screen although you have not pressed that key.
This is probably the second shell prompt, requesting
supplementary information. This may also appear on
your screen if you use an apostrophe or inverted commas: ' or ". The problem may be further complicated by
the fact that you can alter the display of the prompt. A
humorous system manager may change the second
prompt (requesting supplementary information) to the
message 'And now?'. If you decide that the prompt has
appeared without due cause, press <Del>. Your normal
prompt appears again.

```
$'
><Del>
$[]
```

In the raw mode, the <Del> key will be of no assistance. Then you should type the same character again, conclude the line by pressing <Return> and the normal prompt appears once more. This is also the case in the canonical mode, but there the <Del> key is more convenient. Alternatively, type <Ctrl-C> instead of pressing the <Del> key.

If your screen turns into a pandemonium of phrases, snippets and messages, do not fear the worst. The most obvious cause is that the echo of your input is being disturbed by system messages and messages from other users. The result is mostly that you have no idea precisely where you were with your input. In that case, press the <Del> key or <Ctrl-C>.

However, if you do know where you were, you can proceed as normally. The garbage shown on your screen exists only there, not in the computer. In the computer, the input and output ranges are neatly separated. The input is not contaminated. The echo function of the terminal interface is only doing what it should. All instructions to show anything on the screen, whether it is the echo of the input, system messages or messages from other users are implemented.

To clear the garbage from your screen, either press <Return> several times (or hold it down for a couple of seconds) or else give the command: **clear**, which clears the screen instantly.

In this way, malicious colleagues can obstruct your work considerably, and therefore there are functions which enable you to regulate the output to your screen.

Messages from other users can be suppressed using the command **mesg -n** This is an abbreviation for 'message, no'. Statements from the system and messages from the system manager are not suppressed. Enter the command:

```
$mesg -n
$
```

The hyphen in front of the n indicates to the shell that an *option* follows instead of an address. An option is a supplementary instruction for the execution of the original command. Programs often provide various facilities or instructions. By means of option selections or different program names for the same program, it is possible to indicate to the program which facility should be run.

If you wish to allow messages from other users, type the same command, **mesg** but this time with the '**y**' for 'yes'.

```
$mesg -y
$
```

If you type the instruction **mesg** without specifying any options, the shell will indicate which mode is active: **message is no** or **message is yes**.

Error messages directed to the screen display might also cause confusion. Therefore it is possible to redirect them to a harddisk or to a printer.

5.4   Entering commands

The input for a command is concluded by pressing <Return>. The user interface changes the ASCII value of <Return> into that of a new line. This indicates the completion of input and subsequently the user interface submits the line to the program.

We have already discussed the principle of a command line:

```
program name <input data >output data
```

Due to the fact that UNIX regards all program names, collections of data, directories and devices as being files, this syntax for the command line is always valid. This makes working with UNIX a great deal easier.

If a program can be run in different modes, you should specify the option required. Options are almost always preceded by a hyphen. **ls -al** is an example of this kind of command.

```
Program name -option <input data >output
data
```

For this reason, file names may not begin with a hyphen. In order to increase the processing speed, a number of standard situations occur by default:

- As standard, the input comes from the keyboard. Output and error messages are normally sent to the screen.
- The standard options differ according to command. They have been formulated when the command was created and you are not able to alter them. For example, the command **ls** only produces a list of file names without any further information. You cannot change the **-l** option, which produces extended file data, into a standard value. However, UNIX recognizes other possibilities to solve this problem. We shall return to this topic later.
- If a standard value is meaningless, for instance, standard input in the command **ls** (display files in a directory), then a value has to be specified in the program. For **ls** this is the current directory. And with the print command **lp**, a certain printer has to be specified instead of standard output.

Thus, the actual structure of a command, especially with regard to the question which parameter is necessary or possible, depends on the commands of the program. Each program and its command structure is described in the manuals according to the following framework:

NAME	Command name, short description of the function.
SYNTAX/ SYNOPSIS	The basic structure of the command:

```
program_name [option...] name...
```

The square brackets indicate that the argument is optional. The points indicate that the parameter may be repeated several times. In its shortest form, the above command will be:

```
program_name
```

DESCRIPTION	Detailed description of the command functions.
EXAMPLES	Examples.
FILES	Files containing data which are important for the execution of the command.
SEE ALSO	Programs which have a resemblance to this one.
DIAGNOSTICS	Relevant error messages.
BUGS	Known errors in the program itself. Not all mistakes which occur can be easily explained.

Not all of these features are dealt with in every book. Sometimes authors add other features such as HINTS, WARNING, NOTE or AUTHOR. Examples are often omitted or are presented minimally. Help can be gained from the system itself by typing the instruction **help** or **man**, which stands for manual.

The command **man** is, of course, only useful when the relevant file is *online*, which means available on disk. This is not the case with all installations. The basic PC version of XENIX, for instance, is not supplied with an online manual. This has a practical reason: the manuals are so voluminous that they demand an enormous amount of disk space, in fact much more than is generally present on a normal PC.

If your version has a **man** file, you can activate it using the command:

```
$man topic
```

where 'topic' can be any UNIX command.

If you press <Return>, the screen will scroll line by line. If you press the spacebar, the information is displayed screen by screen. Do not be overwhelmed by the almost unlimited information. No-one expects you to apply it all or even remember it all. There is a large chance you will not even understand everything which is written, even though English is your native language. This is due to the fact that this type of manual is written as a supplement for experienced UNIX users.

In some UNIX systems, *help* will be present. The information is somewhat more concise compared to **man**. You can activate **help** using the command:

```
$help ls
```

If you are in a situation where you do not know how to proceed, you can activate the **help** feature with the option **stuck**.

```
$help stuck
```

We shall deal with the most important error messages before moving to the next section. We shall do this using the instruction **cal**. The correct syntax for the command is:

```
$cal [[month] year]
```

If you only specify the command **cal**, you will be shown a diary for the current month, perhaps supplemented by diaries for the previous and subsequent months, depending on which UNIX version you are using. We shall force an error message by deliberately using **cal** with invalid arguments.

```
$cal 9 9 9
usage: cal [[month] year]
$
```

The statement 'usage' indicates that you have specified
the wrong structure, in this case three arguments while
only two are permitted.

```
$cal 99999
Bad argument
$
```

In this case, you have specified an invalid parameter.
The highest year which you may enter is 9999.

```
$Cal 9 9999
Cal: not found
$
```

The program '*Cal*' does not exist. We have already
mentioned that UNIX distinguishes between capitals
and small letters. In this case, UNIX does not search for
the program *cal* but for one with the name *Cal*.

5.5   Using a second terminal to discontinue programs

Occasionally, you will find yourself in a situation where
you wish to discontinue a program running at your terminal. The command **KILL** is applicable here. Of
course, a precondition is that you are able to reach the
processor. If the current process blocks your terminal,
you will have to move to another terminal, since your
own user interface is inaccessible. If you are using a
PC, switch over to the second screen.

First activate the *cat* program on your screen.

```
$cat
```

Using <Alt-F2>, switch over to the second screen at your PC or move to a second terminal. Log in again using the same user name.

```
login: guest
Password:        <Return>

$who
guest      tty02   Dec 25 12.27
guest      tty01   Dec 25 12.25
```

Because more than one process is running, you must clearly indicate in the **KILL** command which process is to be discontinued. Each process has its own number, the *PID number*. You can find out this number by using the command **ps** (process status). If you enter this command without any options, a list of all current processes belonging to you will appear.

```
$ps
     PID   TTY   TIME COMMAND
      96    02   0:01 sh
     173    02   0:00 ps
$
```

In this case, what you require are the numbers of the processes at terminal tty01. This is done using the command **ps -t list**. Here 'list' represents a list of terminal numbers, for example, **01,02**. You may also use a space as a separator instead of a comma, if you place the list between inverted commas: **"01 02"**. The number of the terminal is sufficient. The terminal of the system manager, 'con' is also regarded as a number.

```
$ps -t 01
     PID   TTY   TIME COMMAND
      42    01   0:01 sh
     169    01   0:00 cat
$
```

The actual syntax of **ps** varies according to the system. On some, the terminal number must follow the **-t** without an intervening space and comma-separated lists are not permitted.

The program we wish to discontinue is *cat* with 169 as PID.

```
$KILL 168
KILL: no such process
$KILL 169
$
```

You made an unintentional typing error. Fortunately, there were no processes with PID 168. If that was the case, the wrong process would have been discontinued. The second attempt was successful. Return to the first terminal or go back to the first screen on your PC using <Alt-F2>. A message will be displayed there:

```
$cat
Terminated
$
```

The program has been ended. The prompt indicates that you can enter commands and data once more using this terminal.

The process is not ended by **KILL** itself. This sends a signal to the process. Normally, that is the signal **TERM** with the signal number 15. This represents a polite request to the current program to discontinue itself. Stubborn programs ignore such polite requests. In that case, you can intervene more directly. Give the command

```
KILL -9 PID_number
```

and a different signal will be sent to the current program, namely **KILL**, which has signal number 9. Subsequently, your screen will not display 'Terminated' but 'Killed'. It is self-evident that brutal conduct like this may have painful consequences. The current program has not been able to shut down its processes as it should. If this is a word processing program, you may lose your text. Recursive programs which start new processes themselves, are completely confused by the command **KILL -9**.

If you wish to end all processes, including those processes which have activated your processes, select zero as the process identification number. In this way, the signal number from the **KILL** command will be sent to all processes. If you give the command **KILL -9 0**, your shell is also ended and you will be logged out at the same time.

Unfortunately, even the KILL signal cannot always stop the current processes. If a process is jammed or frozen due to a hardware fault or faults in the device driver, the process is not able to discontinue itself.

The mischievous idea of discontinuing a process of another user has probably occurred to you in the meantime, even if it was only to see the surprise on your colleague's face. The option **-a** in conjuction with the command **ps** shows all current applications. Moreover, the option **-f** displays from whom the process is. The order of sequence when you specify the options makes no difference: **-fa** has the same significance as **-af**. If you are working alone on your computer, you will require a second user. We shall call him *Jasper*. Log in on the third screen as *Jasper* and activate the *cat* program. Switch back to the first screen (*tty01*) and try to terminate the process.

```
$ps -af
    UID   PID  PPID  C    STIME   TTY   TIME  COMMAND
Jasper   182   171  0  12:22:58   03   0:00  cat
 guest   185    42  4  12:23:10   01   0:00  ps -af
$KILL 182
KILL: 182: permission denied
```

As you may expect, you cannot just terminate the processes of other users. Only the system manager has that right. The abbreviations in the above example have the following significance:

UID   User Identification, the name or the num-
                 ber of the user.

PPID   Parent PID, the number of the process
                 which has activated the current process.

STIME   Start time, the time at which the process
                 began.

TIME   The amount of calculation time used by
                 the process up until now.

COMMAND   The command used to activate the pro-
                 cess.

The terms *program*, *process* and *command* have slightly different meanings. A **program** is a series of instructions which the computer can understand. These exist
as files on the harddisk. A **command** consists of the activation of a program by means of the user interface: the
program name with all the arguments which you type in
order to execute all kinds of tasks, is a command. The
execution of the program in the central unit may consist
of a number of **processes**, each of which implements a
separate program instruction.

Another option of the **ps** command which may be useful
to you is **-u user name**. If you log in at several terminals, you can use this option to get a survey of all the
processes which you have activated.

```
$who
Jasper     tty03   Dec 25 09.10
guest      tty02   Dec 25 08.00
guest      tty01   Dec 25 07.30
$ps -u guest
   PID    TTY    TIME   COMMAND
    42    01    0:01   sh
    96    02    0:01   sh
   187    01    0:00   ps
```

Caution   It has already been mentioned now and
                 again, but some extra emphasis will do no
                 harm: some UNIX systems only allow the
                 system manager to log in at one specific
                 terminal. It is of enormous importance that

this terminal does not hang. Do not be enticed into trying something out quickly at this terminal. Instead, log in as a normal user at another terminal, so that you are always able to gain access to the system as the system manager.

6   The harddisk

6.1   Saving text

The harddisk is used for storing programs, device drivers and collections of data. All this information is stored in *files*. A file must have a name so that you will always be able to retrieve it. For the sake of an orderly organization, the files are stored on the harddisk in *directories*, in which the file name and other information concerning the files is stored. The directories which are created by the operating system are also regarded as files: they have names and are part of another directory.

You are already familiar with the command which transports data from one device to another, for example, from the keyboard to the screen:

```
program name <input device >output device
```

Caution   **Under no circumstances should you use the above command structure to write data to the harddisk. Even if you had the right to do this, it could have extremely dire consequences.**

Various UNIX versions use different names for the harddisk. For example, **hd** (harddisk) means the same as **w** (Winchester drive) or **dsk** (disk). Many UNIX versions work with more than one harddisk: *hd0, hd1* or *dsk/0s0, dsk/1s0*. Each harddisk is again subdivided in partitions: *hd0a, hd0b* or *dsk/0s0, dsk/0s1*. Each of these patitions is regarded as a separate device.

Each partition on the harddisk (and on some diskettes) has its own file structure. Under UNIX, the file systems of these 'drives', depending on the circumstances, are united in one integrated, structured file system. In contrast to single-user systems (for example MS-DOS) UNIX does not recognize drives. Thus, when retrieving or saving files, you do not need to specify a drive. You only need to specify the file name in order to read the file, or, as in the example below, to save it:

```
program name <input device >file name
```

We shall now try this out using the command **cat**.

```
$cat>ebir
The early bird catches the worm.
<Ctrl-D>
$
```

The file name *ebir* stands for 'Early bird'. We advise you to always assign names to files so that you can remember the contents later without too much difficulty. The length of UNIX file names is system-dependent. On early systems they were limited to 14 characters but modern systems permit 256 characters or more. Accordingly, we could have named the file 'early bird'. However, lengthy file names are not really convenient and increase the chances of typing errors.

Caution   UNIX does allow invisible characters in file names, but it is advisable to avoid these since after several months you probably will forget precisely which character or characters you have employed in the file name. It is also advisable not to use spaces in file names as the UNIX shell will interpret a file name containing a space as two names.

If your system states that it is not able to create a file, this means that you are currently in a directory where you have no writing rights.

```
$cat>ebir
ebir: cannot create
$
```

If you are working on a PC, this should not happen if you have installed *Jasper* and *guest* as users from your position as system manager. On large UNIX systems, this problem may have a number of causes. We shall discuss these shortly. In the meantime, the best thing to do is ask the system manager for assistance.

Check if the *ebir* file has actually been saved on the harddisk. Use the command **cat** once more to do this.

```
$cat <ebir
The early bird catches the worm.
$
```

In this command, you may omit the smaller-than sign. If you omit one of the signs '<' or '>' in a command, UNIX will interpret the file name as input.

You can also send a saved text to another terminal. It is not essential that another user has logged in there.

```
$cat ebir >/dev/tty02
```

You can also use cat to copy a file:

```
$cat ebir >early
```

If you give the command

```
$cat eary
```

the system will state

```
cat: cannot open eary
```

You have made a typing error. The *eary* file cannot be opened because it does not exist.
The same situation arises if you press <Return> after **cat**, prior to specifying the file name. You have linked the standard input to the standard output, thus the keyboard to the screen. Do you remember? This is an existing command which we have discussed in section 5.1: press <Ctrl-D> (EOF) to indicate the completion of input. You may also press <Del> or <Ctrl-C> to discontinue the

current process. The prompt reappears and you can type the command again.

```
$cat early
The early bird catches the worm.
```

Before using a file name, you should check whether it already exists. Imagine a file already exists with the name 'early' - for example 'early to bed and early to rise makes hay while the sun shines'. If you now wish to save another text under the name 'early' using the **cat** command, you will irretrievably lose the original text.

```
$cat >early
What about the early worm?
<Ctrl-D>
$cat early
What about the early worm?
$
```

UNIX has carried out your instructions without any further warning. You have now lost the original proverb. Single-user systems frequently have all kinds of utilities to restore lost file contents. However, the multi-user UNIX system does not have this capability.

If you wish to add text to an existing file, use a double output sign: >>.

```
$cat ebir >> early
$cat early
The early bird catches the worm.
What about the early worm?
$
```

You can also create empty files under UNIX. The file name is then registered, but there is nothing (as yet) in the file.

```
$cat empfile
<Ctrl-D>
$
```

You can now check whether the file really exists.

```
$cat empfile
$
```

The command is implemented without any problem. This is indicated by the absence of the error message **cannot open empfile**.

6.2   The contents of directories

There is yet another way of checking whether the *empfile* file from the previous section actually exists. Using the **ls** command, you can have a list of all files in the current directory (the directory in which you are working) displayed on the standard output device, the screen.

```
$ls
early
ebir
empfile
$
```

The file names are shown in alphabetical order. In order to examine whether empfile really is empty, you require additional information concerning the files. Using the option **-l** (long) you can display this.

```
$ls -l
-rw-r--r--  1 guest   guests    26 Dec 25 10:47 early
-rw-r--r--  1 guest   guests    32 Dec 25 10:43 ebir
-rw-r--r--  1 guest   guests     0 Dec 25 10:49 empfile
$
```

The empfile contains no characters, early contains 26 and ebir contains 32. All files belong to the *guest* user who belongs to the *guests user group*. The *empfile* file was most recently saved on the 25th of December at 11 minutes to 11. The system does not show whether the file already existed previously.

At the extreme left-hand side there are codes which indicate the sort of files being shown. A single dash indicates a normal file. Normal files are programs or texts.

Subsequently, there are nine signs made up of three
groups of three. These represent the reading, writing
and execution rights in relation to these files.

sign	significance	explanation
r	reading allowed	'r' for *read*
w	writing allowed	'w' for *write*
x	usage allowed	'x' for *execute*

If a dash is shown instead of a letter, this means that the
corresponding right is not available.

The three groups show the rights of various users.

sign	user entitlement
1-3	the owner
4-6	other users from the same user group
7-9	other users

The term 'owner' has mere technical significance here,
legally it has no value.

The user rights for a program could be, for instance:
rw-r--r-x. This means that the owner and the other users
from his/her group may not use the program in contrast to
all other users. This is, of course, an absurd situation, but
it does make it plain that the owner is not automatically entitled to rights of usage which other users may have.

A text can always be distinguished from a program by
the absence of the code x, which indicates that the file is
a program which can be executed. A text can never be
executed independently.

The number '*1*' which is placed between the rights of access and the owner's name indicates the amount of

names which the file has. In fact, a file may have several names in the system. You can link a second name to a file using the **ln** command. In the example shown below, we have linked a second name *morning* to the *ebir* file.

```
$ln ebir morning
$ls -l
-rw-r--r--  1 guest     guests     26 Dec 25 10:47 early
-rw-r--r--  2 guest     guests     32 Dec 25 10:43 ebir
-rw-r--r--  1 guest     guests      0 Dec 25 10:49 empfile
-rw-r--r--  2 guest     guests     32 Dec 25 10:43 morning
$
```

Thus, the syntax for the command is

```
ln first name second name
```

The construction indicates a fundamental difference between a multi-user and a single-user system. In the latter, you can only create a **new** file with **identical** contents if you wish to have a file with two names. However, this costs disk capacity, while the possibilities remain limited. When one program can have and can recognize several files names, the specific name used to activate the program can eliminate the necessity of of defining options.

UNIX itself makes extensive use of this. The commands **ln** and **mv** both activate the same program. What exactly happens then depends on the command: **mv** (move) assigns a file to another directory and/or alters the name of the file if required. This depends on the arguments which you specify along with the command. Both **mv** and **ln** have the same syntax:

```
mv first_name second_name
```

In the example below, we shall use the command to change the name *morning* to *catch*. We shall not specify a new directory, thus the file will remain in the current directory.

```
$mv morning catch
$ls -l
-rw-r--r--  2 guest    guests    32 Dec 25 10:43 catch
-rw-r--r--  1 guest    guests    26 Dec 25 10:47 early
-rw-r--r--  2 guest    guests    32 Dec 25 10:43 ebir
-rw-r--r--  1 guest    guests     0 Dec 25 10:49 empfile
$
```

UNIX treats files differently than single-user systems do. In order to understand **ln** and **mv** you should know that UNIX separates the information concerning a file from the file name. The data are stored in two locations: all file data excepting the file name are stored in the first location; the second location, for instance, your own directory, contains the file name and a reference number for the data. A memory location like this, containing information about a file, is called an *i-node* (identification node) under UNIX. Using the option **-i**, you can display the reference numbers of your files.

```
$ls -i
 110 catch
1147 early
 110 ebir
 421 empfile
```

This lists clearly indicates that the names *catch* (previously *morning*) and *ebir* refer to the same file. What you now see on the screen is all that is in your own directory. File names are linked to file numbers. The file number refers to the i-node in the *i-node list*.

/usr/guest		i-node-list

catch	110
early	1147
ebir	110
empfile	421

| 107 |
| 108 |
| 109 |
| 110 | aa bb cc dd ee ff gg hh ii |
| 111 |

The *inode* contains all information about a file:

- The file mode which indicates the type of file and the way the rights are regulated.
- The link counter which indicates the amount of names under which the file is stored.
- The user number of the owner.
- The group number.
- The size of the file in bytes.
- The addresses of the disk sectors in which the file is stored.
- The date when the file was most recently used, i.e. was read or executed.
- The date when the file was created or most recently modified.
- The date when the inode was most recently modified because something was written to the file or because the user rights, the owner or the user group were altered.

Thus, the **-l** option does not display all stored data. Matters such as sector addresses where a file is stored are really of no interest to the user. The only factor which may be important is that on early versions of UNIX only the first 10 Kb of data are addressed via the inode. This means that you can read these 10 Kb very quickly. The larger the file, the longer it takes to gain access to the data, since this occurs in two, three or four stages.

In order to discover when the *ebir* file was last used, add the option **-u** (used) to the **ls** command. You can also use this option to request a survey of the entire directory, but now you only wish to display the one file. For this reason, you should now add the file name.

```
$ls -lu ebir
-rw-r--r--  2 guest    guests    32 Dec 25 12:03 ebir
$
```

The date when the inode was last altered can be shown by applying the option **-c** (changed). In our example, you

altered the inode when you linked a second name to the
file, and when you subsequently changed the name.

```
$ls -lc ebir
-rw-r--r-- 2 guest   guests      32 Dec 25 10:50 ebir
$
```

Compare this time to the moment when you created or
modified the *ebir* file.

```
$ls -l ebir
-rw-r--r-- 2 guest   guests      32 Dec 25 10:43 vrvo
$
```

You may use all characters in a file name including invisible ones. This causes problems when you wish to
address the file. Create a file with a name containing an
invisible character, for example, <Ctrl-a>. If you request a
directory using the instruction **ls**, there is no trace of any
invisible characters. The example below illustrates this.

```
$cat >abc<Ctrl-a>d
This is a test
<Ctrl-D>
$ls
abcd
...
$
```

We have specified the operating code <Ctrl-a> in the file
name, but it appears as though the file is just called
abcd. If you attempt to open the file using the name on
the screen, UNIX will be unable to do so.

```
$cat abcd
cat: cannot open abcd
$
```

Probably after an error message such as this, you will
remember that you have included an invisible character

in the name. But if that is not the case, you will have to search. In this, the option **-q** may help you. This replaces all invisible signs with question marks.

```
$ls -q
abc?d
...
$
```

Using the option **-b**, you can find out the missing character. This option displays the invisible characters in octal value.

```
$ls -b
abc\001d
...
$
```

In appendix B, there is a table in which you can find the significance of the octal values: under ASCII values in the octal column, you will find the operating code <Ctrl-a> next to 001. Using the command **mv**, you can now assign another name to the file, for example abcd (without the operating code). Do not be disconcerted by the display on the screen. Although you type *mv abc<Ctrl-a>d abcd*, on the screen you will see *mv abcd abcd*, since <Ctrl-a> does not generate a visible character.

```
$mv abc<Ctrl-a>d abcd
$cat abcd
This is a test
$
```

Finally, we shall discuss a hidden file. The option **-A** displays that on the screen. Pay attention to the exceptional way of typing this option - with a capital letter.

```
$ls -lA
-rw-r-----  1 guest    guests    509 Sep 28 18:47 .profile
-rw-r--r--  2 guest    guests     32 Dec 25 10:43 ebir
...
$
```

The *.profile* file has not appeared on your screen as yet because the file name begins with a dot. File names which begin with a dot are normally not shown on the screen. We shall discuss the convenience of this construction shortly. The *.profile* file has an exceptional function: it is a program which is executed when you log in. For this reason, no *x* may be placed next to the rights of access. If you were to start this part of the login procedure while you are already logged in, some strange things could occur.

6.3   Directories

Directories are themselves part of other directories. The position of your own directory has also been determined. Using the **-d** option together with the **ls** command, you can display information about the current directory on the screen.

```
$ls -ld
drwxr-x--x  2 guest  guests  160 Dec 25
07.45 .
```

The first character (*d*) indicates that we are dealing with a directory here. You can gain information concerning the current directory by specifying the option **-d**. Most data files with which you will be working are located in your own directory (the working directory).

Your programs will mostly find the data with which you wish to work, in the working directory. The processed data will probably be stored here also.

There is no need to assign a name to the working directory. A dot (.) is used to represent the name of the current directory. This is a very practical arrangement, since no items with a dot are displayed. In addition, typing is very easy.

The above directory belongs to the *guest* user. He may, as can be seen by referring to the user rights, execute programs, read files and write to files.

The right of access to a directory implies the right to switch to this directory from another directory. Of course, the right of access to a directory does not mean that you are entitled to read, write or execute a file. For this, you must have the appropriate rights to the file itself. If you have these rights for a file, the absence of the right of access to a directory can override these. You cannot read, alter or execute any of the files in this directory or switch to this directory or any of its subdirectories. The right of access to a directory is often referred to, a little confusingly, as 'search right'. Here, the term 'user right' is applied.

Although the other users in the *guests* user group may execute programs and read files, they may not write data to files in this directory. Other users may only execute programs from this directory; they are not even allowed to request a list of the files in this directory on the screen. In practice, this implies that they must know in advance exactly what they are looking for. We shall discuss this topic in more depth in section 6.8.

There are ten files stored in the directory. This is indicated by the size of the directory: 160 bytes. You may be surprised that the registration of ten files only occupies 160 bytes, although much information is stored in these files. But you have forgotten that this registration is only a specification of the i-nodes. Each file requires 16 bytes for the registration of the name and the number which refers to the inode.

The link counter shows 2 since the current directory is a subdirectory. Thus there is also a registration in the parent directory. UNIX makes use of this: in the directory itself, the name appears as a dot in the parent directory (the directory of which our directory is a subdirectory) the 'real' name is given.

This real name (a relative concept, of course) can be discovered using the command **pwd** (print working directory).

```
$pwd
/usr/guest
$
```

The result */usr/guest* is not very surprising.
If, for any reason, you are not in your own directory, use
the command **cd** (change directory) without arguments.
This returns you to the directory into which you were
placed when you logged in. That is the directory which
the system manager has assigned to you as *HOME*. In
chapter 8, we shall deal more extensively with the environment in which you are working as a user. If you give
the **pwd** command once more, the response must be
/usr/guest.

The last option which we shall deal with is **-a**. A list of all
files on the directory is displayed using this command,
thus including the directory names.

```
$ls -la
drwxr-x--x   2 guest    guests    160 Dec 25 07.45 .
drwxr-xr-x  15 bin      bin       256 Sep 27 09:23 ..
-rw-r-----   1 guest    guests    509 Sep 28 18:47 .profile
-rw-r--r--   1 guest    guests     14 Dec 25 11:15 abcd
-rw-r--r--   1 guest    guests     26 Dec 25 10:47 early
-rw-r--r--   1 guest    guests      0 Dec 25 10:49 empfile
-rw-r--r--   2 guest    guests     32 Dec 25 10:43 catch
-rw-r--r--   2 guest    guests     32 Dec 25 10:43 ebir
$
```

A new element here is the directory indicated by the two
dots. This is the directory of which the current directory
is a subdirectory. These are called the *parent directory*
and the *child directory*.

Here is a summary of the **ls** command with all options:

command	result
ls -l	Display the contents of the current directory (without .names).
ls -ld	Display data about the current directory itself.
ls -la	Display all files in the directory, including directory names.
ls -l dir.name	Display contents of named directory.
ls -ld dir.name	Display data about named directory.
ls -la dir.name	Display all files in the named directory.
ls -i	Display the file names and file numbers.
ls -l file	Display information about the named file.
ls -lu file	Display the time when the file (name) was last modified.
ls -lc file	Display the time when the file (name) inode was last changed.
ls -q	Display all files including invisible characters (which are shown as question marks).
ls -b	Display all files including invisible characters (which are shown as octal numbers).
ls -lA	Show all files including hidden files.

Other UNIX systems may have slightly different options. Type **man ls** to see these.

6.4   The UNIX directory tree

In appearance, UNIX has a directory structure in which all files are neatly arranged, providing the user with an orderly view. The reality is, in fact, otherwise: UNIX stores files wherever there is room on the diskette or on the harddisk. The data concerning these addresses is then saved in the inode list where all files on a diskette or a slice of the harddisk are registered. Each diskette and each slice of the harddisk has its own inode list.

6.4.1 The hierarchical structure of directories

When you activate a file, this is done via a directory. This appears to contain the whole file but it is only the file name and a reference number for the inode. The user sees only the directory. The file system seems to be a neatly ordered entity: the root directory is at the top with a number of subdirectories under it. Under these are more subdirectories. As a whole, this structure resembles an inverted tree, which explains the name, *directory tree*. This division into levels characterizes the structure as a hierarchical system.

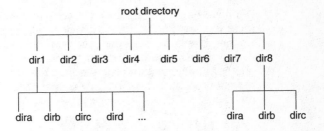

The structure of the directory tree still remains intact when you add new disks. Each new disk has its own structure, but this is appended to the tree as a whole. In the example above, *dr8* for instance could be a new disk. As a user, you will not notice anything of this process: UNIX does not recognize drives as single-user systems do.

Imagine that *dira* is your working directory, then *dir1* is the directory *usr*. The root directory is represented by the first slash (/) and the full directory name is indeed: */usr/guest*. A full name always contains, in addition to the name, the *path* from the root directory to the file: */usr/guest/ebir*, for example. The first slash represents the *root* directory, the other slashes are no more than separators.

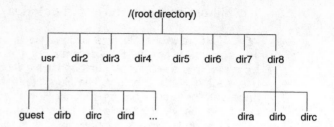

6.4.2   Switching to a parent directory

We have defined the parent directory as being the directory of which the current directory, your own *guest* working directory, is a subdirectory. In this case, thus, that is the *usr* directory. The command used to move to another directory is **cd**. The parent directory is always represented by two points. Thus the complete command is

```
$cd ..
$
```

The system does not display any changes, and this can be tedious since you do not know whether the command has been implemented or not. However, using the command **pwd**, you can discover the name of the current directory.

```
$pwd
/usr
```

The command has indeed been executed. In general, UNIX only displays messages when something has gone wrong. If you give the command **cd** once more, this time without including a space between the command and the directory name, the following will occur:

```
$cd..
cd..: not found
```

In this respect, UNIX is much more strict than, for example, MS-DOS where you may type the two points immediately behind the command. Accordingly, you should type

```
$cd ..
$pwd
/
```

6.4.3   The root directory

You are now in the root directory. The abbreviated way of writing this is using only a slash. You could have moved immediately to this directory by typing the command **cd /.** Specify the instruction **ls -l** in order to examine the files in the root.

```
$ls -l
drwxr-xr-x    2 bin    bin      2032 Feb 22   1989 bin
drwxr-xr-x    5 bin    bin      2272 Feb 22   1989 dev
drwxr-xr-x    5 bin    bin      1504 Aug 25  19:00 etc
drwxr-xr-x    2 bin    bin        64 Feb 22   1989 lib
drwx------    2 bin    bin      1024 Feb 22   1989 lost+found
drwxr-xr-x    2 bin    bin        32 Feb 22   1989 mnt
drwxrwxrwx    2 bin    bin       336 Nov 20  15:06 tmp
drwxr-xr-x   15 bin    bin       256 Nov 19  18:00 usr
-rw-r--r--    1 bin    bin    349625 Feb 22   1989 UNIX
$
```

We can now complete the directory tree.

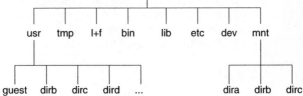

We have greatly simplified the directory tree. In a well-organized system, you will find many more directories. However, the directories shown in the example are always part of the structure. They form the basic set supplied along with UNIX. The *usr* directory will probably deviate much more. The way the structure ultimately appears depends entirely on the manner in which UNIX has been installed on your computer. Nevertheless, the structure illustrated above can always be recognized.

In general, only the operating system is stored in the root. When the system is well-managed, you will encounter no other files in this directory, unless the operating system requires a couple of supplementary files. For instance, XENIX makes use of the *boot*, *dos* and *sfmt* programs in addition to the operating system.

The **boot** program is automatically activated as the first program, and this asks whether DOS or XENIX should be loaded. The letters **sfmt** represent system file maintenance. This program has the function of controlling the file management. A system crash, due for instance to a power failure, is recognized by this program and it then attempts to repair the damage caused by this. The programs are loaded and activated by the system itself. No *x* will be displayed at the rights of access position, in order to prevent the system manager starting them while the system is already running.

The other items in the root directory are directories. We shall deal with them below.

Since files and directories must always have an owner under UNIX, a pseudo-owner *bin* has been created for those files which are accessible to everyone. *Bin* is an abbreviation of binary, the language in which machine code is written. In addition to *bin* there are more of this type of user. We shall discuss this later.

6.4.4 The directory /lost+found

You will not be successful if you try to activate the lost+found directory:

```
$cd lost+found
lost+found: bad directory
$
```

In this case, the error message **bad directory** does not indicate that the directory does not exist, it means you have no right of access. If you examine the rights of access in the list in the previous section, you will see that only the system manager is allowed to work in this directory. Normally, this directory is empty. If the system manager uses the *fsck* (file system check) program to check the entire file system, programs without names or containing faults are stored in this directory.

6.4.5 The directories /tmp and /usr/tmp

The second directory which deviates from the others with respect to rights of access is the */tmp* directory. The name represents 'temporary'.
In this directory, data is stored temporarily while you are working with programs. You will not notice this, it all takes place in the dark recesses of the machine. Many programs, *vi* for instance, have been developed in such a way that they automatically make a backup of texts on which you are working so that a power failure need not be disastrous. In a situation like this, you will then only lose the most recent modifications. That is also the reason that all users have all rights of access to this directory. You will also find yet another */tmp* directory in the */usr* directory.

The remaining directories in the root only provide users with rights of executing and reading files. The only person entitled to write in these directories is the system manager.
You are already familiar with two of these directories:

/usr and */dev*. All device drivers are located in */dev*. The */usr* directory contains many subdirectories. We shall deal with these in the following sections.

6.4.6   The /dev directory

Type the following commands to enter the */dev* directory and to examine its contents:

```
$cd dev
$ls -l
. . .
$[]
```

The system provides a survey of all device drivers and directories with device drivers. This list is so large that the first lines scroll off your screen before you have had time to read them. You can freeze the display using <Ctrl-s>. You can continue using <Ctrl-q> (and sometimes using a random key).

The device drivers are not very important to you as user in general. In order to give you some idea of what they do, we shall quickly discuss a few basic principles.

In the /dev directory you will encounter two new types of file:

```
brw-------    2 sysinfo  sysinfo    1, 0 Feb 22 1993   hd00
crw--w--w-    1 guest    guests     0, 0 Dec 25 11:38 tty01
```

These are called 'special files' and refer to devices which tranport data either in blocks, or character by character. The former type transports data in exact blocks, for example, blocks of 512 bytes. These are indicated by a '**b**'.
In the XENIX version of UNIX, this is, for example, the device *hd00*, in other systems this may be *hd0a* or *w0a*. This refers to the first partition of the first harddisk (hd stands for harddisk, w for winchester disk). The link

counter for this disk partition is two in the case of XENIX since the more recent reference to this partition is dsk/0s0. In the /dsk directory there is a list of all partitions on the harddisk. 0s0 refers to: the first harddisk (0), first partition (slice 0).

Devices which transport data character by character are indicated by a 'c'. Terminals and printers, for instance, work in this way.

You may already know that data transport takes place either serial or parallel. Terminals are linked to the computer via a *serial interface* and printers are generally linked to the computer via a *parallel interface*. This deals with the way a **single character** is transported. A character is composed of an eight-bit structure. In the case of a serial interface, the *bits* are transported consecutively through one cable. In the case of a parallel interface, all eight bits are transported simultaneously along eight cables.
Thus, data transport has at least two aspects: the technical (physical) aspect determines how the transport occurs, and the organizational (logical) aspect determines how many characters are transmitted at one time.

This has no bearing on the */dev* directory list. Here, only the *logical* aspect of the transport is important.

Examine the device specification more closely. Between the registration of user group and the date of the most recent modification, there are two device numbers which are separated by a comma. The first number represents the type of device, the second number represents the specific device in that group.

The special files for diskette stations are called, for example, *fd0* and *fd1* or *fdsk/0* and *fdsk/1*. Printers are registered under the names *1p0* or *printer0* for example. These indications differ according to the system. The working memory for the user is */dev/mem*, and the memory which is reserved for the *kernel*, thus the working memory range for the operating system, is called *kmem.* We shall discuss the specification of the *swap device* extensively in the section dealing with the installation of UNIX/XENIX.

The device driver */dev/null* has practical significance. If you send the input from */dev/null* to a file, only an EOF character will be placed in that file. Thus, a file is created but nothing is written to it. If this file actually exists and contains data, the contents will be lost as a result of this action. If you wish to try this out, you should return to your own directory temporarily.

```
$cd
$pwd
/usr/guest
$ls -l abcd
-rw-r--r--    1  guest   guests  18  Dec 25  11:15  abcd
$cat </dev/null >abcd
-rw-r--r--    1  guest   guests   0  Dec 25  14:13  abcd
$cd /dev
```

/dev/null is also useful if this process is reversed and it is used as an output device. Imagine you wish to test a program which produces a mass of data. The output is unimportant since you are only concerned with the smooth operation of the program itself. *stdout* and *stderr* are the screen: this means that output and error messages are displayed on the screen together. If you send the output to *>/dev/null* it will disappear into nothing and only the error messages, if any, will be shown on the screen.

If you are working on a PC, you will encounter special files for the screen: *mono, cga, ega,* and *vga* are all special files for the video part of the system. The cga device has three categories: *color, colour* and *pga.* Accordingly, with *cga,* the link counter shows 4. All four special files are identical and so are the device numbers. In this example they are 52 and 2. The rights of access at the extreme left are also the same in all cases.

```
crw-rw-rw-   2 bin    bin    52,  1 Feb 22  1989 mono
crw-rw-rw-   2 bin    bin    52,  1 Feb 22  1989 mono-
chrome
crw-rw-rw-   4 bin    bin    52,  2 Feb 22  1989 cga
crw-rw-rw-   4 bin    bin    52,  2 Feb 22  1989 color
crw-rw-rw-   4 bin    bin    52,  2 Feb 22  1989 colour
crw-rw-rw-   4 bin    bin    52,  2 Feb 22  1989 pga
crw-rw-rw-   1 bin    bin    52,  4 Feb 22  1989 ega
crw-rw-rw-   1 bin    bin    52,  5 Feb 22  1989 vga
```

6.4.7   The /mnt directory

Quit the */dev* directory and activate the */mnt* directory.
The most easy way to do this is to give the command **cd
/mnt** directly from */dev*.

```
$cd /mnt
$pwd
/mnt
$
```

You can check the contents of the directory using the
command **ls -la**.
The PC UNIX user will immediately notice that the directory only contains two items, since the volume is a
mere 32 bytes. This means that the directory is empty;
these items consist of the names of the directory itself
and that of the parent directory.

The */mnt* directory is a mounting point for another harddisk partition or for a diskette. The command used by
the system manager to make this connection is called
mount.
The system manager has the freedom to choose any
name for the mount directories.

If you are working in a larger system, the other slices of
the harddisk are undoubtedly linked via other directory
names. In that case, you probably will not find a */mnt* directory.

6.4.8   The /etc directory

The *etc* directory is reserved for the system manager.
The programs and data required for system management are stored in this directory. A list of the stored files
can be displayed by giving the command **ls**. Because
this will scroll at enormous speed over your screen, add
the option **-C**. The output is then arranged in columns.
The option **-F** provides an indication of the type of files.
Programs are indicated by an asterisk, directories by a
slash. Files without further signs are data files.

```
$cd /etc
$pwd
/etc
$ls -CF
...
```

The program *mount** for example, which we mentioned
in the previous section, should be located here in the
middle of the files. If you installed XENIX yourself, you
will recognize the programs *fdisk*, badtrk*, divvy** and
custom*. If you have followed this book as system manager, you will also recognize *cron*, shutdown** and *halt-
sys**.

You will also find the user file *passwd* among the files.
Examine the contents of this file. Alas, this will not help
you very much since the passwords are registered in
coded form. If the file is very lengthy, and when you
apply the command **cat passwd** the information scrolls
off your screen before the end has been reached, you
can use the options **more** or **pg**. The **more** command
displays the file (not directory) contents on the screen
page by page. By pressing the <Return> key, you can
move the file over the screen one line at a time and by
pressing the spacebar you can display a new page on
the screen.

```
$more passwd
...
bin:NOLOGIN:3:3:System file administration:/:
```

```
guest:.SkNzvAnG0JbA:2001:51::/usr/guest:/bin/sh
$
```

The command **pg** is more convenient than **more** but it is not available on all systems. The program also provides help if you type an **h** behind the colon and then press <Return>. The following line is shown by specifying **l**, the first page by specifying **1**, and a new page is displayed on the screen by pressing <Return>.

```
$pg passwd
...
bin:NOLOGIN:3:3:System file administration:/:
guest:.SkNzvAnG0JbA:2001:51::/usr/guest:/bin/sh
(EOF):
```

You conclude **pg** by pressing <Return> after the statement (EOF). The help screen is closed by specifying **\n** or pressing <Return>.

The user input consists of seven fields, separated by colons.

1   The first field contains the user name, *guest*.
2   The coded password. Each password is coded independently of the others, therefore it is useless to try to find similarities in order to discover the key. Even identical passwords are coded differently.
3   The user number.
4   The group number.
5   The comment field. Your comment field is empty.
6   The login directory.
7   The program started at the login procedure is the Bourne shell (*sh*) in your case.

There is another file called *group* in this directory, which gives a summary of all user groups and all their users.

```
$more group
...
bin:x:3:bin,lp
guests::51:guest,Jasper
```

A message, *motd* (message of the day), is shown on the screen every time you log in. The message is also stored in this directory. You can examine it by giving the command **cat motd**.

If you are the system manager, you can change this message. The message which is supplied by the manufacturer will probably irritate you eventually. Log in as system manager (root) at the second terminal and enter the */etc* directory. Then assign another name to the motd file, for instance, motd.org. From this moment onwards, the message will no longer appear on the screen. Of course, you can always create a message of the day yourself using the command **cat>motd**.

```
#cd /etc
#mv motd motd.org
#cat >motd
And now for something completely different!
<Ctrl-D>
#
```

If you also wish to get rid of the *systemid*, the name of your system, proceed in the same way.

```
#cat systemid
xenix 386
#mv systemid systemid.org
#cat >systemid
early worm inc.
<Ctrl-D>
#
```

Using **cat systemid** or **cat /etc/systemid**, as a normal user, you can find out the name of your system.

```
$cat systemid
early worm inc.
```

You have also probably discovered the *profile* file. A similar file, preceded by a dot, is also located in your own directory. All commands which are located in that

file are automatically executed during the login procedure. However, the profile file in */etc,* containing commands which apply to all users, is executed prior to
login.

6.4.9   The /lib and /usr/lib directories

The abbreviation *lib* represents library. In both directories you will find a library containing program mod-
ules. These are the building bricks with which programs
are constructed. You should imagine programs, text
and tables when thinking of these building bricks. It is
not very meaningful to discuss these as yet at this stage
in this book.

Before dealing with the following two directories, we
wish to offer a word of advice: do not become disheart-
ened by the abundance of directories, programs and
data files which are discussed. You do not need to remember them all in order to be able to work with the
system. What you should retain from this survey is an
insight into the way in which the system is constructed.
This is an important precondition of getting to grips with
the system.

6.4.10   The /bin and /usr/bin directories

Change to the */bin* directory and display a list of files on
the screen.

The programs with which you are already acquainted
are shown in bold letters. Now enter the */usr/bin* directory.

```
$cd /usr/bin
$pwd
/usr/bin
$ls -CF
. . .
$
```

```
$cd /bin
$ls -C
STTY      cp        dump      grep      lr        ps        sh        tty
[         cpio      dumpdir   grpcheck  ls        pstat     sleep     uname
awk       csh       echo      hd        lx        pwadmin   sort      uniq
backup    csplit    ed        head      mesg      pwcheck   stty      vedit
banner    date      edit      hello     mkdir     pwd       su        vi
basename  dc        egrep     id        mv        red       sum       vidi
cal       dd        enable    ipcrm     ncheck    restor    sync      view
cat       df        env       ipcs      newgrp    restore   tail      wc
chgrp     diff      ex        join      nice      rm        tar       who
chmod     diff3     expr      kill      nl        rmdir     tee       whodo
chown     dircmp    false     l         nohup     rsh       telinit   write
chroot    dirname   fgrep     lc        od        sddate    test      xargs
cmchk     disable   file      ld        passwd    sdiff     touch     yes
cmp       dparam    find      lf        pg        sed       tr
comm      dtype     fsck      line      pr        setkey    true
copy      du        getopt    ln        printenv  settime   tset
```

You will again see approximately 100 programs, including *help* and *more* and, if you are on a XENIX system,
also the program *sysadmsh* which is the menu-operated user interface for the system manager. The programs in this directory are all application programs.

It is self-evident that we cannot discuss all these programs just in case you might need one of them some-
time. It is sufficient to know where you can find them. In
the course of time, you will learn to use a number of
these.

You will soon see that you can link the workings of
these programs by means of the shell. In addition, due
to the fact that the working of some of these programs
may be programmed and the shell has a powerful programming language available, you can carry out many
programming tasks without having to use Pascal, C or
another higher programming language.

6.4.11   The /usr directory

Activate the */usr* directory and display a survey on the
screen. In this, you should use the **-x** and **-F** options.
The -x option displays information in adjacent columns
on the screen, -C places the information in a list.

```
$cd /usr
$pwd
/usr
$ls -xF
adm/    backup/    bin/    guest/    lib/    news/
pub/    spool/     sys/    sysadm/   tmp/    Jasper/
$[]
```

Jasper and *guest* are user directories. We have already mentioned the *tmp*, *bin* and *lib* directories. *Adm, backup* and *sysadm* are used in the system management. The *pub* directory contains characters sets. Messages are stored in *news* which is accessible to everyone. Finally, *sys* is used in order to reconfigure the system.

The *spool* directory has a number of subdirectories which serve as temporary storage depots for data.

```
$cd spool
$ls -xF
cron/   lp/   lpd/     mail/    uucp/     uucppublic/
$
```

- ■ You can find post which is addressed to you in */usr/spool/**mail**/*guest.
- ■ Data which are waiting to be processed by the printer are temporarily stored in */usr/spool/**lp***.
- ■ Tables which are used to activate programs at a certain time are located in */usr/spool/**cron***.
- ■ The */usr/spool/**uucp*** directory serves as support for data exchange with other UNIX systems (***uucp*** is an abbreviation for UNIX to UNIX copy).

6.4.12   The complete directory tree

We introduced a diagrammatic directory tree in section 6.4.1. We can now fill it in completely.

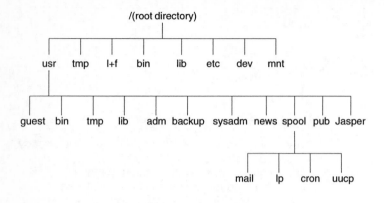

6.5   Your own directory tree

Return to your own directory by giving the command **cd**
without arguments. You can then create as many subdirectories as you wish, and also subdirectories of these
subdirectories. The number of directories you create
depends, of course, on what you intend to do. It is advisable to avoid both extremes. If you restrict yourself to
making two or three directories to store all your files,
you will soon lose your overview: the only way to display
all files is to print them; they will not all fit onto the
screen if the directory is too full.
But too many directories also has its disadvantages.
You can't see the wood for the trees, and you will have
to spend en excessive amount of time looking before
you find the right file. Compare this to an office in which
all letters, dossiers, reminders and memos are stored in
either two gigantic drawers which is chaotic, or each in
its own drawer along the wall which is neat and orderly
but unworkable.

Accordingly, it is sensible to spend time and effort in de-
signing a suitable directory structure. You may create
as many levels as you require. Keep in mind that the
path names will become increasingly lengthy. For this
reason alone, it is advisable to make the directory
names as short as possible.

The command used to create a new directory is **mkdir** (make directory). The syntax is:

```
mkdir name [name...]
```

To begin with, create directories for letters (*let*), games (*game*) and ready-made programs (*bin*, since they are in binary code). Make a directory (*prov*) for your collection of proverbs.

```
$cd
$pwd
/usr/guest
$mkdir let bin game prov
ls -l
-rw-r--r--  1 guest    guests      0 Dec 25 14:13 abcd
drwxr-xr-x  2 guest    guests     32 Dec 25 07:50 bin
-rw-r--r--  2 guest    guests     32 Dec 25 10:43 catch
-rw-r--r--  1 guest    guests     26 Dec 25 10:47 early
-rw-r--r--  2 guest    guests     32 Dec 25 10:43 ebir
-rw-r--r--  1 guest    guests      0 Dec 25 10:49 empfile
drwxr-xr-x  2 guest    guests     32 Dec 25 07:50 game
drwxr-xr-x  2 guest    guests     32 Dec 25 07:50 let
drwxr-xr-x  2 guest    guests     32 Dec 25 07:50 prov
$
```

6.6   Reorganizing the directory tree

Good management entails continually removing that which does not belong in your directories or which has become superfluous, for instance, the *empfile* file which is not in use, and the *games* directory. In order to delete a directory, use the command **rmdir** (remove directory). The syntax is

```
$rmdir name [name...]
```

If you only type the command on its own, you will receive an error message which indicates the correct syntax:

```
$rmdir
rmdir: usage: rmdir dirname...
```

Many programs give indications like this as to the proper usage of commands. If you wish to know more about this command, consult the help screen or manual using **help rmdir** or **man rmdir**.

Prior to really deleting a directory, we shall first deal with two common error messages:

1   You have specified a file name instead of a directory:

```
$rmdir early
rmdir: early not a directory
```

2   You have used the **rm** command, which is used to delete files, to try to delete a directory instead of **rmdir**. Fortunately, there is no file called *game* otherwise you would have lost it irretrievably without warning.

```
$rm game
rm: game non-existent
```

Now delete the game directory.

```
$rmdir game
```

If you now display a survey of the contents of the directory on the screen using the command **ls -l**, the *game* directory will have disappeared. An examination to check this is not necessary since the **rmdir** command only deletes empty directories. Subsequently, delete the empfile file.

```
$rm empfile
```

If you make a typing mistake, an error message will appear.

```
$rm impfile
rm: impfile non-existent
```

If you wish to prevent accidental deletion of the wrong file, add the **-i** option to the **rm** command. Answer the safeguard question by typing 'y' if you are sure. Any other keystroke cancels the command.

The *catch* file is identical to the *ebir* file and therefore may be deleted. The *abcd* file is also an empty file and it too can be deleted.

```
$rm -i catch abcd
catch? y
abcd? y
$ls catch abcd
catch not found
abcd not found
```

The two remaining files, *early* and *ebir*, form the beginning of a new collection of proverbs. You can move them to the prov directory using the **mv** command.

```
$mv ebir prov
$ls -l
...
drwxr-xr-x  2 guest    guests     48 Dec 26 08:20 prov
```

The *ebir* file has probably been moved to the *prov* directory since it has disappeared from the current directory and no error message has been given. In addition, the *prov* directory has become larger: 48 instead of 32 bytes and the time of the most recent modification has altered.

The *early* file should also be moved to the *prov* directory but because you wish to have an oversight of all proverbs there, you wish to change the name.

```
$mv early prov/allprov
$ls -l
drwxr-xr-x  2 guest    guests     32 Dec 27 07:50 bin
drwxr-xr-x  2 guest    guests     32 Dec 27 07:50 let
drwxr-xr-x  2 guest    guests     64 Dec 27 07:50 prov
```

This looks more orderly; you can easily work with this. Enter the *prov* directory in order to examine the contents.

```
$cd prov
$ls -l
-rw-r--r--  1 guest    guests     52 Dec 27 20 10:47 all-
prov
-rw-r--r--  1 guest    guests     32 Dec 25 20 10:43 ebir
$
```

Prior to working with texts, you should make backups of these. Backups can always be recognized if you use the filename extension *.bak*. There are several of this type of extension to indicate the file contents or task. You will find a table of the most common of these in Appendix C.

In contrast to a single-user system such as MS-DOS, the dot is not a separator in file names under UNIX. It is a character just like all others. You may also use more characters behind the dot which is not permitted under MS-DOS. You may also use two, three or more dots in a file name.

Use of underlining, hyphenation or a single capital brings even more clarity in file and directory names, for instance Snt.Cls or Snw.Wht. The underline character is not always usable since it is occasionally used in word processing to prevent a wordwrap. In word processors like these, the underline character is not displayed.

You can copy files using the **cat** command:

```
$cat <allprov >allprov.bak
```

The order of sequence for input and output is not important in this case. The command

```
$cat >allprov.bak <allprov
```

has exactly the same effect. If you find it tedious to have to type the arrows, use the command **cp** (copy).

```
$cp previous_file_name new_file_name
```

As you see, **cp** has the same syntax as the commands **mv** and **ln**. The command also executes the same program. But now the order of sequence of input and output is important: the program interprets what the input is and what the output by this order.

```
cp old_file new_file
mv old_name new_name
ln first_name second_name
```

This is a good reason to maintain this order of sequence, even when using the **cat** instruction. This will help prevent errors.

Now make a backup of both files.

```
$cp allprov allprov.bak
$cp ebir ebir.bak
```

There are now four files in the prov directory. How do you know that *ebir* and *ebir.bak* are two separate *files* and not just a link, i.e. two *names* for the same file? After all, **cp** makes use of the same program as **ln** which is used to make a link, in other words, to give a file a second name (see section 6.2). The commands **cat ebir** and **cat ebir.bak** cannot help since the contents of both files are identical. The solution to this problem lies in the file number: if *ebir.bak* is really another file, it will have its own file number referring to its own inode.

```
$ls -i e*
1147 ebir
1158 ebir.bak
$
```

The asterisk in the command has special significance: it
replaces all the subsequent characters in the file names
beginning with e. If you wish a survey of all backups, type:

```
$ls *.bak
allprov.bak
ebir.bak
$
```

Caution   The asterisk is a dangerous instrument.
The **rm *** command deletes all files in the
directory irretrievably (except those that
begin with a dot), without safeguard questions!

Perhaps you find the name *prov* a little too serious,
owing to the biblical connotations. Using the **mv** command, you can also assign other names to directories
without any problem. The */prov* directory is a subdirectory of */guest*. As long as you remain in */prov*, the directory is called '..'. Without quitting the directory, you can
assign another name to it, for instance '*sayings*'.

```
$mv ../prov ../sayings
$ls -l..
...
$
```

You can examine the parent directory using the command **ls -l** ... The instruction contains a *relative pathname*. A relative pathname takes the current directory
as its starting point and always refers to either the parent (..) or subdirectory, in contrast to a *full pathname*
which always begins at the root directory, for example
/usr/guest/sayings. Do not place a slash in front of the
name of a subdirectory since this is the beginning of a
full pathname.

If you wish to change to the *let* directory, you can address it in two ways: **cd /usr/guest/let** or **cd ../let**. It is more convenient to use the relative address when you are working at a deeper level and the target directory is near to the current directory.

Unfortunately, the commands **ln, mv** and **cp** cannot perform all tasks:

- Early versions of **cp** cannot copy a directory; the **copy**, **cpio** or **tar** commands do this. However, later versions have an **-r** option which copies 'recursively' complete file hierarchies.
- **mv** cannot relocate directories; the **mvdir** command does this.
- **ln** and **mv** do not work across devices. However, **ln** has an **-s** option to create a 'symbolic' link which can link files across devices.

Imagine you wish to create, beginning at your own directory, a subdirectory in which you can store all files which do not require further processing, thus, a directory containing archive files.

```
$mkdir ../arch
$ls -l ..
...
$
```

The command **ls -l ..** shows that the directory now exists. Imagine that you have concluded work on the *ebir* and *allprov* files and you wish to copy them to the new directory.

```
$cp ebir allprov ../arch
$
```

You can copy more than one file at a time to another directory. You can now delete the backups.

```
$rm * .bak
rm: .bak non-existent
$
```

This statement may surprise you: a moment ago there
were two files with the appendix *.bak*. If you look carefully, you will observe that your command has been executed precisely. Your directory is empty. Instead of
typing ***.bak**, you have typed *** .bak** with a space in between! The command first deletes *all* files (due to the
asterisk), subsequently the program searches for .bak
files. These do not exist anymore and an error message
follows.

Accordingly, always apply the command **rm *** in conjunction with the option **-i** which ensures that you are
asked to confirm the command. The **i** is an abbreviation
for 'interactive'. Each time a file is to be deleted, the
name of the file is displayed on the screen with a question mark. The file is only deleted when you press **y** to
confirm the command.

Using this method, you can easily delete files whose
names partly consist of invisible characters. Create a
file like this using the invisible character <Ctrl-a>.

```
$cat >sup<ctrl-a>per
One swallow doesn't make a supper
<Ctrl-D>
$ls
allprov
ebir
supper
$cat supper
cat: cannot open supper
$ls -q
allprov
ebir
sup?per
$rm -i su*
supper:? y<Return>
$
```

The command **ls** may make you think that a file called
supper actually exists. This is untrue, as you will observe by using the command **ls -q** which replaces an in-

visible character with a question mark. The command **rm -i** in combination with the initial letter(s) and the asterisk quickly produces the required file on the screen. You can discontinue the process by pressing the <Del> key or <Ctrl-C>.

Your hobby has become an addiction: by interviewing people on the street, you have collected countless sayings which you had never previously encountered. Moreover, the */arch* directory has also grown disproportionately. You have saved everything indiscriminately. You have now reached the point in the */arch* directory where you no longer know what to retain and what to discard. You finally decide that all really important sayings can be found elsewhere and the entire directory can be deleted. Change to the parent directory */usr/guest* and give the command

```
$rmdir arch
rmdir: arch not empty
```

The command **rmdir** does not work, because the directory is not empty. You must specify the option **-r** in order to delete a directory containing files. The command is then as follows:

```
$rm -r arch
```

Caution   This option is rather dangerous: everything in the */arch* directory will be deleted, including all subdirectories of */arch*, if they exist, and their contents.

The **-r** option works in a recursive manner. This means that it descends into the directory to be deleted, works through all subdirectory levels to delete files, before climbing back up to the current directory, leaving a void behind it. You must be extremely careful in the use of the **rm *** command, and it is advisable never to use the command **rm -r ***.

6.7   Deleting files is easy

You can easily overwrite files using the commands **cp**,
mv and **ln**. This generally occurs without you noticing it.
You are already familiar with the command structure:

command	source file	target file
cp	old_file	new_file
mv	old_name	new_name
ln	first_name	second_name

If a file already exists with the name new_file or sec-
ond_name, it will be overwritten without a safeguard
question. You will not notice this. When the **cp** command is used, the copy acquires the file mode and thus,
in fact, the rights of access of the existing file.

The diagram below illustrates the effect of the three
commands when there is already a destination file of
the same name:

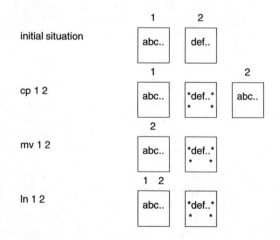

Unfortunately, it is all too easy to delete a file unintentionally. Imagine you are in the directory *xy* and you
wish to create a new file with a name which you have al-

ready used in another directory. Since the full name of a file always consists of the whole path, no conflict will arise between both files. However, imagine that you make an error about which directory you are in (which occurs more frequently than you think!); an accident can easily take place. An existing file is easily overwritten. Therefore, you should use the **ls** command in order to check whether the file you wish to create already exists in the current directory.

In order to create a file, it makes no difference whether you use the relative or the full pathname. But it does make a difference in terms of safety: The command **cat >../../let/fil** is so complex that it remains to be seen whether the file will be created at the required place. Perhaps you have several directories called let. Or perhaps you have directory names which resemble one another, so that a typing error can make the file almost untraceable. For example, **cat >../chap1/fil** instead of **cat >../chap11/fil**.
It is safer to specify the entire path name.

Imagine you wish to remove the second line from the *allprov* file. The **head** command is a convenient command which allows you to read the first part of a file. The name refers to the beginning of the file. However, you may easily make a mistake here: you should not use the same file name for input and output. We shall illustrate this using the *allprov* file.

Using the **head** command, you direct a number of lines, which you have specified as an option, to the standard output device, in this case the screen.

```
$head -1 allprov
The early bird catches the worm.
```

Hopefully, the importance of a backup of a file which you are going to edit has now become obvious. Accordingly, first make a backup of the *allprov* file.

```
$cp allprov allprov.bak
$
```

Now you can give the command **head -1** and simultaneously redirect the command output from the screen to
the file itself. Subsequently, examine the file.

```
$head -1 allprov >allprov
$ls -l allprov
-rw-r--r--  1 guest   guests     0 Dec 27 22.45 allprov
     $
```

The file is empty! You have used the file for both input
and output in one command and, although that is indeed permitted (otherwise you will receive an error
message), it always leads to loss of file contents.

The command will succeed if you use the backup.

```
$head -1 allprov.bak >allprov
la -l allprov
-rw-r--r--  1 guest   guests    58 Dec 27 22.47 allprov
$cat allprov
The early bird catches the worm.
$rm allprov.bak
$
```

File names which are too lengthy can lead to similar
problems. Imagine you have files with the names New-
Book.chapt1 to NewBook.chapt9. You decide to add a
tenth chapter, and because you wish to keep the list orderly, you rename the first nine files:

```
$mv NewBook.chapt1 NewBook.chapt01
$mv NewBook.chapt2 NewBook.chapt02
   . . .
$
```

The command appear to be executed properly, since no
error messages are shown on the screen. But now
examine the contents of the directory:

```
$ls
NewBook.chapt0
```

There is only one file. If you examine its contents, you will observe that this is chapter 9, the last chapter which you renamed. What happened is the following: file names may consist of a maximum of fourteen characters. The new file names have fifteen characters. In that case, UNIX ignores the fifteenth character. Accordingly, you have renamed all the files NewBook.chapt0 and, in doing so, repeatedly deleted the old file. Fortunately, this problem does not occur on more recent versions of UNIX which permit longer file names.

Caution   Only edit and delete files if you have a backup on tape or diskette. This sounds a bit exaggerated, but keep in mind that it is easier to delete a file stored on a magnetic surface where you see only the name than it is to delete, for instance, sheets of paper with the same contents. This requires a number of physical manoeuvres which demand more involvement, so that deletion occurs less readily.

If you wish to guard yourself against unpleasant surprises, check each copy process before continuing with the next. In addition, you should assign write-protection to important files. We shall outline exactly how to do this at the end of the following section.

6.8   Changing user rights for files and directories

6.8.1   User rights under UNIX

Read, write and user rights are assigned to three user groups: the owner of the file, the group to which he/she belongs and the other users in the system. In order to keep control over the user rights, UNIX registers the owner and the group to which he/she belongs in the file data.

There is a distinction between the *user rights* and the *rights of access*. Right of access determines access to the system in general, user right specifies who may make use of a particular file. Only the owner and the system manager may alter the user rights, the name of the owner and the name of the group. This takes place using three commands:

chown   change owner
chgrp   change group
chmod   change mode, (change user right)

The syntax of the three commands is similar:

```
$ch... new_owner_or_group file_name
$ch... new_right file_name
$ch... new_right directory_name
```

6.8.2   Changing user rights of files

There are two files in your directory with the following user rights:

```
$cd /usr/guest/sayings
$ls -l
-rw-r--r--  1 guest  guests    58 Dec 27 22.47 allprov
-rw-r--r--  1 guest  guests    32 Dec 25 10:43 ebir
$
```

We shall now change the user rights of the files in such a way that the user group receives the right to alter the files: the group (g) may (+) write (w).

```
$chmod g+w allprov ebir
$ls -l
-rw-rw-r--  1 guest  guests    58 Dec 27 23 22.47 allprov
-rw-rw-r--  1 guest  guests    32 Dec 25 10:43 ebir
$
```

In addition, we do not wish to allow other users to even be able to examine these files: others (o) may not (-) read (r).

```
$chmod o-r *
$ls -l
-rw-rw----  1 guest   guests    58 Dec 27 22.47 allprov
-rw-rw----  1 guest   guests    32 Dec 25 10:43 ebir
$
```

If you are the system manager, you should under no circumstances change rights by applying an asterisk: you will lose your overview. Both examples will make it plain that you are able to change the rights of several or all files in a directory simultaneously. If you wish to assign the same rights (=) to the owner (also called the *user*, thus you yourself) as to the other users (o), give the following command:

```
$chmod ug=o *
$ls -l
----------  1 guest   guests    58 Dec 27 22.47 allprov
----------  1 guest   guests    32 Dec 25 10:43 ebir
        $
```

Now nobody has any rights for the files. You can also invert this: everyone (a for all) may (+) perform everything (rwx): read (r), write (w) and execute (x).

```
$chmod a+rwx *
$ls -l
-rwxrwxrwx  1 guest   guests    58 Dec 27 22.47 allprov
-rwxrwxrwx  1 guest   guests    32 Dec 25 10:43 ebir
$
```

We shall summarize the user rights again below.

who	**may**	**what**
u owner	+ may	r (read)
	- may not	w (write)
g group	= may also	x (execute)
o others		u the owner
		g the group
a all		o the others

6.8.3   A text is not a program

Allocating the user right *x* to users for a text file has little use: a text file is not executable - it contains no commands which UNIX can carry out. Try to do this using the ebir file.

```
$ebir<Return>
ebir: The: not found
```

The system has actually tried to execute the file as a program, since the user right to do this has been specified. It has sought the command 'The' since this is the first word of the file.

If this first word had been a command, UNIX would have executed the command. If, subsequently, a second command had followed, the system would have carried this out too. Realization of this puts you on the route towards your first own command program under UNIX, prog1.

```
$cat >prog1
clear
echo "clear: clears the screen"
echo
echo "echo: directs the text to the standard output device"
<Ctrl-D>
ls -l prog1
-rw-r--r--    1 guest   guests    104 Dec 28 12:20 prog1
$
```

If you attempt to execute the program, you will observe that you have no user rights for doing this.

```
$prog1
prog1: execute permission denied
```

You will first have to assign yourself this right using the command **chmod**.

```
$chmod u+x prog1
ls -l prog1
-rwxr--r--   1 guest  guests    104 Dec 28 12:20 prog1
$prog1

clear: clears the screen

echo: directs the text to the standard output device
$
```

6.8.4 Changing the user rights of directories

Change to the */usr/guest/sayings* directory. You have all rights in this directory. If you now change your user rights for this directory, something unusual occurs. Try this out by suspending your right to read the directory.

```
$chmod u-r ../sayings
ls -ld
d-wxr-xr-x  2 guest   guests    64 Dec 27 07:50 prov
$
```

Now you are unable to display the contents of the directory on the screen.

```
$ls
. unreadable
```

However, you are able to read the files themselves since you have not changed the user rights for these.

```
$cat ebir
The early bird catches the worm.
$
```

You are able to read files but not directories. In the
same way, you can still write to files or execute programs such as prog1 for instance. But you wish to know
the contains of the directory. Now change the user
rights once more so that you can now read but not write.

```
$chmod u+r ../sayings
$chmod u-w ../sayings
$ls -ld
dr-xr-xr-x  2 guest   guests     64 Dec 27 23 07:50
sayings
$echo "write attempt 1" >attempt
attempt: cannot create
$rm allprov
rm: allprov not removed.:Permission denied
$mv allprov manyprov
mv: cannot unlink allprov
$
```

UNIX cannot create the *attempt* file. This is self-evident
since you do not have any writing rights in the directory.
What is perhaps less obvious is that you cannot remove
or rename a file, for which you have writing rights, if you
do not have writing rights in the relevant directory.
This is caused by the fact that these procedures try to
change the file name and the file name is located in a directory where you have no writing rights. But contents
of the file are stored elsewhere therefore you are able to
alter these. You can change the contents of a file which
can amount to much the same as deletion:

```
$cat<dev/null>allprov
$ls -l allprov
-rwxr--r--  1 guest  guests      0 Dec 28  16.10 all-
prov
$
```

The *allprov* file is empty. This indicates that you can delete files without having writing rights (which also means the right to delete) for the directory.

Restore the writing rights for the directory and then examine the possibilities when you deny yourself execution rights.

```
$chmod u+w ../sayings
$chmod u-x ../sayings
$ls -ld
drw-r-xr-x  2 guest  guests    64 Dec 28 07:50 sayings
$ls -l
. not found
$echo "write attempt 2" >attempt
attempt: cannot create
$cd ..
..:bad directory
$
```

You cannot read or write in your directory. You cannot even quit your directory if you use a relative pathname. There are two other ways of changing to the parent directory: using **cd** or **cd /usr/guest**. Then try to return to the */sayings* directory.

```
$cd
$pwd
/usr/guest
$cd sayings
sayings: bad directory
$
```

This seems impossible. Perhaps you are not able to read the directory because you have no execute permission for the directory.

```
$ls sayings
allprov
prog1
ebir
```

```
$ls -l sayings
sayings/allprov not found
sayings/prog1 not found
sayings/ebir not found
$
```

You are able to display a listing, but details are denied you with the statement **not found** because you have no execute permission. Because you do have the reading and writing rights for the directory and the files, you should be able to to read existing files or create new ones.

```
$cat sayings/allprov
cat:cannot open sayings/allprov
$echo "write attempt 3" >attempt
sayings/attempt: cannot create
$sayings/prog1
sayings/prog1: cannot execute
$
```

Summary   If you have reading and writing rights but you do not have execute permission for a directory, you cannot read, create, modify, delete, rename or implement files in that directory. You can only carry out manipulate the *names* of the files.

6.8.5   Changing the user group

The file */etc/group* contains a list of all user groups and the users in the groups. To examine it, use **cat /etc/group**. By using the command **chgrp** you can change the user group which has right of access to files or directories. For example, if there was a group called fisbook, as system manager you could make the balance available to all your bookkeepers by applying the command **chgrp fisbook bal**.

6.8.6   Changing ownership

A directory of which you are the owner may be handed over to someone else.

```
$cd /usr/guest
$mkdir Jasper
$cd Jasper
$cat >hypothesis
If Henry the Eighth were alive today, he would turn in
                                              his grave.
<Ctrl-D>
$ls -l hypothesis
-rwxr-xr-x   1 guest   guests   66 Dec 27 09:06 hypothesis
$cd..
$chown Jasper Jasper
$ls -ld Jasper
drwxr-xr-x   2 Jasper  guests   48 Dec 27 09:08 Jasper
$
```

An attempt to reassume ownership of the file will fail. You have relinquished your authority over it.

```
$chown guest Jasper
Jasper: Not owner
```

UNIX makes it clear that you have no entitlement. Under these circumstances, you would rather remove the directory from your directory tree (after copying the file to another directory).

```
$cp Jasper/hypothesis sayings/hypothesis
$rm -r Jasper
rm: Jasper/hypothesis not removed.: Permission denied.
rmdir: Jasper not empty
$
```

Since you have the right to execute programs in the directory and, moreover, the right to read the file, you may copy the hypothesis file. However, you cannot delete

the directory using **rm -r**. The directory is protected
against you. However, this does not apply to subdirectories which you might attach to *Jasper.* as long as you
have not adjusted the rights for each individual directory, it may be deleted.

6.9   File protection

In order to prevent a file being unintentionally deleted or
written over, you can apply *write-protection* to files. This
does not provide an absolute guarantee that nothing will
happen to your files and, accordingly, we shall discuss
in some depth exactly how a program reacts to a file
with write-protection. We shall use the *allprov* file as an
example. It is important that you have all user rights for
the directory.

```
$cd /usr/guest/sayings
$pwd
/usr/guest/sayings
$ls -ld
drw-r-xr-x  2 guest   guests   128 Dec 27 09:25 .
$chmod a-w allprov
$ls -l
-r-xr-xr-x  1 guest   guests    58 Dec 27 22.47 allprov
-rwxr--r--  1 guest   guests   104 Dec 28 12:20 prog1
-rwxrwxrwx  1 guest   guests    32 Dec 25 10:43 ebir
```

First try to copy *ebir* to *allprov.*

```
$cp ebir allprov
cp: cannot create allprov
$
```

Thus, the **cp** command cannot write to a protected file.
The command makes use of the same program as **mv**
and **ln**, but does not produce the same results in this respect.

```
$mv ebir allprov
mv: allprov: 555 mode ?[]
```

The cursor remains behind the word *mode* indicating that you can can proceed with the command: if you press **y**, the command will be executed, any other key discontinues the procedure. The same applies to the command **ln**. We shall outline the significance of '555 mode' in the following section.

You will also not succeed in writing over a write-protected file using the redirection sign >.

```
$cat </dev/null >allprov
allprov: cannot create
$
```

The command **rm** produces the same statement as **mv**.

```
$rm allprov
allprov: 555 mode ? []
```

If you press y, the file will be deleted. In short: the write-protection only works absolutely for the commands **cp** and **cat**. Other commands produce a safeguard question, **555 mode**, which can even be suppressed if you use them with the option **-f** (force).

First make a copy of the file before trying out this option. The copy acquires the same rights as the original file. (Exception: if the destination file already exists, the new destination file retains the same rights as the old one.)

```
cp allprov allprov.bak
$ls -l all*
-r-xr-xr-x  1 guest  guests    58 Dec 27 22.47 allprov
-r-xr-xr-x  1 guest  guests    58 Dec 28 09:51 allprov.bak
$rm -f allprov.bak
$ls -l all*
-r-xr-xr-x  1 guest  guests    58 Dec 27 22.47 allprov
$
```

You wish to know whether this 'half' permission can be denied when one assumes the writing rights to the directory.

```
$chmod u-w
$ls-ld
dr-xr-xr-x  2 guest  guests  128 Dec 27 09:25 .
$rm alleprov
allprov: 555 mode ? y
rm: allprov not removed.: Permission denied
$
```

The safeguard question is automatic. The system realizes that deletion is not allowed only after you have pressed 'y'. If you use the -f option, it seems as though the file is actually deleted.

```
$rm -f allprov
$
```

But if you examine the contents of the directory, you will observe that nothing has occurred.

```
ls -l all*
-r-xr-xr-x  1 guest  guests   58 Dec 27 22.47 allprov
```

In short: if you write-protect both the directory and the file, you cannot delete the file using the commands **rm** or **rm -f**.

If you block the writing rights to your directory for yourself and all others, the files are relatively safe. However, if anyone has writing rights to your files, these can be altered using **cp** or by linking. Only write-protection for both directory and files works absolutely.

6.10   Coding user rights

The safeguard question in the commands **rm**, **ln** and **mv** contains the user rights in code: 555 mode. Each number represents a set of user rights from one of the following three groups: owner, user group and other users. Because you can specify the user rights as required, there are eight possible combinations.

code	rights		
	(4	+2	+1)
7	r	w	x
6	r	w	-
5	r	-	x
4	r	-	-
3	-	w	x
2	-	w	-
1	-	-	x
0	-	-	-

By allocating a value to each possible combination of user rights, all rights of all users can be represented by three numbers. The reading right is always represented by a 4, the writing right by a 2 and the right to execute programs by a 1. Accordingly, the code can easily be interpreted. In our example '555 mode', the 2 is absent throughout, which means there are no writing rights. A very common code is 755, which means that the owner has all rights (4+2+1), the group and other users are only allowed to read and execute programs (4+1).

As soon as you come to grips with this coding process, you can use it to change user rights. You adjust the entire mode according to the syntax outlined below:

```
chmod code file_name
chmod code directory_name
```

We shall conclude this chapter with an example of this procedure: we shall assign the standard user rights (755) to the directory and files once more.

```
$ls -ld
dr-xr-xr-x  2 guest   guests   128 Dec 28 09:25 .
$chmod 755 .
$ls -ld
drwxr-xr-x  2 guest   guests   128 Dec 28 09:25 .
$ls -l
-r-xr-xr-x  1 guest   guests    58 Dec 27 22.47 allprov
-rwxr--r--  1 guest   guests   104 Dec 27 12:20 prog1
-rwxrwxrwx  1 guest   guests    32 Dec 25 10:43 ebir
$chmod 755 *
-rwxr-xr-x  1 guest   guests    58 Dec 27 22.47 allprov
-rwxr-xr-x  1 guest   guests   104 Dec 27 12:20 prog1
-rwxr-xr-x  1 guest   guests    32 Dec 25 10:43 ebir
$
```

The error message **cannot create ...** may occasionally
surprise you, but you now possess the know-how to discover the cause of it. Either:

■ there already is a target file with the same name and
  that file is write-protected, or
■ you have no writing rights in the directory: check if
  you are in the proper directory and who has which
  rights.

7   The printer

If you are have installed UNIX on a PC yourself, you should also install the printer spooling system before printing. Read this chapter before you begin, assisted by the information in chapter 13, to install the printer under UNIX.

7.1   Selecting the printer

In previous chapters you have learned that the **cat** command enables you to regulate almost all data transport. This also applies to output via the printer. The first thing needed here is the special file name for the hardware device to which the actual printer is connected. This can be found in the */dev* directory: either *printer* or *lp* (line printer), supplemented by a number in both cases.

```
$ls -l /dev/pr* /dev/lp*
/dev/pr* not found
c-w--w--w-   1 bin     bin     6, 0 Dec 28 17:00 /dev/lp0
. . .
$
```

If your printer device is called */dev/printer0*, the error message will state '*/dev/lp0* not found'. Using the information which you acquire here, you can formulate the relevant command to print a file.

```
$cat allprov >/dev/lp0
```

If you are working in the system on your own, you will encounter no problems. However, if you wish to transport data to the printer at the same time as other users, the *time-sharing* system (see section 3.1) will throw everything into confusion. Your file, and those of others, will be cut to pieces and all these snippets will be printed hotch-potch on the same page. This will produce admirable collages but tends to be somewhat inconvenient.

For this reason, there is a special program for printer management: **lpsched**. Anyone wishing to print something makes use of this program. The *scheduler* registers the print requests in a list which is neatly worked through in order of sequence. This process is also often referred to as spooling and the management program as the *spooler*.

As soon as it is the turn for your print job, the spooler passes your request to a program which actually carries out the printing. All the print options which you have specified are then processed: number of copies, special fonts, headers and footers etc.

It is often convenient to manage printing in more than one way so that you can print texts in several standard forms. This applies even if you always make use of the same printing device. The printer operating program is notified of multiple virtual printers (*lp0, lp1* etc) so that it seems as if more than one printer is connected. If there are several real printers connected to the system, there may be one or more virtual printers for each actual device. In that case, you should know which virtual printer corresponds to which printer device.

In this matter, the best thing to do is request a list of all virtual printers and real devices. This is done using the **lpstat** command (line printer status). If you use lpstat without parameters, the command displays the current output status. If you add the **-v** option, you will receive a survey of all connected printers.

```
$lpstat -v
device for pr1: /dev/lp0
$
```

The virtual printer is called *pr1*, the real printer device file is *lp0*. Do not be surprised if your system states: *device for lp1: /dev/printer0*. The names may be freely chosen. Accordingly, you may encounter *lp printer* and other names.

7.2   Printing

The program which receives your print command and passes it on to the scheduler is called **lp** or **lpr** on some systems. Since there may be several virtual printers although there is actually only one real printer, you may specify a virtual printer in the command. This is done using the option **-d** (for destination) to **lp** or the **-P** option to **lpr**.

If you now type the complete command, the scheduler will confirm your command.

```
$lp -dpr1 allprov
request id is pr1-15 (1 file)
$
```

The message indicates that a number has been assigned to the command at your request: *pr1-15*. This number is composed of the name of the virtual printer (pr1) and a sequence number. In order to find your own printout among the many when the printer is shared, an information page is printed with relevant information: the user name, the command number, the virtual printer in use, the date and time, and the type of printer.

```
xxxxxxxxxxxxxxxxxxxxxxxxxxxxxxxxxxxxxx
G U E S T
xxxxxxxxxxxxxxxxxxxxxxxxxxxxxxxxxxxxxx
Request id: pr1-15
Printer: pr1
Mon Dec 28 20:44:05 GMT 1992
Machine: uxschool
```

The exact appearance of the information page depends on the operating program of your virtual printer. That can almost always be adapted by the system manager to the requirements of the individual users. These also differ according to system.

It is rather laborious to have to specify the name of virtual printer time and again if you are making use of a certain printer. For this reason, it is possible to have the system manager install a default printer. The command **lpstat -d** displays which printer has been defined as the default printer.

```
$lpstat -d
system default destination: pr1
```

In this case, you can restrict your print command to **lp allprov**.

It is a waste of time and paper to print an information page when you are alone or when there are few users in the system and it is easy to distinguish between the printouts. For this reason, there is an option which suppresses this page. In fact, several of this type of option are possible with the lp command. Printer dependent options begin with **-o**.

For instance, the command **lp -ob -olq -o12** means that the text should be printed without the information page (-ob), in letter quality (-olq) with 12 characters per inch (-o12).

The most important options with the **lp** command are the following:

-n Specifies the number of copies of a text to be printed; n represents the number here.

-t Enables you to add a header to a print command; enter the text behind the t. Not all systems recognize this option.

-w In a large system with many users, it may take some time before your print command is implemented. In the meantime, you will continue working and perhaps you will forget to look for your output in the tray. This option will display a message on your screen as soon as the print command has been carried out. Enter the contents of the message behind the w. If you have logged out in the meantime, the contents will be sent to your mailbox.

-m This option works just as **-ow**, except it sends the message directly to your mailbox so that you will not be disturbed.

-c If you wish to remove the text from memory immediately after the print command has been executed, or if you wish to edit it further, use this option to make a copy of the file to be printed. The copy is then printed and then automatically deleted.

As you see, a print command can assume a rather complicated appearance:

```
$lp -ow -n2 -tAll Proverbs -olq allprov
request id is: pr1-16 (1 file)
$
```

7.3   Cancelling a print command

Owing to the fact that your print command is placed in a print queue, you will generally have some time to reconsider before the file is actually printed. Then the **cancel** command can be very convenient.

```
$cancel pr1-16
```

A print command which is waiting to be executed can be cancelled by using the **cancel** command along with the name of the virtual printer.

```
$cancel pr1
$
```

However, if your printer performs quickly and there are few print commands in the queue, this command may come too late.

7.4   Print command refused, printer out of order

It may occur that the print command produces to the following error message:

```
$lp allprov
lp: can't accept requests for destination "pr1" -
    The printer is out of order.
$
```

If the virtual printers *pr1* and *pr2* both refer to the same physical printer, it will not help if you try *pr2* in this case.

```
$lpstat -v
device for pr1: /dev/lp0
device for pr2: /dev/lp0
device for las: /dev/lp1
$
```

In these circumstances, you will have to use the laser printer, presuming that you have user rights for the laser printer. The system manager may restrict user rights in the printer management system.

If you have been waiting for some time for the execution of your print command without having received a printout or error message, you can request the printer status using the command **lpstat -t**.

```
$lpstat -t
scheduler is running
system default destination: pr1
device for pr1: /dev/lp0
pr1 accepting requests since Dec 28 21:08
printer pr1 disabled since Dec 28 21:14 -
    The printer cartridge is being replaced.
pr1-18                    guest           58  Dec 28 21:14
```

The scheduler is operational but pr1 is out of use because a new printer cartridge is being inserted. Your command is in the queue.

When the printer has been reinstated *online*, in other words, it is again capable of accepting instructions from the system, it should implement your command. However, if it does not react and does not carry out your command, something may have gone wrong during the cartridge replacement: printers which are temporarily interrupted during their work occasionally react in a troublesome manner. First check the the system status once more.

```
lpstat -t
...
printer pr1 is idle, enabled since Nov 27 21:16
$
```

The printer is again online (enabled) but is idle, while your command has disappeared. This may be unfair, intolerable, illogical and ridiculous but it is nevertheless true. You will have to specify your command once more. You may even have to check the printer connection cables. A connector may have been shifted during the cartridge replacement.

There are many options with the **lpstat** command. All the information shown by the command **lpstat -t** can be displayed individually. However, you will seldom need to do this, and thus we shall not deal with this option in depth here. In addition, any required information is just as quickly gained from a survey using **lpstat** as from a manual or using the command **help lpstat**. If you only wish to find out if all print commands have been implemented, type the command **lpstat** without parameters.

If you, as system manager, are busy with the installation of the system, proceed to chapter 13.

8   The user environment

In a multi-user system, all users have their *own* directories in which they manage their *own* files which are
displayed on their *own* screens. Users determine themselves the way their *own* user interfaces react.

Thus, there are many elements, including those mentioned above and others, which together form the user
environment. Actually, this description is not entirely
correct: it is the user process which has an environment, the so-called **process environment**.

8.1   Generating a process

A user process does not just fall from the sky. In order
to discover where it does originate, activate the *process
table*.

```
$ ps -el
  F  S  UID   PID  PPID   C   PRI  NI ADDR  SZ    WCHAN  TTY TIME  CMD
  3  S    0     0     0   0     0  20   78   0     fefe    ? 0:00  swapper
  1  S    0     1     0   0    30  20  181  16     18c8c   ? 0:01  init
  1  S    0    22     1   0    40  20  1b6  12  6000000    ? 0:00  update
  1  S    0    23     1   0    26  24  1ad  16     5854    ? 0:00  logger
  1  S    0    25     1   0    26  20  1df  24     2943e   ? 0:00  cron
  1  S   14    39     1   0    26  20  1fc  24     2a0e6   ? 0:00  lpsched
  1  S    0    42     1   1    30  20  18b  20     18d34  01 0:01  getty
  1  S    0    43     1   0    28  20  1ce  24     e1f4   02 0:00  getty
  1  S    0    44     1   0    28  20  1e2  24     e254   03 0:00  getty
  ..  .   .    ..         ..  ..  ..     .. ..    ...    ..:..  .. ...
  1  S    0    53     1   0    28  20  22f  24     e5b4   12 0:01  getty
$
```

The first two processes, *init* and *swapper*, have been
created by UNIX itself. They have the process numbers
(PID) 0 and 1. The column PPID indicates the number
of the process from which a process originates. This is 0
for *init* and *swapper*, which means that they originate

from UNIX itself. All other processes have a 1 in the PPID column and therefore originate from *init* (PID 1). When the system was started up, the following took place:

Init creates a shell for the superuser. The shell executes the commands from an */etc/rc* program in order to activate *update, logger, cron* and *lpsched*. Then *init* starts a *getty* at all terminals; this is the program which handles your login procedure. All these processes belong to root, the user having UID 0. UID stands for user identification.

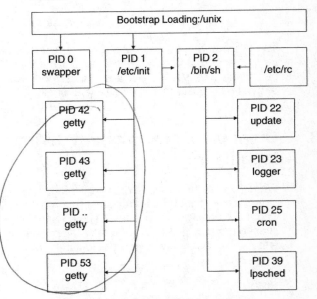

The system processes are not linked to a terminal. The superuser shell ceases to be when the system processes are installed.

A *getty* process, number 42, is running at the terminal where you wish to register, *tty01*. The system displays the prompt for the login process on your screen. Type your name and password. The process table which is

produced by the command **ps -el** is completely different
from the process table previously displayed.

```
$ ps -el
  F  S   UID  PID PPID  C   PRI  NI ADDR  SZ   WCHAN TTY TIME  CMD
  3  S    0    0    0   0    0   20  78    0    fefe   ? 0:00  swapper
  1  S    0    1    0   0   30   20 181   16    18c8c  ? 0:01  init
 ..  .    .    ..       .. ..  .. ..  ...    ...   ..:..  .. ...
  1  S 2001   42    1   1   30   20 18b   20    18d34  01 0:01  sh
 ..  .    .    ..       .. ..  .. ..  ...    ...   ..:..  .. ...
  1  S    0   53    1   0   28   20 22f   24    e5b4   12 0:01  getty
  1  R 2001   56   42   5   52   20 26a   24           01 0:00  ps
$
```

The process with number 42 still exists, but is it is radi-
cally changed. It is now owned by user number 2001,
i.e. guest, thus you. In addition, this is no longer the
original *getty* process, it is a shell, your shell.

8.3 Creation of environment during logging in

What has taken place? When you have typed your
name in the login procedure, *getty* has replaced itself
with the command **login guest**. Thus, *login* has taken
over process 42 from *getty* and searches in the
/etc/passwd file for the *guest* user registration.

```
$more/etc/passwd
...
guest:.SkNzvAnG0JbA:2001:51::/usr/guest:/bin/sh
...
$
```

Subsequently, *login* requests the appropriate password.
Here the echo function is switched off. Type the proper
password and *login* will transfer the operation to the
program which is located in the last field, the *login* program, in this case */bin/sh*, the Bourne shell. The shell

now assumes process 42 and thus it becomes your process, since *login* has ensured that you have been registered as the new owner.

Login has taken care of even more: process 42 has also been informed of your user group (GID 51) and the directory which you are using, */usr/guest*. All these data collectively form the process environment. They are stored as *variable* values, which means you can alter them if required. The names and values of a number of these *environment variables* can be shown using the command **env** or **printenv**.

Your list of environment variables will look something like this:

```
$printenv
HOME=/usr/guest
HZ=50
PATH=:/bin:/usr/bin
SHELL=/bin/sh
TERM=ansi
TZ=GMT
$
```

You are already familiar with two of the values shown, namely your own directory */usr/guest* and */bin/sh* your user interface. As you see, these values are stored in the variables HOME and SHELL.

You can display the value of a variable on your screen using the command **echo**. You should then place a dollar sign in front of the variable name to let echo know that you do not expect the word HOME on the screen but the value of the variable HOME: **$HOME**.

```
$echo HOME
HOME
$echo $HOME
$/usr/guest
$
```

The next variable is PATH. PATH indicates in which directories the system should look for programs. There is also another important variable, TERM. The TERM variable contains data concerning the type of terminal at which you are working, ansi in this case. This definition is necessary due to the fact that the operation of the diverse sorts of terminals may differ considerably. The terminal interface extracts the proper commands for the terminal from a table. If you connect a different terminal, you must also adjust the variable.

In this section, we began by giving a description of the login process. This process works through a substantial number of commands, which we shall outline briefly below. In many cases, these commands generate environment variables.

In not all UNIX versions but, for instance, in XENIX, the login procedure extracts a number of environment variables from the /etc/default/login directory, which apply to all users. You will find HZ, for example, in the above list. This is the power supply frequency, which is 50 hertz in Europe and 60 hertz in North America. In the XENIX version of UNIX, the value for TZ (time zone) is also extracted from this directory: in Britain this is Greenwich Mean Time (GMT); in other European countries this is often Central European Time (CET) which is one hour earlier. Examine this file using **cat /etc/default/login**.

Subsequently, the login process displays the message of the day on your screen. This message is stored in the /etc directory in the motd file.

The message '**You have mail**' is self-explanatory. The login process examines your mailbox, to see if you have mail. The environment variable MAIL indicates which directory contains your mail.

```
$echo $MAIL
/usr/spool/mail/guest
```

Finally, the login process reads two profile programs: firstly the *profile* file in the */etc* directory which all users require, and subsequently the *.profile* file from your own home directory. UNIX versions which do not have a */etc/default/login* directory, extract the TZ environment variable, for example, from the profile file. Each user has an own .profile file in order to specify, for instance, a required path in PATH.

If you examine the *profile* and *.profile* files, you will certainly not comprehend everything which is shown there. Fortunately, that is not necessary. You only need to know, with respect to both files, which functions they have, so that you can adjust your environment if required. It is even possible that there is no */etc/profile* present in your system since everything is regulated by */etc/default/login.*

```
$pwd
/usr/guest
$cat .profile
...
PATH=/bin:/usr/bin:$HOME/bin:. #set command search path
MAIL=/usr/spool/mail/'logname' #mailbox location
...
export PATH MAIL
$
```

8.4   Exporting environment variables

If you examine the *profile* and *.profile* files, you can observe that the environment variables are not only initiated, they are also *exported*. In order to discover exactly what this means, we shall have to look a little more closely at what happens when you give shell the command to activate a program.

It is obvious that a new process is activated. A process like this is called a *child process*.
Firstly, a copy of the current shell (the process image) is

made. This copy consists of several components just as the process itself. For the moment, we shall refer to this as having a general part and a specific part.

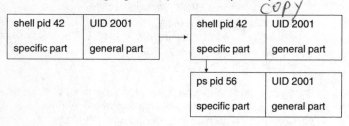

shell pid 42	UID 2001
specific part	general part

shell pid 42	UID 2001
specific part	general part

ps pid 56	UID 2001
specific part	general part

After the copy has been made, the specific part of the copy is replaced by the new program. Take a glance at the process table which was introduced in the previous section.

```
$ ps -el
   F  S   UID   PID  PPID  C   PRI  NI ADDR  SZ   WCHAN  TTY TIME  CMD
  ..  .    ..         ..   .. ..    ..  .. ...  ..:..  .. ...
   1  S 2001    42     1   1   30   20  18b  20   18d34   01 0:01  sh
  ..  .    ..         ..   .. ..    ..  .. ...  ..:..  .. ...
   1  R 2001    56    42   5   52   20  26a  24           01 0:00  ps
$
```

The **ps** program, process 56, is a child of your shell, since its PPID is 42. It is difficult to establish whether **ps** has inherited all the features of the general part of the shell, since **ps** only has a fleeting existence: when it has performed its task it hands back the operation to the original shell. It is better to check the inheritance of features in another way. You can start a new shell, a sub-shell, from your shell.

First display a full list of environment variables on the screen using the command **set**. Subsequently, start up a subshell using the command **sh** and again display a list of the environment variables on the screen using the **set** command. At the moment it is not important to know the significance of all the variables; what we are concerned with here is checking whether both sets are identical, thus inherited.

```
$set
...
$sh
$set
...
$
```

You can confirm that you really have activated a sub-shell, by using the command **ps**.

Using the environment variable PS1 we shall illustrate the significance of exporting. PS is the shell prompt, which is probably defined as *PS1=$* in your system. Define a new prompt using the following command:

```
$PS1="--->"
--->
```

The new prompt is directly valid. Subsequently, start another new shell. This will result in you seeing your old prompt.

```
--->sh
$
```

This subsubshell does not recognize the new prompt. From this fact, you can deduce that a new variable is only valid within the process in which it has been defined: variables are local. In order to give a variable any validity outside that process, you will have to export it; in other words, you will have to transfer it to the general part of the process. Then child processes will also recognize the variable.

In order to try this out, first return to the previous shell. This is done by interrupting the current process (the current shell) by pressing <Ctrl-D>. You will recognize the shell by the special prompt which is located directly behind the normal prompt:

```
$--->
```

Subsequently, place the new PS1 in the general process environment.

```
$--->export PS1
--->
```

By activating a new shell, a subsubshell, you can check
whether the export has taken place properly.

```
--->sh
--->
```

The prompt has been adopted by the new shell, which
means that all child processes inherit the variable. Return to your login shell: press <Ctrl-D> twice and the familiar dollar sign will reappear on your screen.

```
--->--->$
```

If you had pressed <Ctrl-D> thrice, you would have
logged out. The fact that your prompt now appears as a
dollar sign is logical: the inheritance of features can only
occur in a *descending* line.

8.5   The purpose of environment variables

We shall give a summary of situations which can be
easily and satisfactorily regulated using environment
variables:

- Using the environment variables UID, PID and the
  user group, the operating system can quickly check if
  a process has the right to read, write or use a certain
  file.
- Some programs require variables in order to be able
  to execute their tasks; for example, the shell must
  know how to display the prompt.

■ Perhaps you have already discovered the MAIL-CHECK variable. **MAILCHECK=600** results in the system examining your mailbox once every ten minutes.

■ The **date** command makes use of the TZ variable. You can easily check this:

```
$date
Fri Dec 11 23:47:49 GMT 1992
$TZ=
$export TZ
$date
  Fri Dec 11 15:48:17 PDT 1992
$
```

8.6   Details of the user environment

The user

The user is identified by his/her user number (UID), user name (LOGNAME) and user group (GID). In your evironment, the UID and GID are used and not the name of the user or group. Also all specifications in i-nodes work with these numbers.

If you cannot find the LOGNAME environment variable under XENIX, these data are stored in the */etc/utmp* file. Other versions use USER instead of LOGNAME. However, in both cases you can discover the user name using the command **logname**.

```
$logname
guest
```

The process

The last field in the user line of your password file determines which process will be activated for you. This so-called *login* program characterizes your environment from that moment onwards. In the previous section, we described how the general part of this process is inherited by all child processes. The SHELL environment variable has the required data available.

The terminal

To which process terminal this process is connected also belongs to the environment variables. A question using **tty** will indicate this:

```
$tty
/dev/tty01
```

If you wish to be certain that you are owner of the terminal, use the command **ls**.

```
$ls -lg /dev/tty01
crw--w--w-  1  guest    guests    0, 0 Dec 29 13.28 /dev/tty01
```

You can find out the user name and the terminal by applying the command **who**. In addition, the time when you logged in is also registered. The **who** command finds these data in */etc/utmp*, which is modified at each login and log out procedure. Thus, */etc/utmp* always gives a survey of the active users.

```
$who am i
guest    tty01    Dec 29 13:15
```

In the environment variable TERMCAP, data are stored in the form: 'al=\E[L'; these are necessary for the operation of the terminal. The data themselves are stored in the */etc/termcap* file or */etc/terminfo* directory. Of course, they could be sought there with every procedure which is relevant to the terminal, but this is very time-consuming. Instead they are stored in an environment variable.

The user interface

You can display your user interface status using the command **stty** (set tty):

```
$stty
speed 9600 baud; -parity hupcl
swtch = ^@;
brkint -inpck -istrip icrnl onlcr cr0 nl0 tab0 bs0 vt0 ff0
echo echoe echok
$
```

An extensive explanation of the way to specify the interface settings is given later in this book. The values shown in the example are a sample from the entire collection. These are easier to comprehend than you may imagine when you first see them.

Speed indicates the speed of transport of the data between your terminal and the computer.

Parity is switched off, which means that the transmission of data is not checked for possible mistakes.

The abbreviations have the following significance: i represents input, o output, cr <Return> (carriage return), nl new line, bs backspace, and ff form feed. You are already acquainted with tab and echo.

The harddisk

In a multi-user system, you never have free access to the harddisk. Only certain directories are available to you. In any case, the directory containing your mailbox is one of these. The name of this is stored in the MAIL environment variable.

```
$ls -l $MAIL
-rw-r----- 1 guest guests 232 Dec 30 18:47
/usr/spool/mail/guest
```

Your place on the harddisk is determined by your *login* directory, from where you can create as many subdirectories as you wish. This position is not physically determined and cannot be expressed in certain sectors and cylinders of the harddisk. This is a matter of logical (organizational) layout which is dynamically managed. This means that the size of the area is not fixed.

The directory in which you begin working does not have to be your login directory. At your request, the system manager can include another directory in the *passwd* file.

The HOME environment variable assumes the value of the login directory. You can alter this value so that the **cd** command (without parameters) does not return you to the login directory when you have been visiting other directories, but to a directory of your choice.

Work operation

Finally, there are many environment variables actively supporting your work at the terminal. They are linked to your environment when the system is activated or they are exported there in the course of working. These include, for example, PS1 (your shell prompt), HZ, TZ etc.

Perhaps you have discovered IFS already. IFS stands for internal field separator. This is the character which divides fields from each other in one line. This is generally a colon, which is standard with UNIX. If you wish to extract individual specifications from this line, the fields must be separated. A program wishing to make use of these values must first assign the value ':' to IFS. UNIX also allows the use of several separators simultaneously.

We shall discuss a new environment variable in the next chapter: EXINIT which contains the initial parameters for the text editor.

9 Word processing

9.1 Introduction

9.1.1 The demands on word processors

A word processor must have the capability to create and alter text, to adjust the layout of the text and to print it. This may vary from the writing of letters to the production of text for a book. The integration of text, diagrams and pictures is a part of this process.

You will undoubtedly prefer to see the results of your work immediately on the screen. This facility is called WYSIWYG: What You See Is What You Get. However, this requires considerably more in terms of hardware and software than the average word processor provides.

Nowadays a general distinction can be made between four kinds of word processors: editors, text layout programs, word processors and desktop publishing programs.

An editor is the most simple form: using it you can create and modify text.

A text layout program does the subsequent work. Operating codes which you applied using the editor are translated into line wrap, end of paragraph, fonts etc. Using macros, you can lighten the workload substantially when writing form letters for example. Macros are groups of commands in a text layout program which allow you to edit a text easily. A macro is mostly executed by a single keystroke.

A word processor is a combination of an editor and a text layout program. The WYSIWYG feature is often closely approached here.

DTP programs (desktop publishing) are much more involved with the layout of texts. Hardware which sup-

ports graphic display is a precondition of using DTP programs. Several programs are frequently linked to each
other to produce the display of text, diagrams and im-
ages.

As is generally the case with this sort of division, the categories are not absolute. Modern word processors are
often equipped with features which were exclusive to
DTP programs up until now. At the same time, there are
still primitive line editors of roughly the same quality as
an electric typewriter.

9.1.2   The development of word processors

Once upon a time there were only line editors: you
could type a line and conclude it by pressing <Return>.
Subsequently, the line was inaccessible in principle. If
you wanted to make an alteration to a line which had not
been concluded, you had to place the cursor at the position of the mistake and type the rest of the line again
completely. There were relatively elaborate instructions
for the display of lines on the screen. The original UNIX
editor was called **ed**.

A great leap forwards was the introduction of a third
mode in addition to the already existing *input mode* and
command mode: using the cursor, each position in the
text became accessible. Corrections could be made to
the text without laborious instructions. Present-day
UNIX versions are equipped with a text editor of this
type: **vi**.

However, anyone who really wishes to get down to work
with a word processor demands much more. A word
processor must be able to make a second text available
by means of a single keystroke. Interchange of text
blocks must be possible between the texts. A screen
must be able to be divided into windows, so that two
texts can easily be compared or so that a help screen is
permanently available.

A programming language with variables, operating structures and a large number of word processing commands makes it possible to formulate texts using macros or programs. The significance of the keys can be freely chosen. Under UNIX, the programming languages Emacs and MicroEmacs are suitable for this. Both languages are public domain and are also available for PCs, the Atari ST and the Amiga.

Word processors such as WordPerfect which attempt to emulate the WYSIWYG principle also run under UNIX.

9.1.3   Working with applications

Applications are complicated collections of commands used to process data. They include not only commercial programs brought onto the market by software manufacturers, but also programs developed by you personally to organize a chess competition, for example, may also be called applications.

The programs with which we have worked up until now often consisted of no more than a single command. They were implemented by the user interface which subsequently handed the operation back to the shell so that you could continue working. The command **cat** is an exception to this rule - here you must personally indicate that you wish to conclude the input. All other characters which you have entered up until now have been data. A word processor does more than this. It is an interactive program, which means that you not only enter data, you also specify instructions for modifying the data or implementing them in a certain way. Thus, this can be described as a real application.

Programs like these have a visible or invisible user interface. If a program can run in several modes, the interface will generally change along with the mode. Some keystrokes will then suddenly have a different significance. This is almost always the case if you switch from one program to another. However, many keystrokes are more or less standardized so that they do have the same significance in many UNIX programs.

It is self-evident that you have to know something about a program like this before being able to work with it. It is reasonably easy to destroy hours of work with a wrong keystroke or to activate a mode from which you cannot escape owing to lack of know-how. Keep in mind that you may not quit UNIX using a reset: you must always follow the log out procedures mentioned.

9.1.4 Working with word processors

If you have previously worked with a word processor, working with **vi** will probably seem rather strange at first. This is primarily due to the fact that *vi* has evolved from a line editor and this heritage has not completely disappeared. In addition, all the functions for modifying the text or the position of texts can be reached by pressing the normal keys instead of the <Ctrl> keys and that very many of this type of commands are available. No use is made of the <Alt> key. The fact that the text editor has remained line-oriented has the advantage that it is extremely suitable for programming since each line contains a closed expression.

Word processors require skills. Practice should make perfect. However, practice has also shown that it is almost impossible to know two word processors right down to the finest details. Nevertheless, we do recommend you to learn the principles of *vi* since this program is supplied with all versions of UNIX.

Discussing *vi* in great detail is beyond the scope of this book. We shall restrict the explanation to the most important functions. Much of that which we shall skip is aimed at achieving the same objective with less keystrokes. But this know-how is not really necessary to be able to work quickly with UNIX. Practical knowledge of the universal key functions and the repeat commands for searching and replacing in *vi* constitute two of the more important aspects.

9.2 Basic principles of vi

9.2.1 The UNIX standard editor vi

Actually, *vi* is not really the editor itself, it is only the display of the editor geared to the screen. In addition to this *vi mode*, the editor also has an *ex mode* and an *open mode*.

If you activate the editor, which is normally done using the command **vi file_name** and the text appears hotchpotch on the screen, or the message **Using Open Mode** appears, this means that *vi* does not possess the correct information concerning the type of terminal at which you are working.
If the system manager or an experienced *vi* user is around, it is best to request help. Perhaps you can solve the problem yourself assisted by the following tips.

Return to the shell by pressing **:q!**, followed by <Return> or <Del>**:q!**<Return>. Now you must find out the name of the terminal at which you are working. Subsequently specify the TERM environment variable and export the information so that all programs can make use of it:

```
$TERM=vt100
$export TERM
$
```

When you have seen that *vi* now works properly, change to the log in directory and add both commands to your *.profile* file using the command **cat >>.profile**. Be sure to use two greater-than signs consecutively to append the information, otherwise the two commands will be written over the existing contents of the file. Accordingly, as a safety measure, first make a backup of the *.profile* file: **cp .profile .profile.bak**.

9.2.2   Starting up vi

We shall illustrate the use of the text editor using the
calendar. We shall create the text by copying the contents of an existing file called *cal* (last year's calendar)
to an existing calendar. We shall first make a separate
directory for the word processor texts: */usr/guest/texts*.

```
$pwd
/usr/guest
$mkdir /usr/guest/texts
$cd texts
$pwd
/usr/guest/texts
$cal 1992 >calendar
$vi calendar


                                    1992


         Jan                    Feb                    Mar
 M  TU W  TH F  S  S    M  TU W  TH F  S  S    M  TU W  TH F  S  S
       1  2  3  4  5                   1  2                   1  2
 6  7  8  9 10 11 12    3  4  5  6  7  8  9    3  4  5  6  7  8  9
13 14 15 16 17 18 19   10 11 12 13 14 15 16   10 11 12 13 14 15 16
20 21 22 23 24 25 26   17 18 19 20 21 22 23   17 18 19 20 21 22 23
27 28 29 30 31         24 25 26 27 28         24 25 26 27 28 29 30
                                              31


         Apr                    May                    Jun
 M  TU W  TH F  S  S    M  TU W  TH F  S  S    M  TU W  TH F  S  S
    1  2  3  4  5  6             1  2  3  4                      1
 7  8  9 10 11 12 13    5  6  7  8  9 10 11    2  3  4  5  6  7  8
14 15 16 17 18 19 20   12 13 14 15 16 17 18    9 10 11 12 13 14 15
21 22 23 24 25 26 27   19 20 21 22 23 24 25   16 17 18 19 20 21 22
28 29 30               26 27 28 29 30 31      23 24 25 26 27 28 29
                                              30
         Jul                    Aug                    Sep
"calendar" 40 lines, 1991 characters
```

The first section of the calendar is displayed on the screen. The bottom line is reserved as *status line* and *command line*. At this moment, you can see that the calendar file is currently loaded, that it contains 40 lines and consists of 1991 characters.

If no statement is shown on the status line or if only the following appears on your screen

```
~
~

"file name" [New file]
```

something has gone wrong. We shall deal with possible faults in section 9.7.

If you are working with a system with a low baud rate for transferring the data between the terminal and the computer, it may be that only a part of the screen is being used as a word processor. In this case, you do not need to worry: it is simply a matter of too much time being consumed to fill the screen each time.

9.2.3   The vi work modes

vi has three work modes:

- the *insert* or *input* mode, for entering text,
- the *edit mode*, in which you move the cursor to a section of text and make alterations there,
- the *command mode*, which is for commands which pertain to the whole text.

You cannot specify commands in the insert mode; you can only indent lines and make corrections to the current line. In contrast, you cannot enter text in the edit mode or in the command mode.

Various names are used for these modes, depending on which version of UNIX is being used. The insert mode is also referred to as the input mode. The edit mode also occurs under the names 'visual command mode' and (under XENIX) 'command mode'. This may be confusing because 'command mode' refers to the command mode (the third option above) in other versions.

In fact, visual command mode isn't such a bad term since the commands entered in this mode always produce an effect on a part of the text shown on the screen.

Finally, XENIX calls the command mode '*ex* escape mode'. This isn't such a bad term either: it gives an indication of what goes on behind the scenes. When you activate this mode, the editor switches over temporarily to the situation in which you can execute programs and commands.

The program starts off in the edit mode. From there you can switch to the insert mode or the command mode. The edit mode is always half-way house.

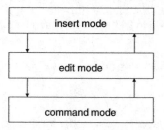

9.2.4 Dealing with malfunctions

In the edit mode, all keystrokes are program instructions. Therefore be very careful: do not try out all sorts of keys while you are not fully aware of what the effects may be.

An acoustic warning signal is produced if a command cannot be implemented. For instance, imagine you have a blank screen before you and the cursor is located on the first line. If you press the k, the cursor should move up one line. In this case, that is impossible and a warning sound is given.

If you have landed in a situation in which you do not have full control over what is happening, you can discontinue the command by pressing the <Del> key. The <Del> key is also used to switch from the insert mode to the edit mode.

The display on your screen can be chaotic due to a technical disturbance or due to messages from other users. When in the edit mode, you can press <Ctrl-L> to remove the display of garbage in your text. Try it out. If you now press <Ctrl-L>, the status line will disappear from your screen.

9.2.5 Moving the cursor

The cursor can be moved across the screen using four keystrokes:

h	one position to the left
j	one line downwards
k	one line upwards
l	one position to the right
spacebar	as l

In addition, if you have the TERM variable correctly set for your terminal and keyboard, you will be able to use the separate keypad containing cursor keys.

9.2.6 Switching between modes

Although there is a whole range of instructions for switching from the edit mode to the insert mode, the following commands are the most important:

i	insert. Text is entered at the current cursor position.

a	append. Text is entered one character to the right of the current cursor position.
O	open new line. Text is entered on the line above the current line.
o	open new line. Text is entered on the line under the current line.

Move the cursor to a position where you wish to insert something, for example a blank line, and press **i**. Nothing visible happens. However, if you press **i** once more, this letter will appear on the screen. The **i** command has carried out exactly what you wished, i.e. switched over to insert mode. The system then waits until you type the characters you wish to insert, in this case the second **i**.

Normally, in the edit mode, *vi* does not give an echo of a command on the screen. This may be disquieting at first. After the first **i**, you were already in the edit mode, although you could not see this. For those who wish to observe the current working mode, *vi* has the **showmode** option. If this has been specified, the words INPUT MODE will be shown in the bottom right hand corner when you are in the input mode.

We now wish to specify the showmode option and at the same time learn how to switch from one mode to the other.

First remove the **i** in the first line using the <Backspace> key. To switch from the insert mode to the edit mode, press <Esc>. To move from the edit mode to the command mode, enter the colon (:).

The command mode has two main functions:

■ implementing commands to alter the form of the text or to look for characters in the text, and
■ activating options which adjust the work environment to one's own requirements.

In the command mode, the commands are specified in the form of text which is then concluded by pressing

<Return>. As long as you have not concluded the com-
mand, you can use the <Backspace> key to make corrections. When the program has implemented the command, it returns to the edit mode automatically.

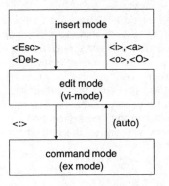

The transfer to the command mode can always be recognized by the fact that the cursor jumps to the status
line. The status line has then become a command line,
which can again be recognized by the colon in the first
column.

If the cursor does not jump to the status line, but a colon
appears in the text at the cursor position, you have forgotten to quit the insert mode. You have not pressed
<Esc> before pressing the colon.

vi is now active in the command mode and you can
switch on the showmode option.

```
    . . .
    . . .
    . . .
:set showmode
```

When you press <Return>, you will return to the edit
mode automatically. Press **i** again and the statement
'INPUT MODE' will appear on the status line.

9.2.7   Making corrections in the insert mode

Now type a text with intentional mistakes in order to become familiar with the *vi* correction keys.

The <Backspace> key deletes the last typed character. You can also press <Ctrl-h> instead of pressing <Backspace>. <Ctrl-w> deletes the last typed word and <Ctrl-u> deletes the whole line. In this case, you will have to type the whole line again. The fact that you can still see the text results from the fact that the screen does not yet mirror the internal memory. 'Deletes' is a relative term: the old text remains on the screen for the time being. In order to save time, *vi* rewrites the line at the moment you conclude it by pressing <Return> or if you press <Esc> to switch to the edit mode.

You are only able to make corrections in the current line, i.e. the line is which the cursor is currently positioned.

9.2.8   Making corrections in the edit mode

You have noticed an error in the first line of your text.

```
You have heart that Armageddon is going to take place on the 7th of
February 1994. Normally, you have appointments on Mondays, Tuesdays and
Thursdays and you want to know whether you will have to shift one of
these. No problem: UNIX will produce calendars on request up to 9999 AD.

...


...

                                                        INPUT MODE
```

The word 'heart' should of course be 'heard'. The mistake is not located in the current line so you will have to switch over to the edit mode in order to correct it. Proceed as follows:

1   Press <Esc> to move to the edit mode; INPUT
     MODE disappears from your screen.
2   Position the cursor on the t in *heart* by using the
     cursor keys or the h,j,k, and I keys.
3   Specify the command **rd**. The r is the abbreviation
     for replace; the d is the letter which will replace the
     t.

Thus, three commands are necessary to change one
letter. *vi* remains in the edit mode after the correction.

9.2.9   Quitting vi and saving texts

You should be careful when closing *vi*. This is primarily
because you could lose your text by specifying the
wrong command. In addition, the correct command will
save the text but it will also write over the original text on
disk.

When you load the text editor using the command **vi file
name**, a copy of the file on the harddisk is made in
working memory.

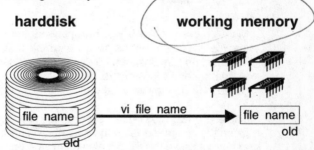

While you are working, you only alter the text in working
memory. If the system fails for any reason (power cut
etc.) you will have lost your alterations, but the original
text remains on the harddisk. In order to prevent you
losing all modifications, *vi* continually makes a backup
in the */tmp* directory of the text in working memory. We
shall explain how to retrieve this copy in section 9.6.3.

harddisk   **working memory**

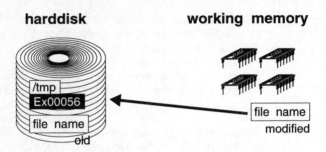

If you finish working and save the modified file under the same name, the original file will be lost.

harddisk   **working memory**

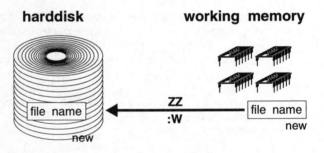

Many (more practical) word processors save the original file under another name, for example *calendar.bak*. The backup remains intact until the altered *calendar* file is again loaded in order to be edited. This extra safeguard is frequently very valuable.

There are two methods to save a file. The easiest is to given the command **ZZ** in the edit mode. This allows you to not only save the file but also to quit the text editor: the familiar shell prompt (*$*) will then appear on the screen.

Load the calendar file in the word processor once more.

```
$vi calendar
```

Use the command **:** to switch to the command mode. The command **q** (quit) followed by <Return> will close *vi*.

The prompt reappears on the screen. Your file has not
been saved and it seems as though you can lose all
your work with a single keystroke. Fortunately, this is
not the case.

Load the *calendar* file once more in the word processor.
Change one character in your text and try again, using
the command **q**, to close the word processor in the
command mode. This is not so easy - on the screen a
message appears:

```
No write since last change (:quit! overrides)
```

vi is alert to the fact that you have made an alteration to
the text and you have not yet saved it. If you really do
not want to save the modified text, give the command
q!.

```
You have heard that Armageddon is going to take place on the 7th of
February 1994. Normally, you have appointments on Mondays, Tuesdays and
Thursdays and you want to know whether you will have to shift one of
these. No problem: UNIX will produce calendars on request up to 9999 AD.
...


...
:q!
$
```

This indicates that you can also save a file interim without having to quit *vi*. The command **w** (write) in the command mode is used for this purpose. You remain in the
editor and can continue working.

```
You have heard that Armageddon is going to take place on the 7th of
February 1994. Normally, you have appointments on Mondays, Tuesdays and
Thursdays and you want to know whether you will have to shift one of
these. No problem: UNIX will produce calendars on request up to 9999 AD.
...


...
:w
```

Keep in mind that UNIX is a multi-user system: perhaps your file will not be immediately stored on the harddisk because other commands may have precedence. If the system fails directly after you have given the command **w**, your command may not be processed as yet. In that case, however, you still have the backup up made by *vi* in the */tmp* directory.

Here is a concise summary of the commands mentioned:

:w	Save the file, replacing the original file; do not quit the editor.
ZZ	Save the file and quit the editor.
:wq	Save the file and quit the editor.
:q!	Do not save the file; quit the editor.

9.2.10   Lost in the command mode

If your status line has suddenly become a command line (a colon is located in the bottom line), you have probably pressed the colon when in the edit mode. You can return to the edit mode by pressing <Return>, <Esc>, <Del> or <Ctrl-C>.

If you press <Return> and the only result is that the screen moves up one line, you have anchored yourself in the command mode by means of the command **Q**. You can only return to the edit mode by giving the command **vi**.

```
You have heard that Armageddon is going to take place on the 7th of
February 1994. Normally, you have appointments on Mondays, Tuesdays and
Thursdays and you want to know whether you will have to shift one of
these. No problem: UNIX will produce calendars on request up to 9999 AD.
...
<Esc><Q>
...
...
:vi<Return>
```

9.2.11 Opening a new file

When you open a new file, the cursor is located on the first line. All other lines contain only a tilde (~), which is an indication that the line is blank. Due to the fact that a tilde is often used as an operating sign, in some versions of UNIX it cannot be used as a tilde in text.

```
$vi new
~
~
~

~
"new" [New file]
```

Quit *vi* once more using the command **:q**.

9.3 Working in the edit mode

Until now we have tried to display all commands and their effects within borders. This cannot be done in the edit mode because the commands have no visible results. Accordingly, we advise you to try out the following examples step by step. If you get stuck, leave the sinking ship by means of <Esc> followed by **:q!** and <Return>. Subsequently, begin again by specifying **vi calendar**. In some cases, <Esc> and <Ctrl-l> will suffice.

9.3.1 Modifying the text window

We require a larger file for the following examples, and therefore we shall link the calendar for 1993 to our existing calendar file.

```
$cal 1993 >>calendar
$vi calendar
```

The screen, excluding the status line, can be regarded as a window behind which you can shift the text up-

wards and downwards. The following keystrokes are
relevant here:

Ctrl-e   one line upwards
Ctrl-f   one page upwards
Ctrl-y   one line downwards
Ctrl-b   one page downwards

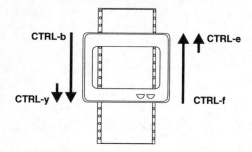

The command **z** is very useful for scrolling the text a required amount:

z<Return>   The current line becomes the top line of
                the window.
z.   The current line becomes the middle line
                of the window.
z-   The current line becomes the bottom line
                of the window.
7z<Return> The seventh line becomes the top line of
                the window.
nz.   The nth line becomes the middle line of
                the window.
nz-   The nth line becomes the bottom line of
                the window.

If you attempt to make the seventh line the bottom line
of the window, you will not succeed. You will also be unable to make the seventh line the middle line of the window. This is due to the fact that your screen probably
has twenty four lines available for text, so that you will
have to specify at least the twenty fourth line as the bottom line. Correspondingly, twelve lines are the minimum

requirements in order to specify a middle line (the twelfth line).

9.3.2 Marking a position

You can mark a position in the text by applying the command **mx**. This x represents any normal letter (not capitals). You will have to remember which position you have marked because this is not displayed on the screen. The command **'x** enables you to jump from any position in the text to the marked position. If you want to jump back again, give the command **''**. You can use these commands as often as you like, thus you can jump back and forward between these positions at will.

mx	marks a position in the text with the letter x (may be any other letter.)
'x	jumps to the position marked by x.
''	jumps to the previous cursor position.

Mark a position in the first line, for instance the d in *heard*, using the command **ma**.

```
You have heard that Armageddon is going to take place on the 7th of
February 1994. Normally, you have appointments on Mondays, Tuesdays and
Thursdays and you want to know whether you will have to shift one of
these. No problem: UNIX will produce calendars on request up to 9999 AD.
...


...
                                              INPUT MODE
```

Press the j to move the cursor a few lines downwards and then try to jump back to the d using the command **'a**.

If this doesn't work, something has gone wrong. It may be that the quote (') is not generated by the key indicated. Examine this as follows: set the cursor on a blank line and activate the insert mode using **i** or **a**. You can now try out the keys. When you have found the appropriate key, delete the line using <Ctrl-u> and switch back to the edit mode using <Esc>.

If you suddenly find yourself in the insert mode, the **ma** command has not worked properly. The m has not been executed correctly and the a has been interpreted as the command to switch to the insert mode. Press <Esc> to return to the edit mode and try again.

9.3.3   Moving the cursor to a certain position

We have already mentioned the four most important keystrokes for moving the cursor.

h   one position to the left
j   one line downwards
k   one line upwards
l   one position to the right

Instead of pressing the l, you can also use the spacebar to move the cursor one position to the right. The following keystrokes are also useful:

$ moves the cursor to the end of the line
^   moves the cursor to the beginning of the text on the
        same line
0   moves the cursor to the first position on the line

You will undoubtedly often use the first two commands. Unfortunately, they are not the most user-oriented keystrokes. In addition, you should keep in mind that the caret symbol (^) sometimes has a special significance and is not always located at the same place on the keyboard.

The commands below always move the cursor to the first position of the relevant line.

H   moves the cursor to the first line of the current
        screen

M moves the cursor to the middle line of the current screen

L moves the cursor to the bottom line of the current screen

G moves the cursor to the last line of the entire text

7G moves the cursor to the seventh line of the entire text

{ moves the cursor to the nearest paragraph break upwards

} moves the cursor to the next paragraph break downwards

vi also has commands allowing larger sections of text to be used as jump intervals:

Ctrl-F moves the cursor forward a window

Ctrl-B moves the cursor backwards a window

Ctrl-D moves the cursor forward part of a window

Ctrl-U moves the cursor backwards part of a window

When *vi* is first activated, the partial-window commands scroll the window half the window size. This amount can be reset by prefixing the partial-window commands by a number. This number regulates the amount of lines to be scrolled. UNIX also remembers this for all future <Ctrl-D> and <Ctrl-U> commands until respecification.

The following commands may be more useful. You can move through the text in a more detailed way.

w moves the cursor to the beginning of the next word

W moves the cursor to the beginning of the next word; ignores non-alphanumeric characters

e moves the cursor to the end of the current word

E moves the cursor to the character before the next space - even if it is not alphanumeric

b moves the cursor back to the beginning of the current word

B moves the cursor back to the character after the previous space - even if it is not alphanumeric

These commands can also be used in combinations with numbers. For example, **4b** will move the cursor 4 words backwards.

When using small letters in commands, the beginning of a word is the first operating sign or the first letter in a string. Now move to the end of your calendar using the command **G** and enter the following text:

```
yes...and...no yes... and..no...no...no
```

Quit the insert mode and type the command **bbBBB**. The cursor should now be at the beginning of the line. Try out other commands in the same way at leisure. The more you practice, the easier it will become when you get down to work.

9.3.4   Searching in the text

All the commands which we have discussed up until now are applicable no matter the current text. However, if you know the text, you can use them to move the cursor to a required position. *vi* has two methods of searching:

■ searching for a character in a line
■ searching for a position in the entire text.

The command used to search for a certain character in the current line is **f**. For example, **fz** means: go to the next character z in the current line. Now move to the beginning of the text using the command **1G**.

```
You have heard that Armageddon is going to
                     take place on the 7th of
```

Now type **fa**. The cursor will jump to the a in have, thus to the first a. Type a semi-colon to repeat the command. The cursor then jumps to the a in heard.

If you wish to look backwards through the text for the same character, use a comma instead of a semi-colon.

If you wish to look for a string in a text, use the slash command. The cursor will then move to the position behind the slash in the command line and you can then type the string which is to be sought.

```
. . .
/31
```

Press <Return> to conclude the command and the search can begin. The function will stop at the first finding. If you type an **n**, the next occurrence will be sought. If you type a capital **N**, the search will be continued in the opposite direction. When the end of the file has been reached, the function will continue at the beginning of the file.

You can also use a question mark to search backwards. You can use the commands **n** and **N** to continue the search as described above.

You can also use wildcards in search strings. These are signs which indicate that at that position a random character may occur. The wildcards are shown in the list below:

.	represents all characters
*****	represents zero or any number of repetitions of the last character
[a-z]	represents small letters
[^a-z]	represents all characters excluding small letters
[ea]	represents only the characters e and a

The last wildcard can be used, for example, to look for all words such as bat and bet.

```
. . .
/b[ea]t
```

Using the following four characters, you can search more precisely.

^	searches at the beginning of the lines
$	searches at the end of the lines
\<	searches at the beginning of words
\>	searches at the end of words

Using the backslash (\), you can switch off the operating functions of the arrows (< and >) and the positioning signs ^ and $ (also referred to as metacharacters). If you wish to completely eliminate these special functions, you can make use of a special option:

```
set nomagic
```

The backslash function is then reversed: for example, a backslash in front of a dollar sign makes it an operating sign again. If you wish to activate the special function of these signs once more, give the command

```
set magic
```

The example below shows the command used to search for all words which begin with a u (both small and capital letters).

```
/\<[uU]
```

You may also combine position signs with wildcards in *vi*. Examples of this are:

```
/^[0-9]$        searches for a line containing only one number
/^[0-9]*$       searches for a line containing only numbers or which is blank
/[0-9][0-9]*    searches for numbers consisting of at least one digit
```

We have now gone rather deeply into the details of *vi*. You will probably only use these in exceptional cases. However, if you begin working with another word processor which does not provide these facilities, you can always work on your text using both word processors.

9.3.5 Deleting text

We advise you to try out the commands in this section yourself. In the following section we shall deal with copy commands which are extremely similar to deletion commands. The difference is, however, that you can see what is being removed in the case of deletion commands, while the result of copy commands remain hidden.

Since chaos will probably arise when you begin experimenting with the deletion commands, the most important command which we shall deal with here is the one which allows you to repair the damage done by all kinds of deletion commands. The command **:e!** deletes the copy of the file in working memory and loads the original file which is still stored on the disk.

The first command enabling you to alter text, and thus delete characters, has already been introduced:

rx   replace the character under the cursor with x

If you specify <Return> for x, a line wrap will be inserted. Place the cursor on the second line of the text behind the full stop and enter the command.

```
You have heard that Armageddon is going to take place on the 7th of
February 1994. Normally, you have appointments on Mondays, Tuesdays and
Thursdays and you want to know whether you will have to shift one of
these. No problem: UNIX will produce calendars on request up to 9999 AD.
...
```

The text is now distributed differently over the lines.

```
You have heard that Armageddon is going to take place on the 7th of
February 1994.
Normally, you have appointments on Mondays, Tuesdays and
Thursdays and you want to know whether you will have to shift one of
these. No problem: UNIX will produce calendars on request up to 9999 AD.
...
```

The line wrap after the first word 'and' is now unnecessary. Remove this using the command **J**. Position the cursor any where on the line and specify the command.

```
You have heard that Armageddon is going to take place on the 7th of
February 1994.
Normally, you have appointments on Mondays, Tuesdays and Thursdays
and you want to know whether you will have to shift one of
these. No problem: UNIX will produce calendars on request up to 9999 AD.
...
```

Now do the same for the line wrap behind 'of' in the fourth line. The text will then appear as desired.

J   joins two lines

Characters in a text are deleted using the command **d**. This is an abbreviation for delete. This command deals with a so-called *operator*, which means you must indicate what is to be deleted. If, for example, you give the command **dw** with the cursor at the start of the word, that word will be deleted. You can use **d** in combination with all position specifications we have mentioned up until now. Here are a few examples:

```
d`a      delete the text from the cursor to the marked position
dw       delete the word at whose start the cursor is positioned
dH       delete the text from the cursor backwards to the top of the screen
dG       delete the text from the cursor to the end of the text
d/bat    delete the text from the cursor to the first occurrence of the word
bat.
```

The last three commands in particular should be applied with a great deal of care. Because *vi* is 'line-oriented', the whole line containing the cursor will be deleted. You can easily delete too much before you realize it. If you wish to delete a text completely, place the cursor at the beginning of the text and give the command **dG**.

If you wish to delete a line, jump to the beginning of the line using **0** and then give the command **d$**. The command **J** enables you to delete the superfluous line wrap and therefore the blank line. All in all, this is rather laborious and a separate command has been developed to replace these three commands: **dd** deletes the current line in one go. The command **D** (instead of **d$**) deletes the rest of the line.

dd	deletes an entire line including the line wrap
D	deletes the line from the cursor position (instead of d$)

Text which you have deleted is not immediately lost. Use can be made of the following commands to restore deleted text:

u	undoes the last deletion; if you press u again, the deletion is again implemented
p	the text which has just been deleted, or is in memory, is inserted after the cursor. If the deletion is a complete line, it is inserted on the line below the cursor.
P	the text which has just been deleted, or is in memory, is inserted before the cursor. If the deletion is a complete line, it is inserted on the line above the cursor.

The buffer in which the deleted text is temporarily stored can hold nine texts which can all be restored using the following command:

"np	insert the nth deleted text behind the cursor

If you specify a capital **P**, the nth text can be restored in front of the cursor. This deletion buffer does have its limitations: individual words are not saved, only entire lines. The dot command (.) is generally used to repeat the last command. This is also the case in these procedures.

If you are looking for a certain text which you have deleted, begin with the command **"1p**. If this is not the required text, undo the insertion using the command **u**. Subsequently, use the point (**.**) to recover the next deleted text etc. The command **.** automatically ensures that the counter relevant to the deleted texts is raised by one.

You can try this out yourself by placing the cursor on the first line of your text and deleting the first nine lines using the command **dd**. Subsequently, search through the deletion buffer using the command range

```
"1p
u
.
u
...
.
```

You will finally find the first line.

If you specify a number in front of a command, you can determine how often the command should be implemented. For example, the command

```
3dw
```

will delete three words. You may also type

```
d3w
```

The result is the same. Other combinations are possible. For example, the command

```
3d3w
```

will delete a total of nine words. In practice this is not very convenient. The command **dw**, repeated twice by specifying **..**, which enables you to delete three words, is just as quick and much clearer. In addition, the command **u** allows you to recover the last word. There is also the command **U** which enables you to undo all alterations to the current line.

U   undoes all alterations to the current line

The command only works, however, as long as you have not quit the current line.

Two combinations of commands which are extremely useful are:

xp   switches two characters
ddp   switches two lines

All information which we have just given concerning the **d** operator, is also applicable to the **c** operator. The command **c** also deletes characters, but then switches immediately to the insert mode.

Caution   Always be alert: it may occur that you begin to enter a deletion command, change your mind and forget to press <Del> to discontinue the deletion command. Imagine you have specified a **d** and then decide to continue at the end of the text by pressing **G**. **dG** deletes everything from the current position to the end of the text. Watch out!

A similar mistake can be made if <CapsLock> is accidentally activated. You may wish to type **d** to delete a single character, but you find that the whole line is deleted. Similarly, **j** may seem not to work properly: instead of the cursor moving to the next line, a line wrap is removed.

9.3.6   Copying sections of text

The operator **y** (yank) is the command used for copying. This does not really copy the text directly: it is placed in one of the deletion buffers. By using the commands **p** and **P**, you can insert it at the required position.

```
yo    place data in deletion buffer 1
```

Owing to the fact that deletion buffers are repeatedly deleted and refilled with new data, there are buffers with names. Letters of the alphabet are used for this. You can address these as "a, "b, "c etc.

In order to copy a section of text, the following two commands are necessary:

```
"a2yy     place two lines in buffer a
"ap       insert the contents of buffer a
          behind the cursor
```

A combination of these commands is also possible:

```
"ay/1992   copy the section of text from the
           cursor position to the line
           containing the number 1992 to buffer a
```

9.3.7   Indenting in the edit mode

Using the instruction > you can indent a line to a certain position: the *shift width*. The operator < enables you to perform the opposite. The default shift width setting is 8 (**sw=8**). You can specify the shift width using the command **set sw=x** where x represents the required width. Both these operators use the same arguments as in the commands **c** and **d**.

We shall illustrate the effect of the command using the initial text.

```
You have heard that Armageddon is going to take place on the 7th of
February 1994.
```

You can indent both lines using the command **2>>**.

```
You have heard that Armageddon is going to take place on the 7th of
February 1994.
```

Restore the previous situation using the command **u** and change the shift width to four.

```
You have heard that Armageddon is going to take place on the 7th of
February 1994.

...

...

set sw=4
```

Give the indent command once more, but now use the search function: **>/1994**. The program will now search for the line containing '1994' and indents all lines up to and including the line containing the specified word.

```
You have heard that Armageddon is going to take place on the 7th of
    February 1994.
```

9.3.8   Search and replace

Using the commands which we have discussed up until now, it is also possible to look for and replace sections of text in the edit mode. For example, you could replace all numbers 31 with 32. Proceed as follows:

1   search for the number 31. The first finding will be the last day of January.

```
                              1992

            Jan                     Feb                     Mar
M   TU W   TH F   S   S     M   TU W   TH F   S   S     M   TU W   TH F   S   S
            1   2   3   4   5                       1   2                       1   2
6   7   8   9   10 11 12     3   4   5   6   7   8   9     3   4   5   6   7   8   9
13 14 15 16 17 18 19     10 11 12 13 14 15 16     10 11 12 13 14 15 16
20 21 22 23 24 25 26     17 18 19 20 21 22 23     17 18 19 20 21 22 23
27 28 29 30 31           24 25 26 27 28           24 25 26 27 28 29 30
                                                   31

...

/31
```

2   The command **cw32**, followed by <Esc>, enables
     you to replace 31 with 32 and then return to the edit
     mode. The operator is **c**, and **w** is the word which is
     to be replaced by the string which follows (32).
     When you have given the command **cw**, a dollar
     sign appears behind the number 31 in order to indi-
     cate that the text has been deleted up to that point.
     You can then enter characters at will. The <Esc> key
     returns you to the edit mode.

3   Using the command **n**, you can then look for the
     next number 31.

4   Repeat the replacement using **.** (thus just the dot).

These last two steps can be repeated as often as you
wish.

9.4   Working in the insert mode

9.4.1   Moving to the insert mode unintentionally

It may occasionally happen that you land in the insert
mode unintentionally. You will always recognize this
due to the fact that your commands will not be carried
out - they appear as characters. If you have activated
the showmode option, the statement INPUT MODE will
appear in the status bar in the lower right-hand corner of
the screen.

There are two methods to remove characters which
have been entered unintentionally from the text:

■ Use the repeat function of the <Backspace> key: hold
  the <Backspace> key down. Only the new characters
  will be deleted, the previous ones will remain. An
  acoustic signal will indicate that all new characters
  have been deleted.
■ Quit the insert mode using <Esc> and when in the edit
  mode press the undo key, **u**.

We have already mentioned that you can activate the insert mode using the commands **i**, **a**, **o** and **O**. This can also be done using the commands **I**, **A**, **R**, **s**, **S** and **C**, which we shall not deal with in this book.

9.4.2   Indenting in the insert mode

The *autoindent mode* is used to indent lines in the insert mode.

```
...
:set autoindent
```

Place the cursor on the second line of the text which we indented in section 9.3.7 and activate the insert mode using **o**.

```
You have heard that Armageddon is going to take place on the 7th of
February 1994.
...
```

You can now indent again using <Ctrl-t>. Type a few words and press <Return>.

```
You have heard that Armageddon is going to take place on the 7th of
February 1994.
   Indented lines provide structure.
...
```

Using <Ctrl-D> at the start of a new line, you return to the previous indent position.

```
You have heard that Armageddon is going to take place on the 7th of
February 1994.
   Indented lines provide structure.
This is the previous indent position.
        ...
```

If you occasionally wish to begin right at the beginning of the line, type ^<Ctrl-D>.

```
You have heard that Armageddon is going to take place on the 7th of
February 1994.
    Indented lines provide structure.
  This is the previous indent position.
This line has no indentation this time.
...
```

If you wish the remove all indentation, press **0** (zero) and then <Ctrl-D>.

9.4.3   Using tabs

A jump to the next tabstop is generated by pressing the Tab key or **<Ctrl-i>**. In text, this is a character like any other. A wide space is placed on the screen up to the point where the next Tabstop is located. The distance between the tabstops is specified using the command **ts**. The default setting of ts is eight. If you define another distance, you can reset the previous standard distance by specifying **ts=8** or **ts=0**. The following command sets the tabs stops at four:

```
...
set ts=4
```

A lesser value has little use if, for instance, you wish to type numbers in columns. Numbers consisting of more than three digits confuse the column structure if the setting **ts=4** is specified. A column will then be skipped.

If you wish to produce the same result on your printer as on the screen, the printer must be able to convert the tabstops to the correct amount of space. In general, you will probably have to define all tabstops individually with regard to your printer. Your printer can probably, just like other word processors, place tabstops at any position as long as the individual tabstop positions for a line are specified concretely.

If the **list** option has been set, no space will be inserted. Instead of this, ^I will be displayed on the screen. The default setting is **nolist**. In order to see this effect on the screen, give the following command:

```
...
set list
```

Move the cursor to the end of the text and switch to the insert mode. Type two or three lines, making use of tab-stops. Then switch off the **list** option and set the tab-stops to ten.

```
...
a^Ib^Ic^Id^Ie
A^IB^IC^ID^IE
1^I2^I3^I4^I5
~
~
:set nolist ts=10
```

nolist hides the tab itself, but does display its effect.

```
...
a         b         c         d         e
A         B         C         D         E
1         2         3         4         5
~
~
```

9.4.4   Entering operating characters

There are three operating characters which you may not enter in the insert mode: <Ctrl-j>, which is used to conclude lines, and <Ctrl-q> and <Ctrl-s> which are both required for use by the operating system.

You may enter all other operating characters. Position the cursor in free space on the screen and type <Ctrl-a>, <Ctrl-b>, <Ctrl-c>, and <Ctrl-D>. The first three characters will be placed on the screen as ^A, ^B, ^C. <Ctrl-D> has no effect on your screen since this keystroke has special significance in the insert mode.

However, if you enter <Ctrl-v> in front of <Ctrl-D>, you can then include this operating character in your text. This also applies to the other operating characters: <Ctrl-t>, <Ctrl-h>, <Ctrl-w>, <Ctrl-u> and <Ctrl-m>. <Ctrl-m> is the operating character for <Return>.

<Ctrl-i> is exceptional: you can include it in the text without having to specify <Ctrl-v> in front of it, while the character itself is not visible in the text. <Ctrl-i> has, in fact, the same function as the <Tab> key and thus generates space on the screen.

If you wish to avoid operating characters slipping into your text due to accidental keystrokes, activate the **beautify** or **bf** option.

```
. . .
:set bf
```

Subsequently, activate the insert mode again. Now try to type <Ctrl-a>. An acoustic signal is given and the character is not accepted. If you wish to enter an operating character in an exceptional case when **bf** is active, specify <Ctrl-v> in front of the operating character.

9.5   Working in the command mode

You are already familiar with some commands in the command mode.

:w	save the current file
:wq	save the current file and quit *vi*
:q!	quit *vi* without saving the file
:e!	open a new file

There is an enormous number of commands in the command mode: all the commands provided by the UNIX *ex-* program are available. We shall only deal with the most important of these in the following sections.

9.5.1 Reading in files and command output

There are two commands used in *vi* to read in the contents of a file or the output of a command.

:r file_name   read in the file with the name *file name* behind the current cursor position

:r!command   implement a command and read the resulting output into *vi*

We shall give an example. First delete the entire text using the commands **1G** and **dG**.

```
. . .
No lines in buffer
```

Then read in the *allprov* file.

```
~
~
:r allprov
```

Now try to read in the output of the **date** command.

```
The early bird catches the worm.
~
. . .
~
:r!date
```

```
The early bird catches the worm.
Fri Jan 01 12:42:59 GMT 1993
~
```

9.5.2 Having the shell implement commands

You can easily activate shell functions from *vi* in the command mode. If, for example, you wish to have an overview of your directory or you wish to know the time, you only have to type the command.

```
...
:!date
Fri Jan 01 12:46:21 GMT 1993
[Press return to continue]
```

On some systems, the command line scrolls one line upwards to make room for the time registration. Then both lines scroll another line upwards to make room for the message that you should press a random key to continue (this does not have to be <Return>). On other systems, the *vi* display disappears and you return to the UNIX command line, with the above message displayed.

If you wish to interrupt your work temporarily in order to carry out other commands, execute a new shell from within *vi*. Just to be sure, you should save your text using **:w**.

```
...
:sh
$ps -f
    UID  PID  PPID  C STIME      TTY   TIME   COMMAND
  guest   44    1   0 08:00:01   03    0:01   -sh
  guest   81   44   0 08:14:45   03    0:00   vi calendar
  guest   84   81   0 08:32:22   03    0:00   sh -i
  guest   90   84   0 08:33:56   03    0:00   ps -f
```

There are four active processes at this moment, one descended from the other except for *shell* which is the senior process. This can be recognized by examining the PIDs and PPIDs. *vi calendar* has been started from shell, a second shell from *vi calendar* and the new command, **ps -f**, is descended from the second shell.

If you press <Ctrl-D>, you will terminate the second shell and you will return to *vi*.

Summarizing:

:!command	Have the command executed by the shell and return to *vi*.
:!!	Repeat the previous command executed by the shell.
:sh	Create a new shell. Return using <Ctrl-D>.

The last command which we implemented was **:!date**. A command can be repeated using **:!!**. The command which is to be repeated is first shown on the screen and then executed.

```
...
:!!
:!date
Fri Jan 01 13:03:12 GMT 1993
```

9.5.3 Automatic replacement

The command **s** (substitute) is used to replace one string1 with another string2. The syntax of the command is simple in principle:

```
s/string1/string2
```

In this command, *vi* betrays its development from the line-oriented editor: it will only work in the line in which the cursor is located and the command is only valid for the first occurrence of the string to be replaced. Accordingly, you must specify the lines in which the command is to be executed and, at the same time, whether it should be applied to all occurrences. We shall give examples of application:

:%s/a/the/g	replace in all lines (%) all (g) words a with the
:1,12s/a/the	replace in the first twelve lines the first occurrence of the word a with the
:%s/22//g	delete in all lines all numbers 22
:%s/^2/B	replace the number 2 at the beginning of all lines with a B

:%s/(.*)//g	delete all brackets in the entire text and the text they contain
:7,14s/^/ /	indent the lines seven to fourteen two spaces
:%s/ .//g	this command deletes everything

In these and in other examples, it is convenient when the lines are numbered. This can be done using the command **:set nu**.

9.5.4   Specifying the work environment

We have already indicated how the *vi* work environment can be adapted. *vi* has many of this kind of options. In principle, they all work as follows:

```
:set option
:set nooption
:set option=value
```

You may set several options simultaneously in one command.
If there is the variable EXINIT in the user environment, the values in this variable are read and implemented when *vi* is activated. Quit *vi*, specify the variable and export it to your environment.

```
$EXINIT="set showmode autoindent sw=4"
$export EXINIT
```

Use the command **set** (without parameters) to check if the variable now exists and then restart *vi*. Activate the insert mode to examine whether everything works as required.

It may be the case that EXINIT is already defined by one of the profile files. If that is so, the setting specified by your own *.profile* file is retained since it is implemented after the */etc/profile* file.

There is also another method: the *.exrc* file serves to

determine the environment when you are working in a certain directory. Place set commands in this file, for instance **set nu**. The commands in this file enjoy precedence over the EXINIT variable.

Unfortunately, XENIX and a number of other UNIX versions do not have this file. Nevertheless, there is a solution: there is a universal method of influencing the environment, namely the command

```
:so file_name
```

In the file with the name *file name* there are commands which have to be executed. Of course, the file need not have the name *.exrc*. You can try this out without having to quit *vi*.

```
...
:!echo set nu >.exrc

...
:so .exrc

  1 The early bird catches the worm.
  2 Fri Jan 01 12:42:59 GMT 1993
```

Using the command **:set all**, you can display a survey of all options which can be applied to adapt your working environment. There are 42 of these in total, arranged alphabetically. The most important of these are shown below. You are already familiar with the following options:

name	significance	(return to) default setting
autoindent	indent all lines	noai
beautify	use of operating signs possible without prior <Ctrl-v>	nobf
number	line numbering	nonu
shiftwidth	indent 8 spaces with autoindent	sw=8
showmode	indicate active mode on status line	noshowmode

Other useful options are:

name	significance	(return to) default setting
autowrite	save text automatically when quitting editor or opening new text	noaw
dir	directory where backups are stored	dir=/tmp
errorbells	acoustic signal with error messages	noeb
list	operating characters visible in text (tabs shown as ^I and line feeds as $)	nolist
nomagic	wildcards are not valid in searches; the positioning signs remain valid; a prior backslash \ determines the significance of the wildcard	magic
ignorecase	when searching, the program makes no distinction between small and capital letters	noic
nomesg	no error messages and statements shown on the screen	mesg
redraw	the screen is adjusted after each alteration	nore
remap	when a macro is activated the text is examined for the occurrence of more macros	remap
tabstop	set the interval between the tabstops (^I)	ts=8
term	*vi* cannot run without the environment variable TERM	term=TERM
warn	you are warned if you try to leave the editor without saving the text	warn
wrapmargin	set automatic line wrap; wm=8 means: automatic line wrap 8 positions before the end of the line	wm=0
wrapscan	when the end of the text is reached in search actions, continue at the beginning	ws

If you wish to know which settings differ from the current default settings, give the command **set** in command mode. A survey of all deviating options will then appear on the status line.

9.6   Other special features of vi

9.6.1   Creating command macros

Macros are series of commands which can be activated by a single keystroke or by starting up a file. Macros are extremely useful if you wish to repeat a number of editing instructions in one or more files.

We have already introduced one method of activating a macro: **:so file_name** opens a file containing a range of commands. The term *so* is an abbreviation of *source*.

The second method makes use of the command **map**, which links a keystroke in edit mode to a series of commands. To link insert mode keystrokes, use **map!**.

```
...
:map #1 :!ls -l<Ctrl-v><Return>
```

The special key combination '#l' provides a survey of the current directory in one go. The number symbol (#) is a pseudo function key. In the edit mode, almost all keys have a function and accordingly, the number symbol is reserved for macros. You can save the command in EXINIT or in a file, for example, the *.exrc* file.

The name of the pseudo function key may consist of ten characters; the range of commands may be 100 characters. As shown in the example, you can only place operating signs in text when they are preceded by <Ctrl-v> (<Return> is also an operating character).

The macro is switched off again using the command

```
unmap function_key name
```

The command

```
map
```

activates a survey of all macros. Once you have discovered how convenient macros can be, you will un-

doubtedly use them a great deal. It is sensible to store
these together in the *.exrc* file, for instance, in your *login*
directory. In that case, you should include the following
lines in your *.profile* file:

```
EXINIT="so/usr/guest/.exrc"
export EXINIT
```

This ensures that the work environment which you have
defined in .exrc is always activated when you start up *vi.*
In addition, this provides the advantage that you can
easily adjust the *.exrc* file to the demands of the current
situation. It does not matter in which directory you are
working; the work environment is always adjusted to
your requirements.

9.6.2   Creating text macros

If you often have to type the same word or series of
words in a text, you can create a macro to perform this
task using the command **ab** (abbreviate). The abbreviation is typed behind the command, and then the string
which should be entered. For example:

```
:ab ysn Yours sincerely
```

The abbreviation is only replaced in the text if it is enclosed by two spaces. The command

```
:unab abbreviation
```

switches the text macro off. A survey of all text macros
can be displayed on the screeen using the command

```
:ab
```

9.6.3   Restoring files

We have already mentioned that *vi* stores all alterations
to a text in a file which is saved in the directory specified

in the dir variable. This is generally the directory */tmp*. You should have write permission on this directory, otherwise an error message will appear:

```
tmp/Ex00057 Permission denied
```

00057 is the PID number of the *vi* process. If you have a backup and you have lost the original in working memory owing to a power cut or system failure, it is easy to retrieve the backup. Activate the directory where you were working and start up *vi* using the option **-r** (recover), followed by the file name.

```
$vi -r file_name
```

9.7   Problems

9.7.1   False start

If you activate *vi* without specifying the file to be opened, only an empty screen will appear. The normal statement concerning which file has been opened will not be shown. If you have not yet entered any text, you can close *vi* using the command **ZZ** or **:q** and start again.

If you have entered text before realizing that no file has been opened, the best thing to do is save this new file under a new name.

```
Reading alone is not enough.
You must try out these commands on your computer.
~
...
~
:w timefile
```

If the *timefile* file already existed, an error message would be shown.

A false start can also originate as follows. You think you have started up *vi* with the proper file name. Nevertheless, the following message appears on the screen:

```
. . .
~
...[New file]
```

Examine the file name closely: there is a good chance that you have made a typing error, for instance, '*calender*' or '*cal endar*' instead of *calendar*. Quit the editor using **ZZ** or **q**. If you accidentally include a space in the middle of the file_name, *vi* warns you with

```
1 more file to edit
```

Subsequently, repeat **ZZ** or **q** in order to quit *vi*.

A special variant of this last mistake will occur if the *cal* file already exists. *vi* will then load that file. Hopefully, you will see immediately that something is not quite right and you will quit the program once more.

However, if you have already added text to cal, proceed as follows. Use the command **:f file_name** to give the text in working memory a new name. Delete the section which originally belonged to the cal file and save the text under a new name. Then load the text which you actually wished to work with and add the text which you have just saved using the command **:r file_name**.

9.7.2   Refusal and chaos

Composure and calm will save you! Banging away on random keys is the worst you can do in *vi*. By doing so, you will undoubtedly alter your text drastically. If you then save the resulting mumbo-jumbo hoping to rescue at least something, you will achieve exactly the opposite effect: you will delete the file which is still intact on the harddisk and also the backup in the */tmp* directory!

Here we describe a situation which occurs if your terminal jams or freezes. First try the <Del> key or <Ctrl-C> once, twice, three times and then <Ctrl-I>. Try to move the cursor. If this doesn't help, press <Ctrl-q>. If this also has no effect, press the <Pause> key once.

Hopefully, you will be able to get *vi* under control again, but your screen has become a collage of text fragments. Save it under a new name, and use this backup of the collage as think-tank. Now restore your file by using **vi**'s **-r** option as described in section 9.6.3.

If none of this helps (in this order of sequence), things are not looking too bright. But all is not yet lost. You are working in a multi-user system: you can attempt to approach the matter via another terminal. If you are working on a PC, activate a second screen using <Alt-F2>. If this terminal has similar problems, the operating system has probably lost control over the computer and you will not be able to avoid a reset. If the second terminal does work, use the command **ps** to find out the cause of the malfunction. If you reach the conclusion that *vi* will have to be discontinued, you can subsequently use the method outlined in section 9.6.3 to restore your file.

9.7.3   Illegal instruction - core dumped

Fortunately, this message has nothing to do with nuclear reactors. It indicates a fault in running the program which may cause the program to crash and your terminal to disconnect. If you are working under XENIX, you can try this out using the following command:

```
. . .
:set hardtabs=0
```

This results in an error message: the cursor, although at a strange place, is still blinking but the keyboard no longer reacts.

```
...
Illegal instruction - core dumped
                                    $
```

You will have to connect your terminal to the computer once more. Proceed as follows:

1   Switch to another screen.
2   Log in under your own name.
3   Using **ps -ef**, find out the process number (PID) of the current process on your jammed terminal.
4   Remove its shell using **KILL -9 PID**.

The number 9 indicates that you wish to discontinue the process under all circumstances and regardless of the consequences. In this case, this is necessary. If you do not specify this option, the previous shell will not be discarded and you will not be given the chance to log in again. Switch back to the previous terminal. The following will be displayed on the screen:

```
...
Illegal instruction - core dumped
                                    $
uxschool!login:
```

When you have logged in, you will find a file called **core** in the directory in which you were working when you were editing the text. This is an image of the program in which the fault occurred. Therefore, you should delete this file in this directory before proceeding further.

This sort of fault is reasonably common. As long as you can emulate the fault, it is mainly quite simple to look for a solution using trial and error. Faults whose cause remains elusive are much more troublesome. These kinds of faults also occur but a great deal can be achieved with a little patience. You will develop a sixth sense allowing you to exorcise these evil spirits in the course of time.

10 Communication within the system

10.1 Direct contact with a fellow user

To carry out the following dialogue, two adjacent terminals are necessary. If you are working under XENIX, you do not even have to leave your chair: using the multi-screen function, you have two screens available at one terminal. Log in under two names, for instance guest and Jasper.

10.1.1 A dialogue with Jasper

You wish to arrange something with Jasper. This isn't absolutely secret, so you can do it using the multi-user system. You can discover whether Jasper is logged in by means of the **who** command.

```
$who
root       tty03    Jan 9   10.39
guest      tty02    Jan 9    9.39
Jasper     tty01    Jan 9    9.38
$
```

Now type a note to Jasper:

```
$write Jasper
```

On Jasper's screen, the following message appears:

```
$

    Message from guest (tty02) [Sat Jan 9 11:00:03]
```

Type your invitation.

```
$write Jasper
Hello Jasper.
```

What about a game of chess?
o

As soon as you conclude a sentence using <Return>, it is
transmitted to your colleague's screen. Prior to this, you
can correct your mistakes using <Ctrl-u> and <Back-
space>. The letter 'o' in the last line is an abbreviation for
'over', well-known from the radio transmission world.
Now Jasper knows that it is his turn and he begins by
addressing *guest.*

```
$
    Message from guest (tty02) [Mon Jan 9 11:00:03]
Hello Jasper.
What about a game of chess?
o
write guest
OK. When?
o
```

You reply:

```
    Message from Jasper (tty01) [Mon Jan 9 11:02:14]
OK. When?
o
This afternoon in the pub?
o
```

As long as neither breaks contact by means of <Ctrl-D>,
you can continue the dialogue. Jasper also concludes
his message with o, so that no chaos is produced by
messages crossing each other. Jasper responds:

```
This afternoon in the pub?
o
No problem, prepare yourself for a lethal Sicilian!
<Ctrl-D>
$
```

Jasper closes the communication with an EOF signal. The line is also broken by means of an EOF signal.

```
No problem, prepare yourself for a lethal Sicilian!
(end of message)
<Ctrl-D>
$
```

Many systems state merely EOF instead of '(end of message)'.

10.1.2 Jasper is working at two terminals

If the user to whom you wish to send a message is working at two terminals simultaneously, you should specify the terminal to which the message should be sent: **write jasper tty04**. If you do not do this, the system will show a message on the console. This message states the terminal to which you are linked and also the additional terminal at which Jasper is logged in.

10.1.3 Jasper does not wish to be disturbed

A couple of days later, you try to send another message to Jasper.

```
$write Jasper
Permission denied
$ls -l /dev/tty02
crw-------   1 Jasper   guests   0, 1 Jan 11 08:50 /dev/tty02
$ls -l /dev/tty01
crw--w--w-   1 guest    guests   0, 0 Jan 11 08:52 /dev/tty01
$
```

After his devastating defeat, Jasper has locked his terminal to messages from the outside world using the command **mesg -n**. You can examine the user rights for his terminal in the */dev* directory: only he may make use of the terminal. This is in contrast to your own terminal for which everyone has writing rights.

Instead of the command **mesg -n**, you can also use **chmod go-w /dev/tty01** to deny others writing rights to your terminal. This command is of a higher order than the **mesg** command: if you subsequently specify the command **mesg -y** this will not be applied.

If you have denied other users writing rights to your terminal but you wish to send a message yourself, the system will remind you that you cannot receive an answer.

Finally, keep this in mind: **Write** is an intrusive command which does not allow the receiver complete control over his/her own environment. If you use this instruction a great deal, the receiver may choose to include the command **mesg -n** in his/her *.profile file* and accordingly make it impossible for you to send messages in this way. This is not the intention, of course. You should use the UNIX internal post (mail) for matters which are not really urgent.

10.1.5   Disturbances caused by another user

1   Imagine you are at work with your new text editor *vi*. You are writing a letter and you have just typed, 'In this situation I would like to register the following:'. Just at that moment Jasper sends you a message which thus appears in your letter on the screen 'Pick up a bacon sandwich for me, please.' As we mentioned in section 5.3, this message is not really included in your letter, but it is tedious. Quit the insert mode using <Esc> and restore the screen display using <Ctrl-l>. In order to prevent further disturbances, activate the command mode and type **:!mesg -n**. Jasper types the following message: 'with mustard please'. Now now he is unlucky; the message

```
Can no longer write to /dev/tty01
```

appears on his screen.

2 You have just exchanged a series of notes with Jasper. Unfortunately, Jasper has forgotten to break the connection at the end of the dialogue by pressing <Ctrl-D>, so that his input still appears on your screen.

```
$ls -l
echo hey!
who am i
```

Jasper is trying in vain to get control of his terminal. You could help him: send him a message using write, telephone him or go even go there. The most simple is to make your terminal inaccessible using **mesg -n**. The next time Jasper attempts to send something, he will receive the statement: 'Can no longer write to */dev/tty01*'. The system will break the connection, so that Jasper will regain his prompt and you your peace of mind.

10.1.5 Activating a subshell

While you are having a dialogue with another user, you or the other user can activate a subshell to carry out a job. This is shown in the example below, although it cannot be seen directly on the screen.

```
$!date
Sat Jan 9 09:35:17 GMT 1993
$write root
Hallo root,
the system clock is not set properly.
!date >/dev/tty03
!
o
Thanks for the tip. I've corrected it.
(end of message)
$!date
Sun Jan 10 09:36:45 GMT 1993
!
```

```
<Ctrl-D>
$<Ctrl-D>

uxschool!login:
```

10.2   Sending post via mail

10.2.1   The mail principles

As you know, each user has his/her own postbox. The *mail* program takes care of sending and receiving the post. Much use is made of this facility and thus, in the course of time, it has been adapted and improved. Besides the standard version there is the more powerful Berkeley version which is used under the name **mail** under XENIX. Other systems use the name *mailx* or *Mail*.

Within the scope of this book, we can only discuss the most important functions which are part of all more recent versions. We shall take the Berkeley version as the point of reference to give examples. Although this version demands a certain amount of training, it is superior to other versions in as much as it indicates clearly who has sent a message, to whom the message is sent and what it concerns. In addition, it provides more support in the long run in terms of practical work.

In order to be able activate the Berkeley version by means of the term '**mail**', you can link this this version to to your directory */usr/guest/bin*.

```
$cd /usr/guest/bin
$ln /usr/guest/bin/mailx mail
$PATH=/usr/guest/bin:/bin:/usr/bin
$export PATH
```

Place the directory */usr/guest/bin* before the other directories in the environment variable PATH, so that messages will be sought there first.

Mail provides two work situations: sending mail and receiving mail. The mode activated depends on the way you start up the program:

mail user name enables you to write and send mail
[user name...] to the specified user(s).
mail activates the receiver mode in which you can process the post received.

10.2.2 Sending post

Sending post will cost you little effort since you are already familiar with the **write** command. Both **mail** and **write** make use of the same program.

```
$mail Jasper
subject: party
We are such stuff as dreams are made on.
Best wishes,
        guest
<Ctrl-D>
(end of message)
$
```

In this way, you enter the message line by line. Type <Ctrl-D> to conclude the message. In contrast to what occurs with **cat** and **write**, the contents are only sent when you have pressed <Ctrl-D>. Thus, the message is not transmitted line by line. Nevertheless, you can only make corrections in the current line. This is tedious if you wish to send lengthy messages. You can delete an entire message using <Del> before it is sent.

```
$mail root
subject: complaint
This is no fun!
Everytime I<Del>
(Interrupt -- one more aborts message)
<Del>
Letter saved in "/usr/guest/dead.letter"[New file]5/53
$
```

Your letter, consisting of five lines and 53 characters, is stored in the *dead.letter* file. Mail also allows you to send files and this solves the problem of having to begin all over again. Write your letter in *vi* first.

```
$vi /let/complaint
```

Subsequently load the letter saved as *dead.letter*.

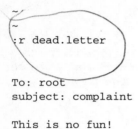

```
~
~
:r dead.letter



To: root
subject: complaint

This is no fun!

~
```

You can now adjust the letter.

```
To: root
subject: complaint


            This is no fun!

Everytime I want to get down to work, someone has tampered with my
settings. Can you help me?

guest
~
```

Quit the editor using **ZZ** and send the letter to the system manager. You suspect your colleague Jasper, so send him a copy to let him know you are aware of his tricks.

```
$mail root Jasper <let/complaint
$
```

Thus, you can send a message to more than one user simultaneously. The great advantage of **mail** in comparison to **write** is that you do not have to disturb anyone who is working and, moreover, you can send messages to users who are not logged in or who have sealed off their terminals to incoming messages.

If you try to send a message to a non-existent user, an error message will appear and the message will be stored in the login directory under the name *dead.letter*.

```
$mail peter
subject: sister
What is your sister's telephone number?

guest
(end of message)
No local user named "peter"
Letter saved in "/usr/guest/dead.letter"[Appended]9/145
$
```

In the Berkeley version of **mail**, each subsequent unsent message is appended to the *dead.letter* file. Other versions write over the previous contents of the file.

You can also send post to yourself. This provides an opportunity to post memos which will appear on your screen the next time you log in.

```
$mail guest
subject: jazz concert
Reserve tickets!!!
(end of message)
$
```

10.2.3   Receiving post

If there is mail for you, UNIX states this when you log in. The system will also do this in between times under certain circumstances when you are at work. Or perhaps there is a stack of mail waiting for you.

```
$mail
mail version 3.0 January 28, 1987. Type ? for help.
3 messages:
  3 guest      Wed  Jan 13 10:14    6/124 "jazz concert"
  2 Jasper     Wed  Jan 13 09:58    8/185 "party"
  1 sysadm     Fri  Dec 11 22:05   10/232 "Welcome to XENIX386"
```

You can now quit the program using **x** or **q** without having modified anything. Commands which are concluded
by pressing <Return> are accepted by mail. The Berkeley
version of mail does not display a prompt on your
screen; other systems use a question mark for this. If
you wish to read a message, type the number which
has been assigned to it and press <Return>. If you only
press <Return>, the contents of the oldest message are
shown on the screen.

```
Message 1:
From sysadm Fri Dec 11  22:04:26 1992
To: guest
Subject: Welcome to XENIX386
Date: Fri Dec 11  22:04:26 1989


                 Welcome to XENIX!

Your login shell is the Bourne shell: please contact
the system adminstrator if you wish this changed.
```

This message was sent when you were registered as
user. The system manager informs you that you can
also get a different user interface (shell) if you wish. You
do not need to save this message indefinitely. Give the
command **d** (delete) to remove the message. You can
recall the list on the screen by pressing **h** (header).

```
h
   3 guest      Wed   Jan 13 10:14    6/124 "jazz concert"
   2 Jasper     Wed   Jan 13 09:58    8/185 "party"
<Return>
-
Message 2:
From Jasper Wed   Jan 13 09:58:09 1993
To: guest
Subject: party
Date: Wed  Jan 13 09:58:09 1993

The next party is coming Saturday at 10 o'clock
Your are very welcome if
```

The message is not complete, so you send an answer
to Jasper by means of the command **r** (reply).

```
r
To: Jasper
Subject: party

Thanks for the invitation which, however, is interrupted at 'if'.
if what?

guest
(end of message)
```

Now you have to wait. In the meantime, you wish to save
the invitation in your */let* directory. In order to be sure that
you will not overwrite another file, you first wish to
examine the contents of the */let* directory. Just as in the
write command, the exclamation mark will help here:
you quit *mail* temporarily and return to the shell.

```
!ls let
complaint
. . .
```

Now using **s** (save), you can save the invitation including the header. The command **w** (write) enables you to

save the text only under a file name. Because you wish
to know who sent the invitation and when, use **s**.

```
s let/invit.Jas
"let/invit.Jas"[New file]8/185
```

You can now delete the message in your post box. You
decide to inform the system manager who is also a jazz
fan, about the coming concert. You send him a message using the command **m**.

```
m root
Subject: jazz concert
Friday evening there is a jazz concert in "The Blow on the Head",
with Porky Blake and Blind Boy Eddie Pass! See you,

guest
(end of message)
```

You will now have to choose whether you leave mail by
means of **x** or **q**. If you use **x** you will retain the post box
in the same condition as it was when you first examined
it: no files deleted, even including those you marked
with **d**. If you quit using **q**, this deletion will take place.
This time, quit using **x** and restart the program directly.

```
x
$mail
mail version 3.0 January 28, 1987. Type ? for help.
3 messages:
   3 guest     Wed  Jan 13 10:14   6/124 "jazz concert"
   2 Jasper    Wed  Jan 13 09:58   8/185 "party"
   1 sysadm    Fri  Dec 11 22:05  10/232 "Welcome to XENIX386"
d
d
h
   3 guest     Wed  Jan 13 10:14   6/124 "jazz concert"
q
held 1 message in /usr/spool/mail/guest
$mail
mail version 3.0 January 28, 1987. Type ? for help.
```

```
1 message:
  1 guest     Wed  Jan 13 10:14   6/124 "jazz concert"
x
you have mail
$
```

Pressing the command **d** twice in succession deletes the two oldest messages. You have checked whether your own memo still exists using the command **h**. You have used **q** to quit mail and confirm the alterations. With a restart, mail will only show one message.

In addition to these commands, mail also provides the following facilities:

p	Display the message on the screen again.
-	Display the previous message on the screen.
RET	Display the following message on the screen.
^	Display the first message on the screen.
$	Display the last message on the screen.
?	Activate the help screen. Sometimes **h** or * is used instead of ?.

10.2.4 Specifying environment variables (Berkeley version)

If you wish to read a message which contains more lines than fit onto the screen, your dexterity will be severely tested: it is not easy to press <Ctrl-s> at just the right moment. For this reason, the Berkeley version is equipped with environment variables which you can activate using the command **set**, just as in *vi*.

By giving the instruction **set?**, you can gain a list of the possibilities on your screen. The **set** command without parameters shows which environment variables have already been specified.

You can define environment variables for mail in the
.mailrc file which can be included in your login directory,
so that mail is always handled in the same way. Commands such as **set page**, for instance are stored in this
directory. This .mailrc file is also checked when you are
working in a directory other than the login directory.

10.2.5   Help with writing messages (Berkeley version)

If you use the question mark to activate the Help
screen, you will also find the command ~**?** under 'HELP
mail commands'. This command enables you to request
help when writing a message. The tilde serves as escape character, allowing you to give commands during
the process of entering text. We have already illustrated
that you can not only send mail in the send mode, you
can also do this in the receiver mode by means of the
commands **m user_name** and **r user_name**. Then mail
switches to the send mode.

Activate **mail** and switch to the send mode using **m
Jasper**. Subsequently display the 'HELP Mail Compose
Escapes' using the command ~**?**. You will already be
familiar with several of these. You can activate vi by typing ~**v**. Now you can write the message. You have
penetrated quite far into the depths of the system; can
you find the way back to the shell? Leave vi by typing
ZZ, then quit the mail send mode by pressing <Ctrl-D>
and then leave mail itself by specifying **q** or **x**. If you are
captured and confused by all this, you can escape using
the <Del> key or <Ctrl-C>, followed by **x**. You should then
regain the prompt on the screen immediately.

```
$mail
mail version 3.0 January 28, 1987. Type ? for help.
1 message:
   1 guest     Wed  Jan 13 10:14   6/124 "jazz concert"
m Jasper
Subject: news?
~v

Any new information?
    guest <Esc><Z><Z>
~
..
"/tmp/...." 3 lines, 32 characters
(continue)
~p
-------
Message contains:
To: Jasper
Subject: news?

Any new information?

    guest
(continue)
<Ctrl-D>
(end of message)
q
Held 1 message in /usr/spool/mail/guest
$
```

PART 2
SYSTEM MANAGEMENT

11 Installing UNIX on a PC

11.1 UNIX versions and PCs

Anyone who wishes to use UNIX requires a powerful computer. This is scarcely a question of cost nowadays. In order to be able to handle the system by oneself, a standard computer should be chosen. 386 and 486 computers with an AT bus (ISA bus) or EISA bus fulfil the requirements.

The following versions are available for a suitable PC (if in doubt consult your dealer):

XENIX 2.3	from Santa Cruz Operation (SCO), USA
UNIX V/386 3.2	from Santa Cruz Operation (SCO), USA
UNIX V/386 3.2	from Interactive Systems, USA
UNIX V/384 4.0	from Consensys, Canada
EURIX V/386	from Generics/ComFood, Münster, Germany
Esix V/386	from Everex Systems, USA

There is also an acceptable price tag on a licence for two users in most versions.

XENIX has been the market leader for a considerable time, providing many applications available which can also generally be run under the above-mentioned UNIX versions. XENIX 2.3 is based upon UNIX System V.3 and contains elements from the Berkely UNIX and previous XENIX versions. SCO has the largest share of the market with its two systems. Interactive, which is a Software manufacturer with a lengthy UNIX tradition, has been taken over by the workstation producer SUN.

Consensys will supply, according to the latest press reports, a new stable release of UNIX version 4.0.

For a long time only those systems supplied by AT&T were allowed to be called UNIX. For this reason, UNIX systems were introduced under all sorts of names.

11.2   Working with several operating systems

The harddisk on a PC can handle four operating systems simultaneously. A pre-condition of this is that the harddisk is divided into so-called *partitions*. The program *fdisk*, available under both DOS and some UNIX systems, enables you to do this.

The first sector on your harddisk, the Master Boot sector, contains the information concerning the individual partitions in a partition table, in addition to the 'bootstrap loader', a program to load programs. This sector itself does not belong to any partition, it deals with the management of the entire harddisk.

Note   In the description of the installation, we shall presume that both a DOS partition and a UNIX partition will be installed on your harddisk. If you do not require a DOS partition, you can skip section 11.5 (Installing a DOS partition).

You probably know that when you start your machine, or after a reset, the operating system will be loaded from your harddisk unless there is a floppy in drive A:. But if there are two or more operating systems on the harddisk, the obvious question is: which system will be activated? Therefore one and only one of the partitions must be marked as 'active'.

This means: if you wish to work under a different operating system, you must first load the operating system which is marked as active, and then apply the *fdisk* program to specify which operating system should be active, and finally start the computer again.

In order to avoid this roundabout procedure if you only occasionally wish to use the DOS operating system, do not activate DOS from the harddisk as described above. It is easier to activate it from a system diskette in diskdrive A:. If diskdrive A: is locked the monitor program will load DOS from the diskette. If A: is not locked, UNIX will be loaded from the harddisk since it is marked as being the active partition.

There are, however, two more convenient alternatives. In order to understand these, you should know a little about loading the operating system: the bootstrap loader does not load the operating system itself. It loads a specific operating system loader located in the first sector of its partition, which in turn boots its operating system.

Thus, the first alternative is: the specific operating system boot program from SCO UNIX and SCO XENIX do not start up by loading the operating system which has been marked as active. Instead, they display a boot prompt:

```
UNIX System V

Boot
:[]
```

By pressing <Return>, UNIX is activated, and by typing **dos** followed by <Return>, MS-DOS is loaded from the harddisk if MS-DOS is the first partition. Older MS-DOS versions could only be installed on the first partition. But the more recent versions can be installed on the second, third or fourth partition as well. However, in these cases, the SCO boot program will not be able to find DOS.

The second alternative is: The bootstrap loader in the Master Boot sector is replaced by a loader such as PAR-

TITIO for example. This type of loader makes it possible
to change the active partition prior to the specific operating system boot program being placed in the ROM and
started up. This method is certainly the most universal
solution - DOS does not have to be the first partition in
this case, as in both SCO versions. In addition, any required operating system can be directly activated from
any of the four partitions, making it also possible to have
several DOS or UNIX versions available simultaneously.

The Interactive UNIX version is supplied with a program
similar to PARTITIO. In other words, it writes a new
bootstrap loader into the Master Boot sector. A problem
does arise if you boot the DOS system in this way and
you use the MKS-Korn-Shell. As soon as you activate
the *ckeygr* program, the system will jam. If you reinstall
PARTITIO and boot DOS, the problem will be solved.

Three remarks concerning PARTITIO:

1. The order of sequence registered in the partition
    table is not necessarily the order of sequence on
    the harddisk.
2. PARTITIO can only be installed or removed when
    DOS has been started up from a diskette in drive
    A:.
3. If an operating system is installed, PARTITIO will
    be overwritten in the Master Boot sector. You
    should first install the new operating system and
    then PARTITIO.

11.3   The principles of the harddisk

Before proceeding further, it is advisable to become acquainted with a number of terms: side, track, byte, sector, head and cylinder.

A harddisk actually consists of a number of disks with
two *sides* coated with a magnetic layer. Each side is
subdivided into several hundred *tracks* which are arranged as a series of concentric circles around the mid-

point. In theses tracks, *bytes* (bit patterns) are are stored consecutively (serially).

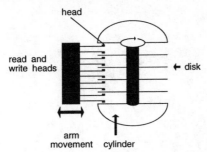

read and write heads

head

← disk

arm movement cylinder

harddisk with read and write heads

Each track is divided into *sectors* by a formatting program. This procedure is called a *low format*. A sector is the smallest unit which can be addressed - individual bytes on a disk cannot be addressed. Of the 570 bytes in each sector, 512 are used for storing data, the other 58 are used for identification of the sector.
512 bytes is the standard size nowadays. There are also systems with 128 or 256 byte sectors.

There is at least one *head* for each side to read and to write data. These read/write heads are located, like the teeth of a comb, on a common arm and thus all move simultaneously. In order to minimize the mechanical movements, all free tracks which are available without having to move the arm are used first for writing the data. When one track is full, the electronic regulator switches over to the next head, thus to another side. This is faster than switching to a neighbouring track. The tracks located exactly above one another form a (conceptual) **cylinder**. The partitioning of a harddisk is always done per cylinder. Technical data generally refer to the number of heads instead of the number of sides. Since the number of tracks per cylinder is the number of sides, the term 'tracks per cylinder' means the same as 'heads per cylinder'.

**Disk side with
tracks and sectors**

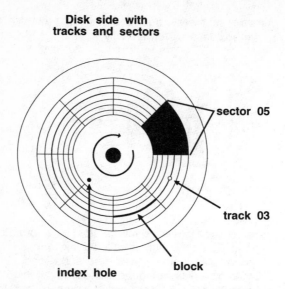

sector 05

track 03

index hole   block

The type of interface greatly influences the workings of
the harddisk. The interface between the computer and
the diskdrive has a double function, namely to control
the diskdrive (controller function) and to manage the
communication with the computer (adapter function).
There are four standards: ST506, ESDI, IDE, and SCSI
of which only two are actually significant nowadays -
IDE and SCSI.

IDE interfaces, also called AT bus drives or ATA (AT At-
tachment), have replaced the previous ST506 standard.
In the old standard, the adapter and controller functions
were managed via a 'controller board'. In the IDE interface, the controller functions are mainly located in the
diskdrive; the adapter functions are regulated by a host
adapter board. These boards are linked to the computer
via the system bus and to the diskdrive via a cable. This
is the most economical solution.

The SCSI interface has become a real standard. It is
more powerful and more modern than the IDE interface.
SCSI devices manage all operating functions them-

selves. These are linked to the computer by a SCSI host adapter. This adapter has its own backend bus which can handle up to seven different SCSI devices such as streamer, scanner, CD ROM and magnetic-optic drives.

Due to the fact that both SCSI and IDE harddisks are supplied already formatted and their device management system automatically eliminates faulty sectors, the installation of UNIX is simpler and faster, when compared to ST506 devices.

If the device management system does not eliminate the faulty sectors, the operating system must adopt this task. During the formatting process with MS-DOS, the faulty sectors are marked in the FAT table as unusable. UNIX deals with this problem via a **map** which allocates a faultless sector to each faulty one. This process is called **mapping**.

Because mapping is not possible during booting, there may be no faulty sectors in the first cylinder of a new partition. Since this problem will not arise with SCSI and IDE devices, a general outline of how to deal with faulty sectors will be given in section 11.7 (PC UNIX installation procedure), but will not be discussed in the specialized sections 11.8 to 11.10.

In order to distinguish between SCSI diskdrives and IDE or ST506 devices, the latter will be referred to as normal harddisks.

Technical data applicable to procedures concerning the harddisk are the number of cylinders, the tracks/heads per cylinder and the sectors per track.

The technical data concerning your harddisk can be found

- on the device itself
- in the setup table (not ESDI and SCSI diskdrives)
- during the installation of UNIX.

In the case of normal devices, the data can be found in the setup table. This table is displayed when the starting up process is discontinued by pressing <Del>. Data concerning the harddisk has been registered here. You should be extremely careful when dealing with the setup table so that no data are lost. Jot down all information (except date and time) before pressing the next key and keep this information in a safe place.

It is more difficult to acquire these data in the case of ESDI and SCSI diskdrives. These devices may not be registered in the setup table when the operating system is located on this harddisk. Otherwise it is impossible to boot the system. However, all UNIX versions find the necessary data at the installation.

Our sample harddisk has the following technical data: 6 sides each with 979 tracks (= cylinder) each with 35 sectors each with 512 bytes. Thus, one track contains 17.5 Kb, one cylinder 105 Kb and the total harddisk 102795 Kb, roughly 102 Mb.

11.4   Preparing the harddisk

In order to prepare the harddisk, you should:

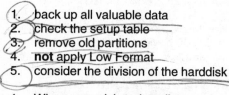

1.   back up all valuable data
2.   check the setup table
3.   remove old partitions
4.   **not** apply Low Format
5.   consider the division of the harddisk

1.   When you wish to install your new operating system on your old computer, you should save the entire contents of your harddisk before beginning. This will prevent a catastrophe if a present partition is accidentally removed. In addition, certain data from a deleted partition sometimes turn out to be useful later, although you may not realize that at the time. Use of a streamer tape here will help keep the costs of storage down.

2. If you have a normal device and you are familiar with its specifications, check the setup table just to be sure. This information will be needed during the installation of UNIX.

3. Present partitions can be removed using the *fdisk* program. The *fdisk* program from DOS 5.0 will also remove non-DOS partitions; *fdisk* from previous DOS versions will not do this. In that case, you will have to activate the operating system pertaining to the partition which is to be removed, and remove the partition using its own *fdisk*. If you apply the *fdisk* program from the new UNIX system to do this, it may occur that the old partition will not be properly deleted.

4. SCSI devices are preformatted and have been tested for faults. If, during installation or the first time UNIX is loaded, you receive error messages in which the word *boot* occurs, you will have to format the harddisk once more and test whether it is faultless. The appropriate program is located in the BIOS of your host adapter. How to apply this program is explained in the guide book to the host adapter.

   IDE devices are also preformatted. They automatically eliminate faulty sectors. An attempt to physically format this device (low format) will often lead to destruction of the disk.

5. The division of the disk should be considered in advance. This requires the information dealt with in section 11.6 (Structure and size of a UNIX partition). For our standard installation, it is sufficient to reserve 31 Mb of the sample harddisk (102 MB) for DOS, so that 71 Mb remain available for UNIX, which will do for a start.

11.5   Installing a DOS partition

The installation of a DOS partition takes place in two stages:

1. Making the DOS partition
2. Installing DOS

1.   Making a DOS partition

If you have an older version of DOS, e.g. DOS 3.3, DOS must be the first partition. If you wish to make use of the DOS boot possibilities of SCO UNIX or SCO XENIX, DOS will have to be the first partition even if it is a more recent version. If you have a program like PARTITIO, a more recent version of DOS can be located on any part of the harddisk.

In order to begin the DOS installation, start up your system by placing the DOS boot diskette in diskdrive A:. As soon as the user interface *command.com* displays its prompt, you can activate *fdisk*.

The DOS 5.0 boot disk automatically leads to a menu-operated installation program.

Caution: If a DOS partition already exists, *fdisk* will not be activated from the installation program, but the old partition will be used. However, you will probably wish to make the new partition larger than the previous one. Then you should proceed as follows:

Select country and keyboard specifications, quit the installation by pressing <F3>, insert diskette 2 and activate *fdisk*.

```
                              FDISK Options

Select one of the following:

1. Create a partition
2. Change Active (Boot from) partition
3. Delete a partition
4. Exit (Update disk configuration and exit)
5. Cancel (Exit without updating disk configuration)


Enter selection: []
```

Remove all superfluous partitions by selecting option 3.

Choose option 1 to create the DOS partition. A submenu will appear. Again select the first option: Create a partition.

The questions as to whether this DOS partition should be given the maximum size and whether this will be the active partition, should be answered negatively, otherwise the entire harddisk will be used.

Three things are then displayed on the screen:

1. The total size of the harddisk is displayed. For our hardisk, this is 100 Mb for the new DOS, or 978 cylinders for the old DOS. Space for operating tasks has been reserved: 2 Mb or 1 cylinder.

2. The possible size of the DOS partition is indicated. In our example, this is 100 Mb for the new DOS (i.e. 100%); for the old DOS this is 312 cylinders which is equivalent to 32.76 Mb. The Consensys UNIX gives a warning if a DOS partition is larger than 31 Mb.

3. In answer to the question regarding the size of the new DOS partition, specify 30 (Mb) or 30%. Then 294 cylinders will be reserved, which is equivalent

to 30.87 Mb. With older DOS versions you have to calculate carefully: one cylinder of our harddisk is equal to roughly 105 Kb. 31000 Kb are necessary. Thus you needed 31000 divided by 105 which is 295 cylinders. We shall opt for 294 cylinders here in order to conform to the example of the new DOS version.

When you have specified the size of the DOS partition and this has been reserved, quit *fdisk* by pressing <Esc>.

2.   Installing DOS

Installing an operating system consists of transferring files and defining environment specifications. However, before files can be transferred, a *file system* must be installed on the new partition. DOS calls this procedure **formatting**. The program used to execute this is *format*. In the case of UNIX, the equivalent program is called *mkfs*, which is an abbreviation for make file system.

Firstly, the DOS boot diskette should be inserted in drive A: and the computer restarted with a reset or by switching it off and then on again (be sure to wait until the harddisk has completely stopped).

The installation process varies according to the DOS version. In all cases, it is restarted from diskdrive A:. The installation is menu-operated in the case of MS-DOS 5.0, including the formatting of the partition. In older versions, diskdrive C: has to be formatted and the system files transferred. This is done by giving the command **format C:/s**. Then the files can be transferred to the harddisk using a copy command.

11.6 Basic structure and size of a UNIX partition

Under UNIX, the partition or handdisk must be divided into divisions (slices, partitions). These divisions are regarded as being independent devices, each (excepting the swap division) having its own file directory.

The first division is called the *root* device because it is the root of the total file system. The file systems of other divisions on the harddisk or of diskettes or other directly addressable data storage media are linked to the root file system in such a way that it seems to the user that there is only one uniform file system.

The term *root* is not only used for the root device with its root file system and the root directory, it is also applied to the superuser as well. *root* is the person who can do everything, for instance, read, delete or execute every file, alter passwords, reassign file ownership or respecify file rights. Under UNIX, files are not only data files or programs, but directories and devices as well.

Up until version V.3, UNIX is loaded from the root device when the system is started up. In version V.4 there is a new division called *stand*. While the system is being loaded, the computer will work *standalone*. All programs and files required for system activation are located in this division.

The second, and in the case of V.4 the third, division which has to be specified is *swap*. Space in working memory is exchanged with space on the harddisk. This will be necessary when the main memory is smaller than the space occupied by all programs which participate in timesharing plus their data. In that case, inactive programs or parts of programs are temporarily stored in the swap space and the program which is next in the list is loaded into working memory. As a result, swap space can be regarded as slow additional working memory.

The swap space should be larger:

- the more applications participating in timesharing,
- the larger the applications,
- the more programs are resident, i.e. are never swapped out of working memory and
- the smaller the working memory itself.

Normally, the swap space should be 1 Mb larger than the working memory. If you use the computer on your own and the working memory is relatively large (in relation to the UNIX version and your applications), 1 to 2 Mb will probably suffice. If large applications are run, for instance databanks or spreadsheet calculations, or if software is being developed, then 0.5 to 1 Mb swap space should be added for each new application. But as some UNIX programs are re-entrant, i.e. one copy in main memory, for a second, third (and so on) use of the program, additional swap space or main memory is only needed for the additional data.

If working memory is too small in relation to the tasks, the system will have to swap a great deal. Accordingly, the throughput will decrease considerably and lengthy delays will occur. The minimum size of working memory should be 2 Mb for the operating system and 0.5 to 1 Mb for each simultaneously active user.

If, subsequently, the swap device proves to be too small, in system V.4 the division can be extended. With older versions, the entire system must be installed once more.

If, while running, a 386 computer does not have sufficient working and swap memory, an error message will be displayed. You will then have to discontinue some processes by giving the **KILL** command.

Instead of placing all programs and data files in the root file system, it is possible to create new divisions. A useful apportioning could be:

■ Root device: only UNIX system software
■ Application device: general application programs
■ User device: user data and programs

In order to be able to save files conveniently, no division should be larger than the longest available streamer tape. However, certain backup and restore utilities allow you to change tapes part way through.

Additional file systems provide vital advantages with regard to:

■ The amount of time required: access to a file is quicker in smaller file systems, because files which belong together according to contents are not so widely dispersed on the harddisk. In addition, the file check of two file systems is faster than that of one large system.

■ Safety: the less a file system is activated, the smaller the risk that this file system will be damaged by a headcrash or by a system breakdown. Since damage to the root file system can have very serious consequences and most activities take place in the user division, it is advisable to separate these two divisions in any case. The separate boot division in system V.4 (*stand*) is a consequence of this point of view.

■ The system administration: if there is a user division, little will change in the root and application divisions. In this case, it will be adequate for the root device to back up, daily, those files which have been altered since the previous complete backup. For the application division, a total backup is appropriate as soon as new applications have been installed, which seldom occurs. For the user division, it is advisable to save the entire division on a streamer tape at least once daily.

The size of each separate division and of the partition itself should now be calculated. The sizes are indicated in megabytes or in blocks (clusters).

A *block* or *cluster* is the amount of data which is read from, or written to, a harddisk at one time. A block corresponds to a sector or a multiple of this. UNIX System V works with a block size of 1024 bytes (1 Kb), which is two sectors.

Previously, a block under UNIX always consisted of 512 bytes. Thus, data sizes measured in blocks 512 bytes long. Even nowadays, you cannot presume that a block always consists of 1 Kb. On the contrary, the size of a file or of available memory is mostly given in terms of 0.5 Kb blocks. Files are read and written in blocks of 2, 4 or even 8 Kb.

Increasing the block size considerably decreases the access time when reading and writing, in other words, reading and writing take place much more quickly. At the same time, the maximum harddisk capacity which can be installed is increased due to the fact that more can be stored under one address. However, a disadvantage of increasing the block size is that more memory capacity is wasted. For instance, when only 23 characters have to be saved, 1024, 2048, 4096 or even 8192 memory places are reserved for this. The rest remains unused.

In this book, the outline of the installation procedure presumes that this is the first time that you are installing a UNIX system and you are not yet familiar with UNIX. Accordingly, the initial installation will be made as easy as possible. In concrete terms, this means that at the installation, additional application and user divisions are not created. That leaves only three specifications to be made: the size of the partition and of the swap division space and, in system V.4, the size of the *stand* file.

1. In our model computer there are 71.4 Mb available for the entire partition. Roughly 1 Mb of this is needed for system tasks.
2. 4 Mb is reserved for the swap space. This is enough for one or two users.
3. 4 Mb is required for the *stand* file.
4. 66.4 or 62.4 Mb remain for the root device.

If you subsequently wish to install the system in a more professional way, you will also have more idea of the software needed, so that you can actually work out the capacity requirements of the individual divisions.

Here are a few tips to calculate the root device capacity:

■ You will mostly find the data concerning the size of the system packages in the UNIX system Release Notes.

■ Many programs require temporary memory on hard-disk. The */tmp* directory in the root file system is the storage depot for these files. With respect to working speed and for safety reasons, it is advisable to create a separate file system for this. In the case of large databank applications, or when working with very large files or when developing programs, 1 Mb is required for each active user and 0.5 Mb for every other simultaneous user.

■ In the root file system, 10 to 20% free memory capacity is needed. If memory capacity becomes too limited here, the working speed decreases drastically.

11.7   UNIX installation procedure and specifications

The installation of particular UNIX versions will be described in the following sections. In order to avoid repetition and to give you an insight into installing other systems, the principles of the procedures which are the same in all systems are outlined below:

1.   Firstly, the new operating system is loaded from diskette and started up. Then the installation begins.

2.   In order to create the new partition, the harddisk data are first checked.

3. The harddisk is partitioned using the program *fdisk*.

4. Faulty sectors must be immediately sought and ex-
    cluded.

5. The new partition is divided into divisions, for each
    of which (excepting the swap division) a file system
    has to be created.

6. The system software can now be transferred to the
    harddisk. In this stage, you will have to specify en-
    vironment variables such as password, keyboard
    definition and time zone.

If you are not yet fully acquainted with the workings of a
computer, here are two remarks before you begin the
installation:

■ We presume you are familiar with chapters 1 to 3.2.
■ When entering data, you must conclude the input
   with <Return>. The program then knows that the input
   is complete.

You can now actually begin with the installation. In addition to the following text, you should also read the instructions which are specific to your UNIX version. You
can find these in one of the following sections, or, if you
do not have one of these versions, in the installation
guide book for your particular UNIX.

Extra measures for normal harddisks will be needed at
one or two places.
These are given in sections headed **For normal harddisks**. If you have a SCSI device, skip that section and
continue with the section headed **Normal and SCSI
harddisks**.

1. Loading the operating system

You have at least one diskette, even when your system
software comes on magnetic tape, in order to start up

the installation procedure. This diskette, used to load
the operating system, has the name **Boot** or **Install ...1**.
Insert this diskette in diskdrive A: and lock the slot.
Switch on the power or perform a reset. The boot program will be loaded. Then - either automatically or after
pressing <Return> - the operating system will be loaded
and the hardware tested. After the automatic start of the
operating system, the installation of a new operating
system on the harddisk will take place. The program will
give instructions how to perform this.

2. Checking the harddisk data

Firstly, the technical data concerning your harddisk will
be made accessible. You now have the opportunity to
adjust these data. If you have an SCSI or IDE device,
you should not alter anything.

Adjustments to the setup table should be carried out if
you have a ST506 harddisk. However, if you have a
harddisk which does not comply with the values specified there **and** the setup table has no line where you can
register the exact data, specify the data concerning your
diskdrive to UNIX in order not to waste any memory capacity.

3. Partitioning the harddisk

Subsequently, *fdisk* will be activated. This enables you
to examine the settings in the partition table and to create, remove or activate partitions. You have to decide
now where the partition should begin and its size.
These data are specified in cylinders or in tracks according to the fdisk version.

Beginning of the partition: specification in cylin-
ders
The partition table indicates the last occupied cylinder.
Select the next one, which is therefore the first free cylinder.

Beginning of the partition: specification in tracks

Fundamentally, each partition begins with a new cylinder. Accordingly, you should check whether the next free track is the beginning of a new cylinder.

Our cylinder has 6 tracks. The first cylinder contains tracks 0 to 5. Since the master boot sector is located in this cylinder, the beginning of a UNIX partition can only occur at track 6, if there is no DOS there.

The next free track in our example is track 1764. If you can divide this number by the number of tracks per cylinder without a remainder, this track is the beginning of a new cylinder: $1764/6 = 294$.

Size of the partition: specification of cylinder requirements

As calculated above, a cylinder contains 105 Kb. If 71 Mb are required, this is equivalent to 71000 Kb/105 Kb = 676 cylinders.

If this is the last partition, you should adopt all remaining cylinders. Thus, a total of 979 cylinders minus 294 for DOS = 685 cylinders. However:

> The last cylinder on the harddisk must remain free for operating system tasks. Although DOS *fdisk* reserves this cylinder automatically, you must do it yourself under UNIX. Thus, decrease the size of the last partition by one cylinder.

Accordingly, the size of the cylinder becomes 694.

Size of the partition: specification of the last cylinder

Calculate the cylinder requirements (see above). Then specify the last cylinder: first cylinder + cylinder requirements - 1 = 294 + 684 = 978.

Size of the partition: specification in tracks

Calculate the cylinder requirements (see above). Then calculate the tracks required: cylinder requirements x tracks = 684 x 6 = 4104.

4. Seeking and eliminating faulty sectors

If you have a harddisk, such as the IDE and SCSI disk-drives, which automatically excludes faulty sectors, you can skip this section.

In the case of other harddisks, the faulty sectors must be found. A thorough check, which you must perform, means that the harddisk will be overwritten. All data will be lost. If your harddisk is not new, have you saved these data?

The faulty sectors are registered in a table. Compare this list to the flaw map which appears on the casing of your harddisk. The faulty sectors which the manufacturer has indicated have probably not been discovered. These are sectors which are only latently faulty, and thus cannot be found by the electronics in your computer under normal circumstances. In any case, you must enter these in the faulty sectors register.

> Check, using the faulty sectors register, whether there are faulty sectors in the first cylinder. If this is the case, you must discontinue the installation and repeat the partition process. Shift the beginning of the partition to the first fault-free cylinder. The reason for this is that when the operating system is loaded, no mapping can yet take place.

5. Creating divisions and establishing the file system

In this stage, the individual divisions of the partition or harddisk are created and, with exception of the swap space, the file system is established. A part of the partition is reserved for operating tasks.

The size of the individual divisions has already been discussed in section 11.6 (Basic structure and size of a UNIX partition). The installation programs split up the partition into divisions using data which is available or which is requested. You can alter this definition immediately, for instance by increasing or decreasing the division sizes, or by adding or removing divisions. The divisions which have to be included in any case are *swap*, *root* and, in System V.4, *stand*. In addition, some space must be specified for the substitution of faulty sectors. Further steps are outlined in the specific relevant section.

6.   Installing UNIX

Prior to or during the transfer of software to the hard-disk, the installation program checks whether you are the legal owner of the software. The required data can be found on the cards supplied or at the beginning of the installation manual. Keep these data in a safe place, in order to be able to reinstall the system in case of need. Problems with specifications usually arise here due to unintentional substitution: an l (letter) for a 1 (number) or an o for a 0 (zero).

Subsequently, depending on the storage medium you had chosen, you will be requested to insert the Streamer cartridge, the CD ROM or the first diskette. The transfer of system software to the harddisk can begin.

In the course of the installation, you will be asked to specify a password for the future system manager. This word must consist of at least five characters and must contain both letters and non-letters. Keep in mind that small and capital letters are distinguished from one another. The characters which you specify are not displayed on the screen. Therefore, the system requires you to enter the password accurately once more. You must remember this password very carefully; without it you will not gain access to the system. You can study how to change your password in section 4.8.

We are subject to Greenwich Mean Time. Summertime is introduced every year, but not always on the same day, thus there can be no fixed regulation for changing the system time. The system time must be changed on the day of the change, using the program *date*.

When the minimal configuration has been transferred, you can transfer additional parts of the system software. However, since this is also possible later, you should go on and complete the installation.

For the installation of your own specific system, refer to one of the following sections:

- 11.8 Installing SCO UNIX or SCO XENIX
- 11.9 Installing Interactive UNIX
- 11.10 Installing Consensys UNIX

11.8 Installing SCO UNIX or SCO XENIX

This description supplements the general outline in sections 11.6 and 11.7. Questions concerning menus and templates are referred to section 14.1 (User guide to menus and templates).

Since the installation of both systems is similar, the description is split into stages and each stage ends at the point where the installation of both systems begins to differ. In the common description the term UNIX is used. Any difference will be indicated between brackets (XENIX...) or by using capitals (ONLY UNIX...).
During installation various programs will be activated. These programs ask you to press <Return> or **q** to quit. If you have finished with a program, press **q** to continue the installation. You can discontinue the installation by pressing <Del>.

If you discontinued the installation by pressing <Del>, do not resume without a reset, otherwise you may encounter problems.

Stage 1: UNIX and XENIX

Start the system from the INSTALLATION N1 (XENIX: BOOT N1) diskette. The boot program will appear after a moment:

```
UNIX System V

Boot
:<Return>

fd(64)UNIX...
```

By pressing <Return>, the operating system will be loaded. The standard program summons has been placed in the boot program. It is the first message to appear on the screen.

ONLY UNIX provides other possibilities:

1. If you wish to repeat the entire installation later, specify restart and press <Return>.

2. In order to operate devices, *drivers* are required. Different devices require different driver programs. There are drivers present in the system for the common devices. You only have to specify which devices you have. If you discover during the installation that your harddisk, tape or CD ROM device is not known and does not correspond to one of the known ones, you will have to repeat the installation and specify *link* at the boot prompt and press <Return> instead of merely pressing <Return>. This presumes that the manufacturer of the device has also supplied a driver along with the diskette. This driver is called BTLD (Boot Time Loadable Driver) by the installation program. It will then also be displayed in the menus under this name.

The additional messages are not significant at the moment. Subsequent to the loading of the operating system, ONLY UNIX will request the INSTALLATION N2 diskette. Then the hardware configuration and the division of working memory are displayed. Capital letters D to M (XENIX: A to Z) are shown. The operating system checks the hardware. If the system breaks off before the letter M (XENIX: Z), this means you have hardware problems. In this case, consult the installation manual.

Stage 2: UNIX

The installation begins with the question whether you are performing a new installation or are updating a previous version:

```
Installation selection:

1. Fresh installation
2. Update installation
3. Exit
```

After selecting the first option (new installation), you will have to specify the keyboard version. You must decide whether the initialization of the first harddisk is to take place automatically, or whether you will personally determine the size of the partition and the divisions.

```
Initialization selection:

1. Fully Configurable Initialization
2. Automatic Initialization
3. Exit Installation
```

Select option 1. Then the program will examine which controller and harddisk you have.

Stage 2: XENIX

```
Z
No single-user login present
Entering System Maintenance Mode
Please press Return
```

After pressing <Return>, you will be able to specify the keyboard version. Then the system will request information concerning your harddisk controller:

```
XENIX System V Hard Disk Initialization
What type of disk controller will be supporting this disk?
1. Standard disk support (ST506, MFM, RLL, ESDI, IDE)
2. OMTI
3. SCSI
```

Specify the appropriate option.

Stage 3: UNIX and XENIX

Under UNIX the technical data concerning your harddisk will be displayed. Under XENIX, this will be done after the next question.

You will be informed that initializing the harddisk may delete all data, and you will be asked: 'Do you wish to continue?'. Answer **y**.

ONLY Normal harddisks
If you have a normal harddisk, you can use the following menu to modify the technical data of your harddisk. Since these values are given in the setup table, continue by pressing **q**, except for the special case mentioned in the general section.

Normal and SCSI harddisks
The installation is then continued using *fdisk* in order to partition the harddisk. The following menus are shown on the screen:

UNIX   XENIX

1. Display partition Table   1. Display partition
                                             Table
2. Use Entire Disk for UNIX   2. Use Entire Disk
                                             for XENIX

3. Use Rest of Disk for UNIX

4. Create UNIX partition
5. Activate partition
6. Delete partition

3. Create XENIX partition
4. Activate partition
5. Delete partition

Do **not** select option 2, otherwise the DOS partition will be overwritten and the entire harddisk prepared for UNIX usage. Using option 4 (XENIX option 3), you create the new partition. The current partition table is shown:

Partition	Status	Type	Start	End	Size
4	Inactive	DOS	1	1763	1763

Total disk size: 5874 (7 reserved for masterboot/diagnostics)

Of the 979 x 6 = 5874 tracks, track 0 is reserved for the master boot sector and the last cylinder, with 6 tracks, for diagnostic tasks. The next free track is 1764. Since this is also the beginning of a new cylinder, you can specify this value as the first free track:

```
Enter starting track number, or 'q' to return: 1764 <Return>
Enter partition size in tracks, or 'q' to return: []
```

As soon as you specify the number of tracks which you have calculated as the partition size, in this case 4104, the partition table is displayed again:

Partition	Status	Type	Start	End	Size
1	Inactive	XENIX	1764	5867	4104
4	Inactive	DOS	1	1763	1763

Caution: It is easy to overlook the warnings which
                 might appear above this table.

■ Keep in mind that the cylinder limits should not be ex-
   ceeded and/or
■ the last cylinder has to be reserved for system operating tasks only.

If these are wrongly specified, you will have to remove
the new partition and enter the correct values.

Return to the *fdisk* menu by pressing <Return>. In order
to activate the new partition, select option 5 (XENIX option 4). Th partition table will be displayed again along
with a request to specify the number of the partition to
be activated:

```
Enter partition number you want to make active or 'q'...
```

When you have made the partition active, check the
table once more (Option 1) before quitting fdisk by
pressing <Return> and **q**.

Normal harddisks
Since a harddisk is seldom completely fault-free, faulty
tracks should be sought using the *badtrk* program and
registered in a list. A menu will appear. Since our model
IDE harddisk automatically eliminates faults, quit this
program using **q**.

```
0 bad tracks have been identified.
Enter the number of bad tracks to allocate space for
or press Return to use the recommended value of 15):[]
```

The program proposes reserving 15 substitute tracks to
replace any current or future faulty tracks. In the case of
IDE harddisks this is already regulated. Thus, specify 0;
otherwise accept this proposal by pressing <Return>. If
this should eventually be too few, you will have to install
the system again completely.

Subsequently, you will be asked if these new values
can be applied to the harddisk. Reply **Yes**.

Normal and SCSI harddisks
The partition must now be divided into divisions using
the program *divy*. This states that the collective UNIX
partition is made up of 71714 blocks, each of 1 Kb. Between 8,000 and 30,000 of these (XENIX between
1,000 and 11,952) should be reserved for the swap
space. The suggested minimum size is probably more
than sufficient, but the program will not accept a smaller
value.

```
Please enter the swap-space allocation, or press Return
to get the default allocation of ... blocks:[]
```

Specify 8000 here. You can adjust this later if you wish.
If the partition is relatively large, the program will need
to know if you wish to create a separate user division */u*
besides the root device. Reply **No**.

Then you will be asked:

```
Do you wish to make any manual adjustments to the size
or the names of the file system or the swap area
before they are created on the harddisk?
(Y/N) y<Return>
```

Answer Yes. In the division table, not only the size or
the desciption of the divisions can be modified, new divisions can be defined or existing divisions removed.

The modifications are implemented via a menu. One of
the options available is *restore* which allows you to restore the previous values, if it becomes confusing.
Overlapping of divisions will be detected, but a gap will
not. You must be careful here in order to waste no disk
capacity.

In order to reduce the swap division, increase the starting block: type **s**. Division?: type **1**. Starting block number?: increase this by 4000. Add the free blocks to the root division. Use the option **e** to increase the last block by 4000, and quit the menu by pressing **q**.

ONLY UNIX provides one last chance to correct everything:

■ press r(eturn) to return to the previous menu to correct the division table, or
■ press i(nstall) to install the division table and continue.

Finally, the message *Making filesystems* appears on the screen.

ONLY UNIX: files can now be copied from the INSTALL N2 diskette to the harddisk. You must now specify the system software storage location: diskette, cartridge tape or CD-ROM. When you have inserted the appropriate medium the system software is transferred.

After some legal advice, you will be asked to

```
Enter your serial number
and press Return abc123456 Return
Enter your activation key
and press Return abcdefgh Return
```

Invalid Activation Key means that either The Activation Key **or** the Serial Number is incorrect. For example, you may have forgotten the three letters in front of the serial number or you have not recognized them as letters.

Stage 4: XENIX (UNIX continues in Stage 5)

Subsequently, you will receive the message:

```
Hard disk initialization procedure completed
...
** Safe to Power Off **
-or-
** Hit Any Key to Reboot**
```

Although XENIX is now installed on the harddisk, the installation is not yet complete. You can interrupt the installation now and switch the computer off.

> If you wish to continue the installation, there should be **no diskette in drive A:.**

As soon as you switch on again or press a random key, the *boot* program is activated. You are already familiar with the boot prompt. By pressing <Return>, XENIX is loaded and started up.

```
XENIX System V

Boot
: Return
hd(40)xenix
...
```

Caution: You should not interrupt the installation until it has finished, otherwise you will have to execute the entire installation all over again.

First the root file system will be checked to see if the contents of the harddisk conform to the entries in the directories of the root device. Subsequent to the statement that there are 94 files in 2272 0.5 Kb blocks, additional files will be transferred to the harddisk.

```
XENIX System V Hard Disk Installation
Checking root file system
/dev/root
**Phase 1 - Check Blocks and Sizes
...


94 files 2272 blocks 131018 free

Insert Operating System (Basic Utilities) volume B1
and press Return <Return>
```

The first diskette to be inserted has the label B1. After
some time, you will be asked:

```
Please assign a password for..."root"
...
New password:      <Return>
Re-enter new password:      <Return>
```

Stage 5: UNIX and XENIX

Then the time zone and other values will have to be
specified.

```
Time zone initialization
Are you in North America? (y/n)n <Return>

What is the abbreviation of your timezone?
Enter 1-9 characters, or 'q' to quit:
GMT <Return>

How many hours west of Greenwich Mean Time are you?
Format: hh[:mm:ss]. (e.g. 10:30:00, use negative numbers
for locations east of GMT) or enter q to quit:0<Return>

Does summertime apply at your location (y/n)? n<Return>
```

Answer no to the summertime question since the date
of change is not always the same; therefore the date
has to be specified manually.
Answer any other questions as appropriate.

Stage 6: UNIX

You will then be asked whether date and time are correct: *Current System Time is... Enter new time
([yymmdd]hhmm):.* When this has been specified correctly, press <Return>. Then the terminfo database is
compiled. With this, the minimal system has been installed. After reporting the current disk usage, the following menu appears:

```
1. Do you wish to install additional software?
(Extended utilities or applications
2. Do you wish to continue with the system configuration?

Enter an option:2 <Return>
```

Option 2 ensures that the installation will be carried on.
The installation of additional software will be discussed
in a separate chapter. Now you must select one of the 4
options dealing with security precautions. If you are the
only user in the system, level 4 (low security) will do.

The next option, namely to execute the first system manager tasks using the system manager interface, should be
ignored in order to bring the installation to an end. How to
use this interface is dealt with in a separate subsection.

```
1.Run System Administration Shell
2.Continue

Enter an option:  2  <Return>
```

Then you are given the choice of picking a password
yourself or having a (pronounceable) word assigned to
you. By pressing <Return>, you choose the first option:

```
1.Pick a password
2.Pronounceable password will be generated for you

Enter choice (default is 1): <Return>
Please enter new password:
New password:     <Return>
Re-enter new password:      <Return>
```

Stage 6: XENIX

Subsequently, the file directories are created. As soon as the current disk usage is displayed, the minimal system has been installed. The question as to whether the installation should be continued actually means, do you wish to transfer additional software? This can be done later. Discontinue the installation:

```
1.Discontinue installation
2.Continue installation

Enter Option:1 <Return>
```

Stage 7: UNIX and XENIX

As soon as you see this message on the screen

```
** Safe to Power Off **
  -or-
** Hit any Key to Reboot **
```

the installation is complete and you can switch off. The following stage can be found in section 12.1 (First management tasks) and in section 12.2 (Working for the first time under SCO UNIX and SCO XENIX).

11.9   Installing Interactive UNIX

This description of the installation completes the general outline in sections 11.6 and 11.7. Questions concerning menus and templates are referred to section 14.1 (User guide to menus and templates).

Begin this installation with the *Boot* and *Install* diskettes. However, you should perform the following actions first:

1.   You should make a copy of the *Boot* diskette and you **must** make a copy of the *Install* diskette, since data is written to these diskettes during the installation. Use these copies to perform the installation. Under DOS, the copies should be made on an HD diskette using the command **diskcopy A: A:**

2.   If the partition which you have reserved for Interactive UNIX still has contents, these should not be removed during the installation using the Interactive *fdisk* program. This should be done prior to the installation using the DOS (5.0) *fdisk* program or the *fdisk* belonging to the operating system which is still on the disk.

The installation begins by loading the system from the *Boot* diskette. After the message *Booting the INTER-ACTIVE UNIX Operating System*, it will take a little time until the operating system is loaded:

```
UNIX System V/386

...


Insert the Install diskette and press <Return> []
```

Insert the **copy** of the *install* diskette and press <Return>.

Caution: If you interrupt the installation without closing down the system in the proper way, the installation diskette will be damaged.

You must specify your serial number and license number. Then you will have to specify the keyboard definition. US International is the most common.

Then register whether your monitor is colour or monochrome. Press <Return>.

The screen will then provide the following information:

■ Pressing <F1> will produce specific context-oriented information. By pressing <F1> twice in succession, you will gain access to the general information system. You can then request information concerning a certain topic from a list of options. <Esc> returns you the program.

■ You can discontinue the installation by pressing <Ctrl-\>. The number sign then appears as prompt. Either repeat the installation from the keyboard definition onwards by specifying **install**, or close down the system properly by giving the command **shutdown** and wait until the message appears that you can reboot the system.

Using <Ctrl-R> you can redraw the screen if something has disappeared or if there is confusion. If this does not work, type some values and try <Ctrl-R> again.

The installation program will then wish to know which of the available packages you have acquired. The label on the diskette casing will provide the necessary information. You can respond negatively to the question whether you wish additional information for each stage of the installation. You already have this book. In addition, specific information can be gained by pressing <F1>. The installation menu will then appear:

```
Install  Help  Shell  Exit
Do full installation
```

The first line shows the option and the second line gives a decription of the currently selected option. Select *Install*.

The technical data concerning your harddisk are first displayed. You do not wish to examine or alter these, in as much as the special case has not been mentioned in the genral section. Accept the values by pressing **Y** for yes.

A template then appears, already filled in. Fields containing values within direction symbols, for example *<read>*, and *y/n* fields are selection fields. The questions deal with the preparation of the harddisk.

1. Execute low format? No
2. Should the harddisk be partitioned? Yes
3. Interleave factor? 0 means none; in other words, that sector 2 follows sector 1 immediately. The current value of the harddisk is shown. Do not change this!
4. Replace faulty sectors? That depends. It is not necessary in the case of IDE and SCSI harddisks. Select *none*.
5. Register known faulty sectors? In the case of IDE and SCSI hardisks the answer is certainly *no*.

By pressing <Esc> you indicate that the template has been completed. Before the process is continued using the specified values, a safeguard question will be posed. By pressing **y** you set the process in motion, with **n** the previous values are reset and with **e** you will return to the place where you stopped.

The installation menu appears again. Select the *Install* option again. The installation is continued using fdisk to create the partition.

```
Available harddisk size: 978 cylinders

Cylinders
```

Partition	Status	Type	Start	End	Length	%
1		DOS16	0	293	294	30
2		UNUSED	0	0	0	0
3		UNUSED	0	0	0	0
4		UNUSED	0	0	0	0

```
Options:
1. Create partition
2. Change active partition
3. Delete partition
4. Specify partition table
5. Exit (update disk configuration and exit)
6. Cancel (exit without updating disk configuration)

Selection: []
```

As soon as you select option 1, you will be asked:

1. Which operating system is to be installed? Enter **u** for UNIX.

2. You can specify the size of the partition either as a percentage of the harddisk capacity or as an amount of cylinders. Enter **c** for cylinders.

   (a) You will be asked: what is the first free cylinder? This is **294**.
   (b) You must then specify the number of cylinders the partition should have. This is **684**.

   Note: *fdisk* cannot be 'persuaded' to use the last cylinder between two partitions. This means that the actual number of cylinders possible must be reduced by one.

Note: if you allocate the last cylinder too, no warning message is given.

3.   Finally, *fdisk* wishes to know if this partition will be the active one:**y**.

Then the partition table is completed. Using option 5, this table will be transferred to the harddisk.

The installation menu appears once more. In order to calculate the number and size of the divisions in the partition automatically, the installation program wishes to know by means of the following form, how the system is going to be used; in other words, how many small (up to 2 Mb), medium (2-3 Mb) and large programs are going to run simultaneously, and if the system is going to be applied as a fileserver.

In the case of a relatively small partition, the program will propose no separate user division. Your specifications will only influence the default size of the swap space. If you accept the default value, a swap space of 11 Mb is defined. You can reduce this, either now or later, to 8 Mb. Even if you set all these values in this table to 0, the swap space is always at least 8 Mb.

As soon as you have specified these values, a table showing the divisions appears on the screen. The first cylinder of the partiton is secretly reserved; it does not appear in the table. One cylinder of the *reserved* division (ALTS type) is required for the replacement of faulty sectors.

If you have a large partition, the table will indicate a user division. You can remove this by removing one of the fields *Mount-point, Size* or *Number of Cylinders*. The capacity which then becomes free is shown at the bottom and can be divided among the other divisions.

If you wish to create an additional division, specify the name and the size of the division either in Mb or in number of cylinders. If there are no or not enough (not yet) assigned) cylinders free, you will have to reduce other

244 Part 2: System Management

divisions first. The start cylinder of each division will be calculated automatically.

As soon as the table displays your specifications, press <Esc> and **Y** to ensure that the divisions are created and the file systems are set up. When the files have been transferred from the installation diskette, the series of diskettes *Core 1* to *Core 4* will be requested. Insert these as directed. Finally, the *Boot* diskette will be requested in order to transfer the operating system kernel. When you have extracted this diskette again, some tasks will be executed and finally the message will appear that you can specify your environment variables.

1. Instead of assigning a password, quit the screen using <Esc>. At the first login, you will be asked to specify a new password.

2. Now check date and time. Set the time zone to Greenwich Mean Time. Reply **N** to *Daylight saving?*. The minutes should be corrected just before the values are written to memory.

3. Select a name for your computer; here that is *uxschool.*

The installation is now complete. The following directions deal with the capabilities of your software and the order of sequence in which you should transfer the software you require: OS -> SDS -> X11 Runtime -> X11 Development ->TCP/IP -> NFS -> TEN PLUS -> VP/ix in the case of the Workstation Developer Package. The following menu will now appear:

```
InstallPkg   Kconfig   Sysadm   Shell   AddDisk   Exit
Install optional packages
```

This enables you to install additional software, to adapt the operating system kernel to certain tasks, to perform the first system administration tasks, to run a shell, to add another harddisk or simply to exit.

Select *Exit*. The system is closed down. After the message *The system is down. Press any key to reboot*, you may switch off.

The following relevant sections are 12.1 (First management tasks) and 12.3 (First management tasks under Interactive UNIX).

11.10 Installing Consensys UNIX

This description of the installation supplements the general outline in sections 11.6 and 11.7. Questions concerning menus and templates are referred to section 14.1 (User guide to menus and templates.

The hardware requirements of System V.4 are more demanding than those of the former systems. You will need 4 Mb working memory and 70 Mb harddisk capacity. In the case of SCSI harddisks, Consensys requires an Adaptec 1540-compatible controller.

To start the installation, you will need both boot diskettes, either of the type *WD* for normal diskdrives or type *SCSI* for SCSI harddisks. Place the first diskette in diskdrive A.

```
As soon as the message
 "Proceeding..."
appears, you can discontinue the booting by pressing the spacebar.
You can then enter the name of a UNIX kernel to be loaded from
the /stand directory.
Otherwise the kernel version /stand/UNIX will be loaded.
Booting the UNIX system...
```

Kernel refers to the kernel of the operating system. The default version *stand/UNIX* will be loaded. The screen will then display a whole division of messages, which we shall deal with presently. If you have the majority of your software on a magnetic tape, pay attention to the following message:

```
...

.........cartridge tape controller was found at address 0300H.


Please insert the UNIX System "Boot Disks"
Disk 2 and then strike <Return>.
```

The magnetic tape controller has been found. In com-
pliance with the last request, insert the second diskette
and press <Return>.

ONLY SCSI bootdisk 2: you will be warned that the active partition is not a UNIX partition. This warning actually comes prematurely, because you are not able to
define and activate a partition at this stage.

```
Please press <Return> to install UNIX on harddisk
or <Del> to discontinue the installation. []
```

If you wish to interrupt the installation and begin again,
you do not need to begin all over again with the first diskette and a reset. Use <Del> to discontinue the installation. A small menu will appear. Select **q** for quit and the
system prompt # will appear. Now specify **INSTALL**
and press <Return> in order to repeat the installation.
The second boot diskette, which is now requested,
should still be in diskdrive A.

Continue the installation by pressing <Return>. The following warning, that all files in the system will be
deleted by the installation, does not mean that all available partitions will be deleted if you continue the installation. But it might happen by accident. After all, you
have saved your files? If so, reply **y** to the next question.
All others keys except Y and N will produce the question
whether you wish to install the new system.

ONLY SCSI boot diskette 2: the program will wish to
know if the harddisk should receive a low format. Defi-
nitely not! Enter **n**.

The validation key, which is requested in the next
screen display, can be found on the first page of the

your installation manual. If the key is correct, the technical data concerning your harddisk will appear, along with the question whether you wish to alter the number of cylinders. Since these values are extracted from the setup table, answer **n** here or press <Return> to continue, unless the special case is not described in the general section.

The following screen will show information concerning *Low-Level Fdisk* which is a little disturbing. However, there are no plans to physically change the harddisk; we only wish to perform a completely normal partitioning.

As soon as you press a key, the current partition table will be shown, perhaps along with two warnings:

■ A warning is given if the DOS partition is larger than 31 Mb (= 312 cylinders on our model harddisk). A DOS 3.3 partition which is created using the default fdisk values is 32 Mb.

■ A warning will be given if there is no active UNIX partition. The partition which you wish to create must be marked as the active one.

Caution: If you already have a UNIX partition on the harddisk and you receive **no** warning, you must pay close attention to activating the partition which you wish to create. If you do not do this, the already existent UNIX partition will be seen as the installation partition and will be overwritten.

```
 Change  Delete  Apply & Exit  Help  Quit

 FDISK - Partitioning - Disk 0 979 Cyls
```

Type	Active	Start	End	Size	(MB)	%
DOS	y	0	0293	30		30
___	___	___	___			
___	___	___	___			
___	___	___	___			

The first line on the screen shows a menu. After the selection of *Change*, the table under this becomes a form in which the new UNIX partition will be entered.

When filling in this table, there are the following deviations from the normal procedure:

1. A specifications table is accepted by pressing <Return> at any field
2. Option lists are made accessible by pressing the <Spacebar> + <Tab> keys.

Go to the first field on the first free line. You must specify here the type of operating system you wish to install: DOS, UNIX,...There is an options list which you can open behind this field. After specifying **u** for UNIX, the following line will appear in the partition table:

UNIX_Sys   n_   ___0   ___0

If you activate this partition (by entering **y** in the second field), the currently active partition will be placed on non-active. In the next field, enter the number of the first cylinder and in the following field, the number of the last cylinder of your partition:

UNIX_Sys   y_   ___294   ___978

The very last cylinder is reserved by Consensys *fdisk* in any case. After having accepted the alterations by pressing <Return>, and the menu is active again, check that your specifications are correct just to be sure. Then write the new partition table on the disk by using the *Apply & Exit* option.

Normal and SCSI harddisks

The new UNIX partition is to be examined for faulty sectors. All current data will be destroyed during this process. You still have time to discontinue the installation in order to save the data if required. You will be asked whether the examination of the harddisk (meaning the partition) should be carried out now. Answer

- **n** if the word **recommended** is shown in the first line. You either have a SCSI harddisk or you answered y to the previous question (the faulty sectors are already known).
- **y** if the word **mandatory** is shown in the first line. Otherwise the entire installation will be discontinued.

Subsequently, the program *v4layout* will be activated. After some initial information, a warning will appear if your partition is smaller than 70 Mb. Then the screen displays a menu and, below it, a division table showing a proposal for the division of the partition. This proposal depends on the size of the working memory and on the size of the partition to be created.

```
Change  Apply  Help  Quit

V4 File System Layout - Disk 0 - 69 Mb
                      Rec'd Actual
```

Name	Description	Type	Rec'd MB	Actual MB
root	Root Filesystem	ufs	55	55
stand	Boot Filesystem	bfs	4	4
swap	Swap Division	none	6	4
...	...	...	..	..
home	User Filesystem	ufs	4	0
home2	2nd User Filesystem	ufs	0	0

By selecting the option *Change*, the table becomes a form. The proposals for our sample computer with 4 Mb working memory and 70 Mb partition, are 4 Mb for the user division and 6 Mb for the swap space. Enter 4 Mb in the *Actual Mb* column for the swap space - this is the minimum size with which the system can work.

Remove the *home* user division by specifying 0. Allocate the newly-available bytes to the root division. The program will discover any calculation errors so that memory will not remain unused, or allocated when not available.

The file system type of the root device and of the *tmp, usr, var, home* and *home2* user divisions can be altered in the table. Instead of the suggested *ufs*, the Berkeley University Fast Filesystem, you can choose the System V Filesystem (*s5*). The *ufs* is more powerful but it does use 10% of the division for administrative tasks.

After pressing <Return>, the menu will be active again. Check the division once more and then, by selecting *Apply & Exit*, write this table onto the the harddisk. The file systems will be created automatically and then the operating system kernel and the first files will be transferred to the harddisk. As soon as the message *Reboot your system* appears, you can discontinue the installation.

Note: At the installation message **A UNIX system will now be installed on your harddisk...**, the message **NOTICE: HD: interrupt with no request queued** may appear if you have a fast harddisk. One has neglected to remove this message, which has had a test function. Ignore it.

If you wish to continue the installation, there should be **no** diskette in diskdrive A. In order to go on, press either <Ctrl-Alt-Del> or the reset button or switch the computer on again.

The system will now boot from the harddisk. You are already familiar with the messages shown here. First you will have to specify the data medium: **C** for Cartridge (magnetic band) or **F** for Floppy disk. <Esc> will discontinue the installation.

If you press C, the program must be informed whether the cartridge driver will be operated via an SCSI device or via a normal diskdrive (qt).

Finally, the cartridge or the diskettes will be requested. The installation from tape takes approximately 10 minutes. Some other tasks will then be executed and

then the data for the most important environment variables will be requested:

1. Passwords must be assigned for *root* and the user
    install.
2. Choose a name for your computer, here *uxschool*.
    This name will be used as both system name and
    address in the node.

Then the software installation program *v4pkg* will be activated. This is used to transfer additional software. This
program must be used if you are installing from
streamer tape since the tape driver will have to be
added in any case.

The *v4pkg* program has the same user interface as described above. The main menu provides the possibility
of listing the contents of individual software packages,
and adding or removing packages.

The interface is a little surprising, since the procedures
are not uniform with the selection of the options:

■ In the case of the *List* and *Remove* options, you remain in the main menu but selecting other options is
   only possible using the cursor keys.
■ After selecting *Add*, a submenu appears containing
   the options *Select* and *Apply*.

To return to the previous level, press <Esc> or select
Quit in the submenu.

After choosing the main function, an option list will appear. This shows the sets (subsystems) from which the
individual packages can be chosen. These packages
contain utility programs and data files. In order to transfer new software, choose *Add* and then *Select* in the
package list:

```
Change   Accept   Help   Quit


ADD PACKAGES - V4 Runtime System


Add   Installed   Name      Description                    Requires


y      no          compat    BSD/SunOS Compatibility
                             Package
y      no          crypt     Security Administration
                             Utilities
y      no          ed        Editing Utilities              terminfo
```

The packages which are to be transferred are already
specified: in the *Add* column, a *y* has been placed. As
soon as a package has been installed, the *no* under Installed changes to *yes*. In the *Requires* column, the
companion programs to these packages are listed.
These also have to be transferred.

You can alter this preselection using the *Change* option.
You will probably not need *crypt*. After changing this (*n*
instead of *y* in the Add column), return to the menu and
choose the *Accept* option. This only means, however,
that the selected packages are included in the list of
packages which are to be adopted; it is not yet transferred. That process occurs one level higher (*Apply*).

When you have used *Quit* to return to the second menu
level, select the required packages from the other sets
in the same way. In the case of a magnetic tape, much
running time can be saved if you first select all the packages you require and then select *Apply*.

After selecting *Apply*, a number of questions will be
asked concerning the hardware. Finally, the *v4pkg* program will activate the *pkgadd* program which actually
does the work. You have already answered the questions posed by this program: *v4pkg* has them available
for application. If you perform the installation from magnetic tape, after giving the **go** signal, you can take a
break for about an hour. However, if you are acting as a

diskjockey, you will have to remain alert to insert the required diskettes.

You have probably not installed the package NSU (Network Support Utilities). In order to be able to use the sendmail program, you must first install NSU and then have the following command executed:

```
# /usr/ucb/newaliases -oA/usr/ucblib
/aliases >/dev/null 2>&1
```

Just before the end of the installation a message will be given: *** *IMPORTANT NOTICE* ***. After the installation, the system must be started up and tested.

Do **not** switch the system off if the following message appears:

```
Tape installation was successful.
Hit <Return> key to continue...[]
```

The installation has been succesful up until now but is not yet complete. Pressing <Return> will return you to the *Add* menu which you leave using *Quit*. You will be informed that you can transfer additional software via the *v4pkg* program.

The operating system kernel must be relinked, in other words, the parts which are necessary for the usage of the adopted programs and hardware data have to be worked in. All alterations to the kernel were deferred during the transfer of the software. The original kernel is stored under the name */stand/mUNIX*. As soon as the message *Reboot the system now* appears, you can switch off the system.

The next relevant sections are 12.1 (First management tasks) and 12.4 (First management tasks under Consensys UNIX).

12   First management tasks for the UNIX PC

This is not a manual for the system manager of a UNIX system. We wish to make you gradually familiar with the UNIX system without you having to go to considerable expense doing special courses. UNIX system V.3 is a stable system so that there need be no fear of system failure and complications. System V.4 has also gained stability in the meantime. Most problems encountered by beginners arise from the fact that manuals often present too much information at one time and as a result the first essential steps are not easily discerned.

UNIX system management is greatly simplified by programs which execute certain instructions, for instance, the registration of a new user. Even the activation of actual management programs can be supported by a system operating menu. This support conceals what exactly has been modified, therefore you do not become familiar with details and correspondences.

The following outline will attempt - despite the availability of these supporting programs - to describe the details of the basic principles, even although you may not yet be able to properly appreciate some parts. Later, when you have worked through chapters 1 to 9, you can return to the computer to deal with them again.

In order to avoid repetition, the information which refers to the management of all systems is given in the first section of this chapter. However, do not continue your work using the following general section, but using the section which specifically applies to your UNIX version:

■ SCO UNIX and SCO XENIX: section 12.2
■ Interactive UNIX: section 12.3
■ Consensys UNIX: section 12.4

In these sections, you will also find repeated references back to the subsections of the general outline.

12.1 First management tasks

12.1.1 Starting up and closing down UNIX systems

This book contains only a description of those stages which are necessary to start up the system on your own and to close it down properly.
Loading the operating system from the harddisk has been discussed extensively in section 11.2.

When you have activated UNIX, you cannot just switch the system off again as you might do with other systems. UNIX **must** be closed down properly.

In order to close down the system, you must be logged in as *root*. This Super User status contains risks:

Caution: As root, you have access to all files. It can easily occur that you may delete a file which is essential for the system. Accordingly, never use the root status unless it is absolutely necessary. **Never** use the wildcards *, ? and [...] to deal with files if you are root.

UNIX can be run in single-user mode or multi-user mode. The system is started up in single-user mode. The system manager determines when UNIX moves to multi-user operation. Certain management tasks must be executed in single-user mode. This is referred to as the maintenance mode. This does not mean, however, that the single-user mode is the proper operating mode when you are working in the system on your own. Even if you are the only user, you should work chiefly in the multi-user mode because:

1. Single-user mode always entails superuser status (see the warning above), and
2. it is useful in practice to log in several times to be able to move back and forth between different applications.

12.1.2   The time function

The system administration programs *sysadm* are frequently not adjusted to the European situation. In order
to specify the timezone and or date/time, it is not
necessary to activate the entire administration program.
The date and time can be specified using the *date* program:

 # date 1752

The above example specifies the time as being 17
hours 52 minutes. In order to specify the date and time,
for instance 8 minutes to six in the evening of the 30th of
June 1993, type:

 # date 0630175293

Our timezone GMT should be stored in the file */etc/TI-
MEZONE*. This information is retrieved from there when
you log in and registered in your work environment.
Change, if necessary, in the */etc/TIMEZONE* directory
the registration TZ=XXX to TZ=GMT as soon as you
can handle **chmod** and an Editor.

12.1.3   Installing new users

Each new user is registered in a user file. This specifies
a HOME directory for the user's own files. Each user in
the file is also automatically given a mailbox file.

Up until now, you have had the choice between various
commands, referred to as the Shell. Specific files belong to each shell and these are executed when the
shell is executed. These files define the user environment and ensure that certain tasks are carried out. The
user may modify these files according to his/her requirements.

A user may be a member of one or more groups. Thus,
he can gain rights to files which do not belong to him.

The user file used to log in the user is called
/etc/passwd. This is often, not quite correctly, referred to
as the password file. Each line, like the example shown
below, consists of the following data:

```
guest:.SkNzvAnGOJbA:2001:51:
:/usr/guest:/bin/sh
(1)   :(2)              :(3) :(4):(5):(6)
:(7)"
```

1. The user name. This must begin with small letters
    and consist of no more than 8 characters. There
    should be no duplication of the name since the sys-
    tem uses the name to find the user identification
    number.

2. The encrypted password. In the more recent ver-
    sions, the password is stored in a separate file to
    which a normal user has no access. In that case,
    this field is marked by an * or an x.

3. The user identification number. The rights which a
    user has to files has are recognized by means of
    this number. This means:

    (a) If the name is altered in the login, this does not
        mean that the rights to the files are lost since
        these are recognized via the identification
        number.

    (b) If the same number is specified along with an-
        other name, this means that the same user has
        two names. Accordingly, either can be used to
        give commands.

4. The user group is registered at the login. One user
    can be registered in the user group file */etc/group*
    as belonging to several groups. However, only one
    of these associations is indicated in the user envi-
    ronment. If the user wishes to gain access to files to
    which the group also has right of access, the
    newgrp program ensures that the required group

membership is indicated within the user environment. Management programs dealing with registration of users generally make it possible to indicate the supplementary groups to which the user belongs.

5. Sometimes a notation. Mostly the full name and telephone number are shown here.

6. The login or HOME directory. Normally in the case of a new user, the log in or Home directory is */usr* or */home* (V.4) and the post box is */usr/mail, /usr/spool/mail* or */var/mail* (V.4) For example, for guest that will be */usr/guest/* or */home/guest* for the login directory and */usr/mail/guest, /usr/spool/guest* or */var/mail/guest* as post box.

7. The shell which is activated at login. This entry can also be modified as soon as you are familiar with the fundaments of the system.

The current standard, the Korn shell is recommended. It is the most powerful and most convenient shell to manage. In addition, it is generally compatible with the previous standard, the Bourne shell.

The start up files are *.profile* in the Bourne shell, *.cshrc* and *.login* in the C shell and in the Korn shell *.profile* plus a file which is defined by the variable *ENV*.
If, when logging in, you activate another program instead of the shell, this program will be started up. This prevents the user moving freely in the system. The program has then only one exit: as soon as the user ends the login program, he/she is simultaneously logged out. The second, less rigorous alternative is to limit the freedom of movement of the user within the system by specifying a 'restricted shell'. The restricted shell in the Bourne shell is *rsh*, and in the Korn shell is either *rksh* or is invoked with the **-r** option: **ksh -r**.

The first user, when you log in, is *guest* with the user number *2001*, belonging to the user group *guests*, a new group yet to be created. The default values apply to the remaining settings.

In order to have contact with anyone, a second user is needed. After all, UNIX is a multi-user system. If you are alone on the computer, you will have to play both roles. But even on a single screen, several different log ins present no problem (see section 12.1.4 Multiple logins and multiple shells). The second user is called *Jasper* with the user number *2002* and he also belongs to the *guests* user group.

12.1.4 Multiple logins and multiple shells

You will probably read this section and the relevant special sections when you are familiar with the system and when you wish to actually begin working with the system.

Normally speaking, one user works at one terminal with one shell. Nevertheless, it is often convenient to have several terminals available at once. You can then log in several times, for example to examine something and to hold it on the screen, or in a PC UNIX system, where the user is also the system manager, to switch quickly between the two roles.

Extra terminals on one desk are expensive and bulky. For this reason, the idea was formulated of using a single screen in a pluriform way. One can switch back and forth between various applications by means of function keys (so-called *hot keys*). The section heading indicates that there are two distinct modes of multiple usage, multiple logins and multiple shells:

- If you can log in under several names via one screen, you refer to **multi-login**.
- If it is possible to run several shells parallel on the same screen, you refer to **multi-shell**. Multi-shell is very convenient if the UNIX version only allows two users.

Each device, thus also each terminal, is registered in the device directory called *dev*. This registration, the 'node' is linked to the device. Since each usage or each case of multi-usage requires its own terminal, several logical terminals must be available instead of one physical terminal. In order to produce several logical screens out of one physical screen, corresponding specifications are required in the device directory. These logical terminals are not really present; accordingly, they are referred to as virtual terminals or pseudo terminals. These represent two forms of logical screens; these concepts are related in the following way:

■ Virtual terminals are those which are registered in the device directory as *vt00, vt01,...* (in SCO as *tty00,...*) and

■ Pseudo terminals which are registered as */dev/sxt...*

In all four UNIX versions, when the system is started up, there are up to eleven additional virtual terminals. Pseudo terminals are only readily available in the Consensys version, but are easily installed in other versions.

In all four UNIX versions, the pseudo terminals */dev/sxt..* are used by the *shl* program for multi-shells and the virtual terminals */dev/vt..* (*/dev/tty..* in SCO) are used for multi-logins. In the Consensys version, not only the virtual terminals are used for multi-logins, but in UNIX System V.4 the program *newvt* (new virtual terminal) and in Consensys the program *v4screens* are also used for multi-logins.

There is a distinction in practical usage between the multi-shells which are activated by *shl* on the one hand and *newvt* or *v4screens* on the other. Using the latter, you can switch back and forth between virtual screens using the hot keys so that the contents of the screen remain displayed. The shells produced by the *shl* program have no screen of their own. They write on the same screen and in doing so, displace the display of the previously-used multi-shell.

Multi-login

A login at a terminal is only possible if a login process is started up for this terminal. The operating systems provide the following default facilities: Consensys has one, Interactive three, and SCO twelve login screens available. If your UNIX is a two-user version, specifying more than two login screens is useless.

In Interactive, you can increase the number of additional login screens to seven by means of management programs.

If you are not assisted by a management program, in order to increase or decrease the number of login screens, it is only necessary, for each screen, to change one word in the table which serves to initialize the system. This table is called */etc/inittab*. In this table you will find the following line for virtual terminal 5.

```
vt05:23:off:/sbin/getty vt05 vt00
```

This line comes from the Consensys inittab: for virtual terminal 05 (vt05) no (off) login process will be activated. The corresponding virtual terminal in Interactive is also called *vt05* and in SCO, *tty05*.

In order to make a login possible at virtual terminal *vt05*, replace *off* with **respawn**:

```
vt05:23:respawn:/sbin/getty vt05 vt00
```

Caution: do not alter anything else! If you alter the line **co:...**, you will lose access to the system. As in the case of all alterations to this sort of file, you must first make make a copy for safety reasons: **cp inittab inittab.org**.

The next time you start up the system or after giving the command **init q** the new screen(s) will be available.

Switching between virtual terminals

After being installed, SCO versions have eleven additional virtual terminals available, Interactive and Consensys, seven. If, under Consensys, you wish to increase the number by four, read the parallel section for the Consensys version.

Operating system/Program		Key combination and continuation	
		Alt-	Alt-SysRequ+
SCO	Multi-Login	-F12	
Interactive	Multi-Login		+F8
Consensys	Multi-Login		+F12
Consensys	v4screens	-F8	+F8
Consensys	newvt		+F12

On PC keyboards *Sysrequest* is produced by pressing <Shift-PrintScreen>. The full key combination is then <Alt-Shift-PrintScreen> followed by <F1>,...

The virtual terminals which are used directly are linked to one another (Interactive and Consensys) in a circle as it were. By pressing <Alt-SysRequ+n> you can move to the next, <Alt-SysRequ+p> brings you to the previous and <Alt-SysRequ+h> brings you to the original (home) terminal.

You will realize by looking at the table that it is not absolutely necessary to use the key combinations <Alt-F1> to <Alt-F12>. This is important since many programs use these key combinations to execute tasks and the switching possibilities are then blocked.

Special cases:

■ In Interactive, the system console is <F8>.
■ If *v4screens* is active in Consensys:
 - <Alt-F1> is the system console and
 - <Alt-SysRequ+F1> is the virtual screen VT1 (vt01) on

which a multi-shell is running which has been produced by *newvt*.
- Both types of activation keys in the range <F2> to
<F8> operate identically: you can switch from *vt02*
to *vt08* since the the user shell of the system console is running there or because a login screen is
created there by means of *inittab*.

Multi-shell via shl

All four UNIX versions contain the *shl* program (shell
layers). This program can activate up to seven shells for
one user. Each shell like this runs at a pseudo terminal
(*/dev/sxt..*). Under Consensys, these devices are readily available, under SCO and Interactive, these nodes
must be created and the operating system altered ap-
propriately. The necessary procedures are quite simple,
but they differ from each other and thus are discussed
in the corresponding parallel sections.

Working with *shl* is easy, although not as comfortable
as working with *newvt* in System V.4. Activate *shl*:

```
# shl
>>>c
(1)[]
```

>>> is the shl prompt and the **c** means create the first
shell.

■ The key which is used to return you to the currently
active *shl*, is called *switch* and is defined by shl as
<Ctrl-Z> if you have not defined it otherwise (-->*stty*).

<Ctrl-Z> activates the *shl* command level. Another **c** will
create a second shell:

```
(1)<Ctrl-Z>
>>>c prompt
prompt []
```

For easier orientation, you could assign names instead
of numbers to the shells. The name then appears as
prompt. If you type **h** (help) after the shell prompt, the
possible shl commands are listed:

block name	block output of non-active shell
create name	create a new shell
delete name	remove a shell
layers-1	show created shells with information
quit	discontinue all shells
toggle	switch between the last two shells
resume name	activate named shell
unblock name	readmit output of a non-active shell

12.2   First management tasks under SCO UNIX and SCO XENIX

This description supplements the general outline given
in the subsections of section 12.1. What menus and
forms are, and how they are operated, can be read in
section 14.1 (User guide to menus and forms).

12.2.1   Starting up and ending UNIX/XENIX

The term 'UNIX' is used here to cover both UNIX and
XENIX. Any difference will be given between brackets
(XENIX:....).

After the computer has been switched on or a reset has
been performed, the **boot** loading program appears:

```
UNIX System V

Boot
:
```

If DOS is located on the first partition of your harddisk,
you can type **dos** and press <Return> in order to activate
this operating system. In order to load UNIX, pressing

<Return> will suffice. The standard address *hd(40)UNIX* is known to the boot program.

UNIX also has an autoboot program: 60 seconds after the appearance of the boot prompt, the operating system is automatically loaded and started up. You can modify this automatic process as soon as you are familiar with an Editor. Go to the */etc/default/boot* file and replace *AUTOBOOT=YES* with *AUTOBOOT=NO* (XENIX: *LOADXENIX=YES* with *LOADXENIX=NO*).

After pressing <Return>, the first statements regarding copyright, version, serial number and list of peripheral devices will appear. Information will also be displayed about the the size of working memory and division of operating systems (kernel) and user. If problems arise at the start, consult your installation manual.

UNIX will then want to know:

- If you wish to execute maintenance tasks in the single-user mode; then specify your root password;
- or whether the multi-user mode should be activated; in this case you only have to press <Ctrl-D>.

```
INIT:SINGLE USER MODE
Type CONTROL-d to proceed with normal startup
(or give root password for system maintenance):
```

If you activate the multi-user mode, the date and local time are displayed. If they are both correct, press <Return> to continue. Otherwise you must in any case specify the hour (hh) and minute (mm). If the year (yy), month (mm) and/or day (dd) have to be adjusted, you must make the specifications in the proper way, namely with two cyphers and without spaces.

```
Current System Time is Thu Jan 28 19:28:00 GMT 1993
Enter new time ([yymmdd]hhmm):<Return>
!*** cron started *** pid = 144 Thu Jan 28 19:28:21 GMT 1993

scosysv!login:[]
```

The following message states that the program *cron* (Gr. cronos = time) has been started up and that this process has the process identification number 144. The *cron* program ensures that programs can be activated regularly at a certain time. The programs to be activated are found by *cron* in the *crontab* table.

The last message is the request to login. In order to close the systen down again in the proper way, you have to be registered as *root*. Of course, you remember your password. Details concerning problems with logging in are discussed in section 3.6 (Problems when logging in).

```
scosysv!login:root <Return>
Password:               <Return>
...
#[]
```

You are welcomed and there may also be the message that You Have Mail. Ignore this for the moment. You will recognize by the prompt # that the Bourne shell is active as the system manager user interface.

Closing down the system is quite simple: apply the **shutdown** program. At the same time, you should specify the number of minutes you assign to the other users to bring their work to an end. At the moment 0 minutes is enough since there is no-one working in the system. In XENIX the command is: **shutdown 0**. In UNIX that is:

```
# shutdown-y-g0

...
Broadcast message from root
...
```

The g stands for grace, representing the time which still remains. The y suppresses any additional questions.

All users receive the message that the system will close down in the specified number of minutes. After this, all running processes will be halted. **Always wait until the following message appears:**

```
*** Safe to power off ***
 -or-
*** Hit Any Key to Reboot ***
```

You can now switch off or restart the system.

There is a second possibility to close down the system: if you are working **alone** as *root* in the system and **no** applications are running, you can close down the system quicker by giving the command **haltsys**.

12.2.2 Switching to the maintenance mode

In order to perform certain maintenance tasks, for instance to examine the root file system, you must switch to the single-user mode. When the system starts up, the following will appear:

```
Type CONTROL-d to proceed with normal startup
(or give root password for system maintenance):
```

Specify your root password. The system then switches to the maintenance mode. Then the system management prompt # will appear:

```
Entering system maintenance mode

#[]
```

XENIX: the statement *TERM = (ansi)* will appear in front of the prompt. This is the question whether your terminal conforms to the ANSI standard. Confirm this by pressing <Return>.

This system mode can be quit in two directions:
(1). Using **haltsys** to close down the system
(2). Using <Ctrl-D> to switch to the multi-user mode

12.2.3   Procedure in the SCO system administration programs

The UNIX and XENIX system administration interface *sysadmsh*, just as the *custom* software installation program, is provided for user operation. The scope of this book makes it possible to deal with only those facets which are necessary to run the management tasks discussed here. In order to become familiar with these aspects, login as *root* and execute the system administration shell, **sysadmsh**.

```
# sysadmsh


                                                              SysAdmSh

System Backups Accounts...Jobs Dirs/Files Filesystem User Quit
Administer and configure system resources and report status
/                                              Thu Jan 28 1993--:--
```

XENIX:

```
                                                              SysAdmSh

Dirs/Files Processes Users Backups System Filesystem Media Quit
Manipulate, modify and store files and directories
28 Jan 93 22:00                        /                       __
```

This interface works with menus and forms. The operating principles of this type of interface are outlined in section 14.1 (User guide to menus and templates).

The remaining four lines shown on the screen are used to select the instructions:
(1) The first line, at the extreme right-hand side, shows where you are in the menu hierarchy. *SysAdmSh* is the highest menu level.
(2) The menu itself is shown in the second line.
(3) The third line explains the current option.
(4) The fourth line is always displayed in the same way. This indicates the date, time and the directory in which you are currently working.

As soon as you have chosen an option, a new screen
will display a similar construction or a form. The following function keys are important:

F1	Help
F2	End this program
F3	Open value table
F10	Form completed - end input

12.2.4   Installing software under UNIX

In order to transfer or remove software, login as *root*
and activate the **custom** program:

```
# custom
```

The program has the same procedure as *sysadmsh* :

```
                                                        Custom
Install Remove List Quit
Install software
/                                        Thu Jan 28 1993 10:09
```

In order to install new software, select *Install*. A template will appear, providing a list of options. The product
from which you wish to transfer additional parts is *SCO
SYSTEM V Operating System*. The next screen provides the following options:

```
Choose an option: Entire Product Services
Service Components
```

Not *Services* but **Service Components** is the proper
choice here, otherwise all system parts will be installed.
Select **Extended Utilities** from the subsequent list of
options, so that *Runtime System* is transferred to the
harddisk.

Then, you must determine the selection level:

```
Choose an option: Entire Product Packages
Files
```

The *Entire Product* consists of *Packages* which in their
turn consist of *individual files.* Select *Packages.* A list indicates which packages are available:

```
Name        Inst      Size      Description

ALL         Part      33962     Entire Operating System set
AIO         Yes       48        Asynchronous raw I/O administration
BACKUP      No        272       System backup and recovery tools
```

Only install what you really need. It is easier to find it
again in the system. To begin with select BASE, DOS,
FILE, KSH, LPR, MAIL, MAN, SYSADM, VI and LINK.
When the list of the required files is completed, the
necessary diskettes will be requested and the software
transferred.

At the installation of the MAIL package, the post address for data transport is determined. This address
and the name of your computer are predefined as *sco-
sysv.* If you wish to specify your own name here as post
address, answer the relevant question with **yes** and
specify the new name. Information will then be given as
to how you can alter this post address and how to give
an internal computer name by specifying **uname-S**. As
soon as the required packages have been transferred,
you can examine whether the correct packages really
have been stored on the harddisk by applying the *List*
option. This can be further checked by examining the
contents of the individual packages by means of the
Files option.

In order to transfer a new product, for instance a fa-
vourite game, to the harddisk, select *Install, New Product, Packages.* The instruction **Insert distribution 1**
means that you should insert the first of perhaps several
diskettes or other storage media. Only the list of available packages will be loaded. You can then select the

required game in the now familiar way. If you then examine the list of products using *List*, you will notice that the *SCO System V/386 Games* list has become more lengthy.

12.2.5   Installing a new user under UNIX

See also section 12.1.3 (Installing new users)

In order to include a new user, log in as root and activate the system administration interface *sysadmsh*. Open the first form by selecting *Accounts, User, Create*:

(1a)   The first field requests the name of the user: *guest*
(1b)   The comment field should not be filled in

By pressing <F10>, you conclude the registration and the new user is installed.
If you do not wish to adopt all default values:

(1c)   answer *Yes* to the question *Modify defaults?* A new form appears.
(2a)   in the login group, select *Specify*. Enter **guests**. Since this group does not yet exist, a new form appears in which you can state that the new group should be created. Accept the default value for the group number.
(2b)   As soon as you move to the second field, a field containing several lines is opened, in which the groups to which the new user will belong are listed. By pressing <F3>, you can also activate a value list here.
(2c)   Subsequently, the (old) standard, the Bourne shell (*sh*) is the proper choice as the login shell.
(2d)   Accept the default value for the login directory.
(2e)   Specify **2001** as user number.
(2f)   SCO UNIX recognizes various types of user. The normal user belongs to the *individual* type. In order to have a quick look at the other types, choose *Specify* and press <F3> to produce a list.

You will recognize that you are dealing with the command range here. Finally, choose *individual*.

(2g) The last field is only relevant if a new user is installed for special tasks, for example a user of the type *sysadm*. In this field, the user name of the *individual* is registered, which is the same as the new user. In this way, you can assign actions under these user names to a certain person. This is important in high security matters.

When you press <Return> or <F10> after specifying the last (appropriate) field, the following menu appears:

```
Please choose one of:Re-examine   Yes   No
```

By selecting *Yes*, the new user is installed.

12.2.6   Installing software under XENIX

In order to transfer or remove software, log in as *root*. Then activate the *custom* program:

```
# custom
```

The following list appears:

```
1.Operating System
2.Development System
3.Text Processing System
4.Add a Support Product

Select a set or 'q' to quit:1
```

Three sets are provided. You can transfer these either partially or totally. Sets consist of packages and these in turn consist of files. Select option **1** in order to transfer additional components of the operating system. This software installation program then transfers some files to the harddisk automatically, and then requests you to insert diskette *X1*. The following menu appears:

```
1.Install one or more packages
2.Remove one or more packages
3.List available packages
4.List files in package
5.Install a single file
6.Select another set
7.Display current harddisk content
8.Help

Select an option or 'q' to quit:[]
```

If you select option **1**, a list of the individual packages in these sets will be shown. You can see whether a package is installed or not by looking at the *Inst* column.

```
Name       Inst      Size      Operating System packages

ALL        Part      12624     Entire Operating System set
LINK       No        1526      The Link kit
RTS        Yes       3832      XENIX run time system
...
```

You should only install those which you really need. It is then easier to find them again in the system. To begin with, choose LINK, BASE, MAN, SYSADM, MAIL, VI, KSH, LPR, and DOS. The required diskettes will be requested.

When transferring SYSADM for the system management and BACKUP for safety tasks, a user *sysadm* and user *backup* will be created for each user. A password must be specified for each. If you, as system manager, regulate this yourself, you should choose the same password. Prior to transferring BACKUP, you should consider how and when you should apply the security and whether BACKUP is really necessary for this.

As soon as the required packages have been transferred, the package menu appears again. You can examine whether these actually have been transferred to the harddisk by selecting option 1.

In conclusion, you can examine the contents of a package using option 4. Option 7 shows the current contents of the harddisk.

Return to the set menu using option 6, in order to install packages from other sets or, using option 4 (Add a Supported Product), to add other software, for example Games. If you do this, the request to **Insert distribution volume 1** will appear. This means that you should insert the first of probably several storage media (diskettes). This will then be included in the list of available packages, but not yet actually loaded. You can then select it in the familiar way and have it loaded. If you then return to the set menu using option 6, you will see via option 5 that the SCO System V/386 Games list has become longer.

Use **q** to quit *custom*. It is self-evident that you can transfer or remove Sets, Packages or Files by means of the same instruction at any time.

12.2.7   Installing a user under XENIX

See also section 12.1.2 (Installing new users)

In order to install a new user, log in as *root* and activate the *mkuser* program. You may discontinue this program at any moment by pressing **q** and then begin again, or first alter some data before the new user is actually installed.

```
# mkuser
...
Do you need context-oriented help? (y/n/q):n
Enter the name of the user:guest
Assign the next free user number? (y/n/q):n
Please enter the user number:2001
Should the user belong to the default user group?
(y/n/q):n
Existing groups are: Group "group":
Assign user to one of these groups? (y/n/q):n
```

```
Enter name of new group:guests
Specify number for new group or press <Return> for next
free number:<Return>
1.sh                                  Standard (Bourne) Shell
...
Select a shell (command mode):1
Enter password:
Re-enter password:
Do you wish to modify anything? n
```

Now the new user will be installed.

- Password file updated: firstly, *guest* is registered in the */etc/passwd* file with all specifications.
- Group file updated: the new user name is also registered in the new line '*guests:*' in the user group file */etc/group*.
- Home directory */usr/guest* created: the login directory */usr/guest* is installed.
- */usr/guest.profile* created: the *.profile* standard file is copied to the login directory.
- Test mail sent to user guest: the postbox */usr/mail/guest* is created and the first message is sent to the postbox. When you log in as *guest*, you will receive on the screen the message that you have mail. Please ignore this message for the time being. Details are discussed in section 10.2 (Sending and receiving post via Mail)

Finally, you will be asked if you wish to install another user. Conclude the program by responding No.

The second user is further installed using the system administration interface *sysadmsh*. The procedure is similar to that described above since *sysadmsh* also activates the *mkuser* program.

12.2.8 Multi-login and multi-shell

As supplement to section 12.1.4 (Multi-login and multi-shell), this section deals with the way in which the pseudo shells for *shl* are created.

Multi-shells via shl

In order to create the pseudo terminals for *shl*, activate, as root, the *mkdev* (make device) program.

```
mkdev shl
```

First the nodes are made, then the kernel of the system must be altered. The Shell Layers Initialization program asks you whether you wish to:

1. add an SL module or
2. remove SL module or
3. alter the number of available pseudo terminals.

As soon as you select option 1, the new kernel will be created and then, after your confirmation, installed as new standard kernel. The next time the system is started up a new kernel environment is created. Then you will be able to use *shl*.

12.3 First management tasks under Interactive UNIX

This description supplements the general outline given in the subsections of section 12.1. What menus and forms are and how they function, can be read in section 14.1 (User guide to menus and templates).

12.3.1 Activating UNIX

After the computer has been switched on or reset, the boot load program will appear:

```
Booting the INTERACTIVE UNIX Operating System in Partition 2

┌─────────────────┬──────────────────────────────────────┐
│ Partition       │ Type                                 │
├─────────────────┼──────────────────────────────────────┤
│ 1               │ DOS                                  │
│ 2               │ UNIX                                 │
│ 3               │ UNUSED OR NON-BOOTABLE               │
│ 4               │ UNUSED OR NON-BOOTABLE               │
└─────────────────┴──────────────────────────────────────┘

Enter the boot partition number: 2
```

By specifying 2, you will load the UNIX which will be confirmed by the message **Booting the INTERACTIVE UNIX Operating System**. The following screen will display various version data, copyright information, memory capacity and memory available, date and time, the message that the *cron* program has been activated and finally welcome greetings.

```
Welcome to the...
System name: uxschool
Console Login:
```

The last line is a request to log in. This request applies to the normal user as well as the system manager, when the system is running in the multi-user mode.

12.3.2   Ending UNIX

See also section 12.1.1. (Starting up and closing down UNIX systems)

In order to close the system down properly, you must be logged in as *root*. Of course, you still remember your password. Details concerning logging in and relevant problems are discussed in section 4.6 (Problems when logging in).

```
Console Login:root <Return>
Password:         <Return>
```

```
...
#[]
```

You will recognize by the prompt # that the system manager shell is active. Closing down the system is simple.
You only need to execute the *shutdown* program. At the
same time, you should specify the number of minutes
you allow the other users to finish off their work. At the
moment 0 minutes is sufficient since there are no other
users active in the system.

```
# shutdown-y-g0

Broadcast message from root...
...
```

The g stands for grace, the time which still remains. The
y (yes) suppresses any additional questions. All users
receive the message that the system will close down in
the specified number of minutes. After this time has
elapsed, all running processes will be stopped. **Wait
until the following message appears**:

```
The system is down.
Press any key to reboot.
```

You can now switch off or reboot the system.

12.3.3 User operation of the Interactive administration programs

The *sysadm* (system administration) program provides
extensive help in basic management tasks.
In order to become familiar with these aspects and the
operation of sysadm, in as much as this is necessary for
the managements tasks dealt with here, log in as *root* at
the Console terminal. Then activate the *sysadm* program:

```
# sysadm
```

The help system is installed along with the first activation. The program must be informed whether you have a colour or monochrome monitor. After a moment, the following screen will appear:

```
Disk  File  Machine  Software  User  Help  Quit
Manage disks and diskettes
```

This interface works with menus and forms. The operating principles of this kind of interface is dealt with in section 14.1 (User guide to menus and templates).

You will be familiar with the appearance of the screen from the installation process. The operation of the help functions <F1> and <F1+F1> is also described there.

A new element is that the help text provides additional help. Certain words are emphasized using colour or shading. One word is already selected. Pressing <Return> produces information concerning this term. The emphasized words can be selected using the <Tab> or cursor keys.

The same options often appear in subsequent frames which are displayed: in this system, you can not only move from upper to lower but also back and forth and even in a circle. This type of menu is called a ring menu. Using the *Go Back* function, it is possible to move back through the same information channel which might otherwise be difficult if you have proceeded in a haphazard way to a certain point.

Fields between brackets (round, sharp, square) are accessed by pressing the spacebar. Filling in forms is concluded by pressing <Esc>, just as in the case of the installation. The following selections take place via buttons. These are the white, framed options such as *OK* and *CANCEL*. You can switch from one button to another by pressing the <Tab> key.

If you are used to typing, you may prefer to use the <Ctrl> keys. Try them out: <Ctrl-J> and <Ctrl-D>, <Ctrl-N> and <Ctrl-P>, <Ctrl-I>, <Ctrl-W>.

12.3.4   Switching to the maintenance mode

In order to execute certain maintenance tasks, for instance to examine the root file system, you must switch to the single-user mode. Log in as *root*. Close down the system as described above, now with the additional specification **-iS**. By specifying **-iS**, you initialize the Single-user Mode after the shutdown.

```
# shutdown-y-g0-iS
```

You are already familiar with the broadcast message. You wll then be asked to enter your root password:

```
INIT:New run level:S
INIT:SINGLE USER MODE
Type CONTROL-d to proceed with normal startup
(or give root password for system maintenance): <Return>
Entering System Maintenance Mode
# []
```

You can leave this system mode in two directions: either close down the system (Run Level 0) using

```
# init 0
```

or run the system in the multi-user mode using

```
# init 2
```

If you press <Ctrl-D> by mistake, you will be asked to specify the required system mode (Run Level):

```
Enter RUN LEVEL (0-6, s or S):
```

As long as you are not really certain of the result, do not use any other value than 0 or 2.

12.3.5 Installing software

In order to install software, activate the management program *sysadm*. A window is opened via the options *Software, Install a package*. Here you must specify the diskdrive and diskette type from which the software will be read in. After pressing *OK*, you will be requested to insert the first diskette and asked if you wish to continue.

■ A summary of all available packages and their functions can be found in Release Notes. The diskettes are labelled correspondingly.

You will first wish to transfer the Help Utilities, Manual Entries and File Management packages. The Kernel Configuration is also necessary. When you have inserted the first diskette and have affirmed the question as to whether you wish to continue (use the *Yes* button), the screen will display a list of the packages which are located on the diskette. In the *Install?* column, all packages are marked **yes**. The Spell Utilities on the first diskette are marked **no** just as the Terminal Utilities package. Move to the *OK* button using <Esc> and confirm your selection. The Help Utilities will then be installed.

■ Pay attention to the messages. They indicate what you have already transferred.

Finally, there is the question if you wish to install more packages. Continue with any additional packages as described. Keep in mind that certain packages require other companion packages. This interdependence is outlined in the *Installation Instructions*, although not fully: The *Manual Entries* require the *File Management* package. This is indicated in the error message which might appear.

12.3.6   Installing a new user

See also section 12.1.3 (Installing new users).

In order to install a new user, log in as *root* and activate *sysadm.*

Since the new user, *guest*, will belong to the new group, *guests*, you must first create the new group. Activate the group template by means of the options *User, Group Management, Add a New Group*.

1.   Specify the name of the new group in the first field: *guests*.
2.   Accept the suggested group number.

Using <Esc>, move to *OK*. The new group will be created.

Now the new user can be installed. Activate the user form by means of the options *User, User Management, Add a New User*.

1.   *Full Name* is the comment field. It requires at least one character.
2.   The name of the user: **guest** should be entered in the *Login ID* field. You can now conclude the definition by pressing *OK* and the new user will be installed. However, because you do not wish to adopt all default values, continue with the other options.
3.   Specify *2001* as the user number (User ID).
4.   Accept the default value for the login directory.
5.   Select the login group, *guests*, from the options list.
6.   The (old) standard, the Bourne shell (*sh*) is the proper choice for the Login shell.
7.   Assign password?: No? This will be demanded and regulated at the first login.

As soon as you conclude the specifications in the form by pressing <Esc> and *OK*, the new user will be installed.

12.3.7 Multi-login and multi-shell

As a supplement to section 12.1.4 (Multi-login and multi-shell), this section will only deal with how to increase the number of multi-logins and how to create the pseudo terminals for *shl*.

Multi-login

Two virtual terminals are predefined. Using *sysadm*, you are able to install up to seven virtual terminals, if the Kernel Configuration Package has been read in. Use the *Machine, Tty Management, Virtual Terminals* options to activate a form in which you can specify the number of terminals. Confirm this by pressing *OK*. Then quit *sysadm*. Because the new setup only comes into force after a restart, give the command **init q**.

Multi-shells using shl

In order to create the pseudo terminals for *shl*, three stages are necessary. These can be implemented using the configuration program *kconfig*. This program has a procedure similar to that of *sysadm*. The three stages are:

1. Selecting the driver
2. Creating the new kernel
3. Installing the new kernel

(1) Open a selection window using the options *Configure, Drivers*. This will indicate that the Shell Layers Driver is not yet installed. In this line, you can select *On* or *Off*. Set the driver status to *On*, quit the form and confirm these choices. These planned modifications to the kernel are first placed in memory.

(2) In order to create the new kernel, use the options *Build, Build a Kernel*. Choose *Yes*. In the comment

field which then appears, give a short description of
what you have changed, as an aid to memory.

(3) In order to install your new UNIX version, activate
the *Install* option, select the only available kernel
and confirm your selection using the *INSTALL* button, in order to be able to work with the new kernel.

12.4   First management tasks under Consensys UNIX

This description is a supplement to the general outline
in the subsections of section 12.1. You can find out
what menus and templates are in section 14.1 (User
guide to menus and templates).

12.4.1   Starting up UNIX

When the computer is switched on or reset, the load
program will appear in the now familiar way:

```
Until the message
"Proceeding..."
appears...
```

You can interrupt the loading process by pressing the
spacebar in order to load another system kernel as
/stand/UNIX.

The following screen will register the size of memory
and the available free capacity. After version specification and other copyright information, data about the
hardware and the name of the system will appear.
Eventually, the following message will appear:

```
Welcome to the At&T 386 UNIX System
System name: uxschool
Console login:[]
```

This last message is the request for you to log in. This request applies to both the normal user and the system manager when the system is running in multi-user mode.

12.4.2 Closing down UNIX

See also section 12.1.1 (Starting up and closing down UNIX systems)

In order to close down the system properly, you must log in as *root*. Hopefully, you will still remember your password. Details concerning and problem concerning logging in are dealt with in section 3.6 (Problems when logging in).

```
Console login: root <Return>
Password:        <Return>
...
#[]
```

The message that you have mail should be ignored for the time being. You will recognize by the prompt that the system manager shell is active. This is the new standard shell, the Korn shell. This book is largely based on the old standard, the Bourne shell; however, since the Korn shell is compatible with the old standard, you will not notice the difference.

Closing down the system is simple. Activate the **shutdown** program. At the same time, specify the number of minutes which you wish to give the other users to finish their work. At this moment, 0 minutes is sufficient since there are no other active users in the system at present. Thus, specify:

```
# shutdown-y-g0
...
Broadcast message from root...
...
```

The **g** stands for grace, the time which still remains. The **y** suppresses any other questions. All users receive the message that the system will be closed down within the specified number of minutes. After this time, all running processes will be stopped. **Wait until the following message appears:**

```
The system is down
Reboot the system now
```

You may either switch the system off or reboot it.

12.4.3   Management of System V.4 administration programs

The program *sysadm* (system administration) provides context-related help for basic management tasks. More extensive information can be found in the manual for System V.4, published by Prentice-Hall. There is a separate issue for 386 systems.

If you are asked, for example when switching over to the maintenance mode, as to the type of terminal, the correct answer is probably **AT386**

In order to become familiar with the aspects and operation of *sysadm* which will be needed to deal with the management tasks described here, first log in as *root* at the console terminal. As soon as you give the command

```
#sysadm
```

the management program will appear:

```
UNIX SystemV/386 Operations, Administration and Maintenance

1                  UNIX System V Administration
applications      -Administration for Available Applications

...
users             -User Login and Group Administration

HELP              ENTER            CANCEL    CMD MENU
```

This interface works with menus and forms. How to work with this kind of interface is described in section 14.1 (User guide to menus and templates).

The current significance of the functions keys <F1> to <F8> is displayed in the bottom line of the screen. The selection options are shown in a list. The active window has a red border which becomes blue as soon as an option is selected. A new window appears which may partially cover a previous window. However, all windows will remain visible. In the window title bars, the hierarchical level is shown at the extreme left-hand side. CANCEL (<F6>) returns you to the previous window. By means of the CMD MENU (<F7>), you can, for example, quit the program using *exit* or remove superfluous windows using *cleanup*.

If you prefer to use the command interface or prefer not to use the function keys, you can produce a prompt by pressing <Ctrl-J>:

```
$exit
```

Instead of ending the program in this way, you can also specify other *sysadm* commands or switch back and forward between the windows using numbers.

The significance of other function keys

SAVE (<F3>)	adopts the value from a list and activates the following function.
CHOICES (<F2>)	opens a value list at an empty field or shows the selection options in the case of a predefined field.
CONT	continue
PRE or PREV	previous. (NEXT stands for next). Used in combination with PAGE or FRM (form).

The main menu provides the following options:

applications	Administration for Available Applications
backup services	Backup Scheduling, Setup and Control
file_systems	File System Creation, Checking and Mounting
machine	Machine Configuration, Display and Shutdown
network_services	Network Services Administration
ports	Port Access Services and Monitors
preSVR4	Peripheral Setup
printers	Printer Configuration and Services
restore_service	Restore from backup data
schedule_task	Schedule Automatic Task
software	Software Installation and Removal
storage_devices	Storage Device Operations and Definitions
system_setup	System Name, Date/Time...
users	User Login and Group Administration

12.4.4 Switching to the maintenance mode

In order to implement some tasks, to check the root file system for example, you will have to switch to the single-user mode. You can do this using the system manager interface. However, the standard method using *shutdown* is more simple. This is described in the parallel section 12.3.4.

12.4.5 Installing software

The software installation program *v4pkg* and its companion program *addpkg* have already been described in conjunction with the installation of the operating system (section 11.11 Installing Consensys UNIX).

12.4.6 Installing a new user

See also section 12.1.3 (Installing new users).

In order to install a new user, log in as *root* and activate *sysadm*. By means of option 1: *users* and option 2: *add*, you will be presented with a form where you should specify whether you wish to install a new user or a new group. Since the new user *guest* is going to belong to the new group *guests*, you will first have to create the new group. Use **CHOICES** to mark *group* and then actually select using **SAVE**.

Outline of the group form:

1. The name of the group should be entered in the first field: ***guests***.
2. The proposed group number should be accepted.
3. Primary members are those who are assigned this group identity at login.
4. The user who is also going to belong to this group, in addition to those just mentioned, can be specified in the fourth field.

As soon as you conclude the specifications in the form by pressing **SAVE**, the new group will be installed.

Now the new user can be installed. Option 1: *users*, option 2: *add* and option 3: *user* present you with a form.

Outline of the user form:

1. The comment field requires at least one character.
2. The name of the user: ***guest*** should be specified in the login field. You can now conclude the specifications by using *SAVE* and the new user will be installed. But because we do not wish to adopt all the default values, we shall continue.
3. Enter ***2001*** as the user number.
4. You can type the login group *guests*, or select it using *CHOICES*.
5. Additional group members: none.

6. Accept the default value for the login directory.
7. The (old) standard, the Bourne shell(*sh*), is the proper choice of shell.

Accept the default values for the remaining three fields. The functions of these values is explained in the Help text.

The following form requires information concerning the way in which the system should handle the password:

1. The status field provides three options:
    (a) password: The system manager determines the password.
    (b) no password: The user specifies the password at the first login.
    (c) lock: The system manager specifies the password later using the *passwd* program.
2. The number of days the password will remain valid. A new password will have to be specified within this time. An empty field means that the password is valid for an unlimited period.
3. The minimum period of validity.
4. The warning time in advance of the password expiry date.

As soon as you press *SAVE*, the user will be installed. The *.profile* file, which copies the *sysadm* to the user login directory is */etc/skel/.profile*. If you wish to create a new *.profile* standard file later, you will have to alter these files.

12.4.7   Multi-login and multi-shell

As a supplement to section 12.1.4 (Multi-login and multi-shell), only a description of how to increase the number of virtual terminals and how you can install the Consensys program *v4screens* is given here.

Increasing the number of virtual terminals

In the */etc/default/workstations* file there is the line:

/dev/vt dev/kd/kd 9

Change the **9** to **13**. When the system has been started up again, four additional terminals will be available.

Multi-login

When you boot the system for the first time, you will notice that there is only one login screen. When you have a two-user version you will wish to create a second facility. You will have to alter *inittab*. Do this as described in the general section.

Multi-shell using v4 screens

When you log in for the first time, seven additional Korn shells will run under your name at the virtual terminals *V2* to *V8*. With colour terminals the screen frame is multi-coloured, which provides a firework effect when the system is closed down. These shells are created by the *v4screens* program which is activated by the */etc/profile* file. However, *v4screens* only works for the system console.

At other login screens, you can use the *newvt* program to make additional terminals available after logging in. This presumes, however, that there are free virtual terminals available. Only *vt01* and, if installed, the new terminals *vt09* to *vt12* are free. In order to create additional free virtual terminals, you might come up with the idea of reducing the number of shells created by *v4screens*. However, this will not produce the desired effect.

If you wish to reserve more free virtual terminals for the multi-shells, register new multi-logins at the virtual terminals *vt02* to *vt08*. This works!

Multi-shell using newvt

The *newvt* program is more powerful than *shl*. In order
to get to know this program, log in as a normal user but
not at the system console where *v4screens* is running.
The **newvt** command will produce the following screen:

```
VT1>[]
```

An extra **newvt** opens the virtual screen *VT9*. Now
three shells are running parallel. You can switch between the screens as explained in the general section.
A VT shell is closed just like a normal one by pressing
<Ctrl-D>.

The procedure using **newvt** can be simplified by giving
the command **vtlmgr -k** which you should include in
your *.profile* file. This **vtlmgr** is a monitor which, when
activated, runs in the background and performs three
tasks:

1. You can move to a specified virtual screeen without
    having to apply the command **newvt**. If there is no
    shell running at this screen, it will be created. Then
    you will only need to use the command **newvt**
    when you do not know which virtual screen is still
    free.

2. When **vtlmgr** creates a new shell, the start up file
    .vtlrc is implemented. There you can, for example,
    specify the command **setcolour -o blue** and all
    new screens will contain blue windows as we al-
    ready know from *vtscreens*.
    When you create a new shell using **newvt**, **vtlmgr** is
    not activated and thus *vtlrc* will not be implemented.

3. As soon as you log out, all running shells will be
    discontinued automatically, when possible. The op-
    tion **-k** ensures this.

13 The printer spooling system

13.1 Introduction

Before working through this chapter, it is advisable to have command of chapters one to six (concerning the harddisk), chapter twelve (First management tasks under UNIX) and to have read through chapter seven.

If you have previously worked with a PC with a single-user system, you will know that connecting a printer poses no problems. If the printer is only to be engaged by one user, no special measures are necessary. However, UNIX is a multi-user system, so that situations arise in which several users may require the services of the printer simultaneously in order to print all kinds of documents. In such cases, it must be possible to refuse instructions if the system is threatening to be over-loaded or if the printer is temporarily out of action. In addition, it must be possible to disable the printer during the time that new paper has to be installed.

If you have just installed UNIX, you should install at least one printer. Log in as system manager and answer the couple of simple questions in order to install the standard printer. However, in the long run, you should try to acquire more insight into the printer system to ensure good management. We shall deal with this in the following sections.

13.2 The principles

A user wishing to print a file, gives the print instruction and specifies at the same time the printer on which this should be done and the number of copies which are to be produced. This instruction is placed in a queue. Directly afterwards, the shell prompt appears on the screen, so that the user can continue working, regardless of what happens to the print job in the meantime. A management program ensures that print jobs are passed on one by one to the required printer. The printer sends this program a message each time a given job has been completed, so that the next print job can be submitted.

This is called *spooling*: the instructions and, if applicable, the files are stored on disk and processed in order of sequence. Normally, UNIX works using time-sharing, but in the case of printing, this is not possible.

13.3   Virtual and real printers

The spooler distinguishes between real and virtual (pseudo) printers. The user only deals with virtual printers. Of course, he knows on which real printer he should seek his printout, but one printer can correspond to several virtual printers. This seems more complicated than it actually is.

The concept 'virtual printer' has been applied in order to enable the user to print different kinds of work on the same printer. Accordingly, a document can first be printed in draft quality and the final product in letter quality by specifying different virtual printers. By means of different printer specifications, different output operating programs are activated which ensure that, as in our example, the real printer is set to produce the required print quality.

The real printer is connected to the back of the computer by means of a cable. A device has been defined in the */dev* directory for each connector at the back of the computer. Printers are *character devices*: they transmit characters either serial or parallel. The *tty* interfaces in the */dev* directory are for the serial output, the parallel output flows via devices with the names *lp0, lp1* etc.

It is no coincidence that the parallel interface is indicated by the letters *lp* (line printer). Most printers nowadays make use of the parallel interface. Since the installation of this type of printer is more simple, the following outline will confine itself to the connection of a printer with a Centronics interface to the printer port */dev/lp0*.

13.4 Printing with E/A instruction

When you have connected your printer to this port, you can then test if the link works properly. Log in as *root*. Change directory to */usr/guest/text* By means of the **cat** command, you can print the *hols* file:

```
#cat hols > /dev/lp0
```

ONLY Interactive:
The print connector to the monochrome adapter is */dev/lp0*. If your first printer connector is located on the motherboard or on a separate card, use */dev/lp1* instead of */dev/lp0*.

ONLY SCO UNIX:
If you receive the error message **cannot create /dev/lp0**, check by means of the command **hwconfig** whether the printer port is actually available in the system kernel. You should then look for the following field:

```
p # hwconfig
...
name=parallel base=0x378 offset=0x2 vec=7 dma=- unit=0
```

If this line is absent, do not activate *sysadmsh* since *sysadmsh* only issues the following command:

```
# mkdev parallel
```

You must first select *Add a parallel port* and then *Serial/parallel adapter #1*. Subsequently, you will be asked about the *Interrupt Vector, 5 or 7*? Since 7 is the default value, simply press <Return>. Answer **y** to the next three questions: whether a new UNIX kernel should be created, whether this is to become your UNIX standard and whether the kernel environment should be suitably adjusted. Now shut down the system and reboot the new UNIX.

For all versions:
It is useful to have a shell script containing this command, applicable to a variable instead of a fixed file name:

```
cat...> /dev/lp0
```

If you name this instruction program *print*, you will be able to print *hols* by giving the command *print hols*. Now the shell must regulate that the *hols* parameter is applied instead of .... This is quite simple. The command arguments are referred to using the names of variables:**$0** refers to the command itself (print), **$1** to the first argument (hols), **$2** to the second argument etc. Our shell script should be as follows:

```
cat $1> /dev/lp0
```

The screen will then appear as follows:

```
# cat>print
cat $1>/dev/lp0
<Ctrl-D>
#chmod a+x dr
#print hols
#print: not found
# []
```

If you receive the error message **print: not found** this means that the shell is not looking for programs in your directory. But there might be a directory for user-created programs, which is public to all, e.g. */usr/xbin*. Then, of course, this directory will be a part of the PATH variable too. Before placing *print* there, you should allocate the general rights so that all applications can use this program when required.

```
# chown bin print
# chgrp bin print
# mv print /usr/xbin
# print hols
#[]
```

You can also use this program to channel your instruction directly to the printer:

```
# print
This text is sent directly to the printer.
This line too.
<Ctrl-D>
# []
```

Since no parameter has been specified and no file name appears in the instruction, *cat* has linked the standard input to your printer. Wait a moment when you have pressed <Ctrl-D>. A second <Ctrl-D> will log you out.

If your printer is not yet ready for operation, it may occur, as it does in many systems, that your user interface will no longer respond. Then you will have to discontinue the process from another terminal using the *KILL* program. However, in most cases, <Ctrl-D> is sufficient to deal with the problem and the print request is discontinued after a short time.

This was not only good practice material allowing you to apply the knowledge gained up until now. You can also use the new command when you are alone in the system and have no additional special wishes. However, when two or more users activate this program simultaneously, this will produce a hotch-potch of text. Accordingly, read through the following section to become acquainted with the advantages that the UNIX System V spooling system provides.
The following does not apply to the spooler administration of Berkeley systems.

13.5 Learning and leaving the spooler management

If you wish to install a virtual printer, the spooler administration program *lpsched*, the so-called scheduler, has to be switched off. The *lp* stands for *line printer* and *sched* for *scheduler*.
Berkeley and XENIX call it 'swapper', the other versions under discussion call it 'sched'.
lpsched has the same kind of job as *sched* but only for **lp** tasks.

Check whether the scheduler *lpsched* is still running. If you wish to know which processes are running and which of these are yours, give the command *ps* along with the options *-e* and *-f*: do not become confused by the mass of processes running. If you ignore all processes on certain terminals, something like the following will remain over:

```
$ ps -ef
UID     PID    PPID    C   STIME        TTY    TIME    COMD
root      0       0    0   22:15:36      ?     0:01    sched
root      1       0    0   22:15:36      ?     0:01
/sbin/init
root    144       1    0   21:23:28      ?     0:00
/usr/sbin/cron
root    152       1    0   21:23:31      ?     0:01
/usr/lib/lpsched
...
```

The processes *sched* (XENIX: *swapper*) and *init* are those created by UNIX. *init* not only creates the login process at the terminals, it also activates *cron* and *lpsched* as you can see by the table. You are already familiar with *cron*. How the program has been activated is indicated at the extreme right-hand side. The program *lpsched* is thus located in the */usr/lib* directory. All programs which belong to the spooler system administration are located here. The program *lpsched* belongs, depending on the UNIX version, to *root* or *lp*, one of the pseudo users from */etc/passwd*.

If *lpsched* refuses to run, this means that it has not been executed during the booting process. Possible causes are:

■ SCO XENIX/SCO UNIX: you have not yet transferred the Printer Spooling package LPR.
■ Interactive UNIX: the instruction to the spooler during booting, must be determined by means of the *sysadm*. Start up *sysadm*. Via the options *Machine, Printer Management, Spooler Management* you will open the form for *Printer Spooler Status*. If you select the START button, the subsequent template will show that the activation of the scheduler during booting is *disabled*. Use the ENABLE button to alter this and quit *sysadm*.

Now switch to the */usr/spool/lp* directory.
Under System V.4, this may be approached via two names, either */var/spool/lp* or the old name */usr/spool/lp*. System V.4 has an improved directory structure. It remains possible, however, to use the old names by means of symbolic links.
Note: If this directory is not available, you have forgotten to transfer the Printer Spooler Software.

Now examine this directory:

```
$ cd /usr/spool/lp
$ ls -l
-rw-rw-r-  1 lp  lp   0 Jul 16 10:33 SCHEDLOCK
...
$ []
```

The *SCHEDLOCK* file only exists when *lpsched* is running. *SCHEDLOCK* has a signalling function: when *lpsched* is activated, this program checks immediately whether this file already exists. If this is the case, it is discontinued thus preventing two schedulers running simultaneously.

In order to install the spooling system, *lpsched* has to be
stopped. This is done by *lpshut*, which is located in
/usr/lib.

```
$ /usr/lib/lpshut
Print services stopped
$ []
```

SCHEDLOCK and *lpsched* do not exist anymore.

13.6   Installing a virtual printer

The installation of a virtual printer consists of three
stages:

1. giving the printer a name; we shall call it *pr* in this
    case
2. specifying an output operating program or "filter"
3. specifying the printer port for the real printer; in
    principle, this is /dev/lp0

The second stage demands most effort. You will find
the printer driver programs in the */usr/lib/lp/model* directory (V.4) or */usr/spool/lib/model*. In the most simple
case, a filter like this ensures that the files which you
have specified in the **lp** command are printed in sequence. However, you can modify these programs so
that:

■ you can print more than one copy of a file
■ a banner can be printed so that each user can identify
  his/her own job
■ a title can be printed on the banner page
■ controls or restrictions are applied which are linked to
  the names of the users
■ you can make allowances for the special wishes of
  the users. These can be linked to the print command
  using the option **-o** (see section 7.2). Much of what is
  possible depends on what the system manager has
  installed in the print filter and that is also dependent
  upon the capabilities of the real printer.

In the *model* directory, you will find the standard operating program *standard* (XENIX: *dumb*). If you examine
the information dealing with **lp** in your manual or request **man lp**, you will discover which **-o** options are
available in this standard filter. The system manager
can install additional options, including those specifically for the printer. The display of additional options
can be done in the form of a summary (**-o nobanner -o
lq**) or in the form of a list (**-o "nobanner lq"**).

```
# ls -l model
-rwxrwxr-x 1 lp    lp   25376 Dec 25 1992 standard
# []
```

You will probably find additional models there, and
probably one which directly corresponds to your printer.

The printer port is */dev/lp0*. The program which regulates the link between the output filter, the printer name
and the printer port is called */usr/lib/lpadmin*. This program contains all three instructions in the form of options, **-m filter, -p printer name** and **-v device**:

```
# /usr/lib/lpadmin/ -m standard -p pr1 -v /dev/lp0
# []
```

A virtual printer *pr1* has now been installed.
Exactly what has occurred?

1. A filter has been installed. In the directories (ac-
    cording to system):

    ■ V.4: */etc/lp/interfaces*
    ■ V.3: */usr/spool/lp/admins/.lp/interfaces*
    ■ XENIX: */usr/spool/lp/interface*

you will find a copy of the driver program *standard* or
dumb under the name *pr1*. This is the interface between
the user and the printer which deals with the requirements of the user in the print commands.

2. The link between the virtual and real printer is registered:

   ■ XENIX: The file *pr1* is created in the */usr/spool/lp/member* directory to contain the name of the real printer */dev/lp0*.
   ■ V.3 and V.4: The directory *pr1* is created in the directory */etc/lp/printers* (V.4) or */usr/spool/lp/admins/lp/printers* (V.3). The *configuration* files are located here. If you examine these files, you will also find the real printer */dev/lp0*.

The program model could be represented as follows:

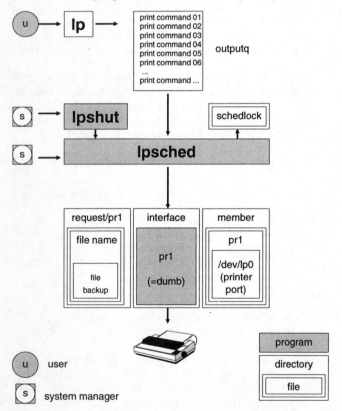

Users give their print commands using **lp**. The print commands are placed in the queue *outputq*. The *lpsched* program ensures that the proper printer and the proper output filter are used.

13.7 Activating the spooler

Restart the scheduler:

```
# /usr/lib/lpsched
```

In order to print the hols file, change directory to */usr/guest/text* or */home/guest/text* (V.4). Now check if the command works by specifying *print*. Have you switched on the printer and arranged the paper?

```
# cd/usr/guest/text
# print hols
```

If this works, you can now try to interrupt the print process using the command *lp*. Specify this using the option **-d printername**. The command is then as follows:

```
# lp -d pr1 hols
```

Instead of the expected printout, you will receive the error message stating that no commands for *pr1* are being accepted. In order to inspect this thoroughly, run the *lpstat* program which provides information about the spooler. If you wish to gain all information about this, specify also the option **-t** (total):

```
# lpstat -t
scheduler is running
no system default destination
device for pr1: /dev/lp0
pr1 not accepting requests since ...
      new destination printer pr1 disabled since
      new printer
# []
```

no system default destination

There is no instruction as yet concerning which printer
will be the default printer. This command is not necessary if you always name the printer to be used in the print
command. We shall examine this using the command
lpadmin in conjunction with the option **-d**. The **d** stands
for destination: the virtual printer. The command is as
follows: **lpadmin -d printername**.
Thus:

```
# /usr/lib/lpadmin -d pr1
# []
```

This specification applies to all users. In order to avoid
this necessity, from System V.3 onwards, the environment variable *LPDEST* has been made available. If you
specify **LPDEST=pr2**, the default printer is not *pr1* but
pr2.

pr1 not accepting requests - new destination

Whether a virtual printer accepts requests or not is
determined by the system manager: **accept pr1** switches on the acceptance of instructions, **reject -r
"printer is being repaired" pr1** switches this off. It is
meaningful to also specify the reason; the user can then
gain information using the command **lpstat -a** and react
accordingly. Both programs are located in */usr/lib*.

```
# /usr/lib/accept pr1
destination pr1 now accepting requests
```

printer disabled - new printer

Perhaps print instructions will be accepted, but will not
be printed. A printer can also be brought into and taken
out of operation (enable/disable) in order to replenish
the paper or replace the ribbon. This is practical but be
alert: both programs are located in the */bin* directory.

They may be used by everyone. The command structure is identical to *accept/reject.* The **disable** command
may also be used with the **-r** option.

```
# enable pr1
printer "pr1" now enabled
```

When you have examined the total situation once more,
you can finally print your *hols* file by specifying **lp hols**.

```
lpstat -t
scheduler is running
system default destination: pr1
device for pr1: /dev/lp0
pr1 accepting requests since ...
printer pr1 is idle, enabled since ...
# lp hols
request id is pr1-1 (1 file)
# []
```

You will probably be surprised that the first page which
is printed looks something like the following:

```
#####
#####
#####      User: uxschool!root
#####
#####      Printed: Sat 07.48 Dec 26, 1992
#####
#####  Job number: pr1-1
#####
#####
#####
```

In a multi-user system, the printer is generally available
to several users. In order to specify your property, this
information is printed first. This page is called the *banner.* The operating program performs this as standard.
This can be suppressed by giving the option **-o nobanner** (XENIX: **-ob**).

13.8   Information concerning the spooler

In the directory */etc/lp* (V.4) or */usr/spool/lp*, you will find
the new *default* file in which *pr1* has been registered as
the default printer:

```
# cat /etc/lp/default
pr1
```

If you wish to know which printers accept commands
and which do not, and the reason why, give the command **lpstat -a**. The command **lpstat -p** shows the
availability of the printer (*enable/disable*). The command **lpstat** shows the system status which is located
in the file */usr/spool/lp/system/pstatus*. XENIX uses two
files for this, *qstatus* and *pstatus*, both of which are located in the directory */usr/spool/lp*.

There is yet another new file:

■ V.4: */usr/spool/lp/tmp/uxschool/.SEQF*
■ V.3: */usr/spool/lp/temp/.SEQF*
■ XENIX: */usr/spool/lp/seqfile*

seq stands for *sequential*. The scheduler finds the sequence number of the previous print instruction in this
file and thus calculates the number of the following instruction. The last of the three ones in the following
example is the counter. XENIX shows only one number.

```
# cat /usr/spool/lp/tmp/uxschool/.SEQF
1:999999:1:1
```

A **spooling list** is made for the remaining instructions:

■ V.4: System V.4 creates a directory for each com-
  puter, here that is */usr/spool/lp/tmp/uxschool*
■ V.3: */usr/spool/lp/requests*
■ XENIX: */usr/spool/lp/outpq*

The files to be printed are located either in the original
directories or **copies** are placed in separate directories.
These directories are:

- V.4: System V.4 creates a directory for each computer, here that is */usr/spool/lp/requests/uxschool*
- V.3: */usr/spool/lp/temp*
- XENIX: XENIX creates a directory for all virtual printers, here that is */usr/spool/lp/request/pr1*

The commands which have been implemented are registered in a **log**:

- V.4: */var/lp/logs/requests*
- V.3: */usr/spool/lp/logs/requests*
- XENIX: */usr/spool/lp/log*. These files are transferred to */usr/spool/lp/oldlog* each time the scheduler is activated.

A complete model of the scheduler working looks something like this:

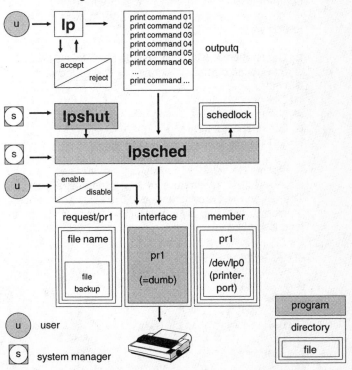

13.9   The print filter

An examination of the print filter will help clarify the instructions in these programs. We are not really concerned with the details at the moment, but more with the
principles: which data does the filter adopt when it is activated by *lpsched* and how does it deal with these?

In a shell script, the fields which begin with # are comment
fields. The other fields are commands which are executed
by the shell, line by line. As you can see by examining the
filter, the shell can also make decisions itself: *if [...] then ...
fi*. This means that the shell is not only a command inter-
preter but also a programming language.

The scheduler passes a line to the operating program,
containing all the information which you have specified
in the **lp** instruction. This line is constructed in the following way:

■ Destination printer (option **-d** or default value)
■ Instruction number (assigned by the scheduler)
■ User name
■ Title (option **-t**)
■ Number of copies (option **-n**)
■ List of special requests (option **-o**)
■ List of files to be printed

The separate fields in this line can be accessed, as you
already know, by means of the variables $0, $1, ...
These variables are expanded to the values of the fields
passed to them as arguments. The filter for this interface looks like this:

```
printer=`basename $0'
request_id=$1
user_name=$2
title=$3
copies=$4
option_list=$5     #$5 is a list with -o options
shift 5
files="$*"
```

The first argument which is expanded is the name of the virtual printer required by the user, for example *pr1*. Since *lpsched* defines the printer as *interfaces(s)/pr1*, *interface(s)* must be separated from *$0*. The *basename* program does this.
The *request* variable is assigned the value of the first argument (*$1*). The remaining options are self-explanatory.

Using **shift**, you can shift all arguments *n* positions (here 5) to the left, behind the program name (*$0*). The program name (*$0*) itself does not move. During this shift, the first argument is lost. Since this takes place five times in succession, only a list with the names of the files to be printed remains as an argument. The shell refers to this list as **$***. This is thus the list of the files to be printed. The whole list is assigned to the variable: *files*.

13.10 Changing the output format

This section presumes that you are able to employ a text editor and either have a basic knowledge of the structure of programming languages or have become familiar with the shell as a programming language.

In order to adjust the operating program to your own requirements, install a second printer *pr2* for required tasks. If you are working alone on the system, you do not need to use the scheduler.

```
# /usr/lib/lpadmin -p pr2 -m standard -v /dev/lp0
```

Switch to the *interface(s)* directory and edit the new print filter *pr2*.

First modification

If the option **-o nobanner** (XENIX:**-ob**) is specified, *pr2* will not print the information page. Look for the following line: **nobanner="no"** (XENIX: **banner=yes**). This is the default situation, meaning that the information page will be printed. If you reverse this setting - quite easily done with an editor - no information page will be printed, whether you specify the option **-o nobanner** (XENIX: **-ob**) or not.

If you wish to ensure that the information page is printed when this option is given, you should alter a second line in the operating program. In the **for-do-done** loop which deals with the sequence of all -o options, you will find all the options possible under **case**. There are among others:

```
UNIXversion          Optionname)          Command              ;;
--------------------------------------------------------------
V.3 - V.4            nobanner)            nobanner="yes"   ;;
XENIX                b)                   banner=no        ;;
```

If you switch **yes** and **no** here again, when the **-o no-banner** option is given (XENIX: **-ob**), the information page will be printed, which, except in the case of XENIX, sounds rather absurd.
However, since the *nobanner* variable is being used on other terminals and *banner* is also in use, we shall leave the name assignation as it is.

Further changes

You can use the following options for a NEC P5/6/7 printer:

lq for letter quality
dq for draft quality
12 for a character width of 12 per inch
10 for a character width of 10 per inch
am for the American character definition

In the *for* loop which we just mentioned, these options can be supplemented with the corresponding command which is to be executed:

```
for   i   in...
do
  case $i   in
    nobanner)nobanner="no"  ;;
    ...
    lq)       echo "\033x1"  ;;   # These
    dq)       echo "\033x0"  ;;   # are
    12)       echo "\033M"   ;;   # the
    10)       echo "\033P"   ;;   # new
    am)       echo "\033R0"  ;;   # lines
    ...
  esac
done
```

A test will be carried out for all the elements in the -o options list (adopted from field 5), as to whether the *case*,
(the current condition *$i*), occurs. If this is true, the in-
structions up to the next ;; will be executed.

You will have to activate *accept* and *enable* :

```
# /usr/lib/accept pr2
...
# enable pr2
...
# []
```

Now switch to the */usr/guest/text/* or, if applicable, the
/home/guest/text directory and give the following print
command:

```
# lp -d pr2 hols
request id is pr2-2 (1 file)
# []
```

Now no information page should be printed. For the
next exercise, you should manually set your printer to
the opposite value: *draft quality* and *10 cpi*. Then give
the following command:

```
# lp -d pr2 -o"lq 12"hols
request id is pr2-3 (1 file)
```

Has the test gone smoothly? This means that this operating program and printer *pr1* will suffice in the future. Return to the *interface(s)* directory and copy *pr2* to *pr1*. Pay attention to the syntax, otherwise you may overwrite your new file, by copying *pr1* to *pr2* for example. If you wish to play safe, copy your new output program to the *model* directory as *standard.nec* (XENIX:*dumb.nec*) for example.

```
# cp pr2 ../model/standard.nec
# ls -l ../model
...
# cp pr2 pr1
# []
```

13.11 Removing a virtual printer

You no longer need the virtual printer *pr2*. You are familiar with *lpadmin* in two application areas: using the **-p** option, a new printer is installed and using the **-d** option, the default printer is defined. The third option is **-x printername** which removes an installed printer.

```
# /usr/lib/lpadmin -x pr2
# lpstat -t
scheduler is running
system default destination: pr1
device for pr1: /dev/lp0
pr1 accepting requests since...
printer pr1 is idle, enabled since...
# []
```

PART 3
GENERAL

14 User interfaces

14.1 User guide to menus and templates

Information given here concerning user guidance in management tasks also applies to application instructions or how to deal with an executable program. We shall discuss the selection of functions and the specification of values.

Instructions are executed by programs. This does not only apply to commands which are to be executed by the computer, it also applies to the management of the computer itself.

Computer management encounters two problems:

1. There are a great many administration programs
2. Precise values are necessary

The selection of the proper programs can be done by means of **menus** which support the correct specification of values via **forms** and **values lists**.

If the amount of programs cannot be gathered into one standard menu, the programs with identical or similar instructions are gathered into one menu. Then, in the standard menu, you can choose one of the command areas and you will then move to the corresponding **submenu**. This is an example of a menu hierarchy with two levels. If required, there are other selection levels. The top level is referred to as the **main menu**.

When a submenu is opened, either a totally new screen is formed or a new window is displayed. In the latter case, the previous menu remains partially visible. The new, active menu is in the foreground. In this way, several menus can be viewed simultaneously. Accordingly, you can see where you are in the hierarchy.

The choices provided in a menu or form are called **options**. Options may be placed next to one another in a summary or under one another in a list. Choosing an option takes place in two stages:

1.   An option must be **marked**. This is done by means of one, two or three of the following possibilities:
     (a) the cursor keys, or
     (b) typing the first letter of the required option, or
     (c) pressing the spacebar.

The option chosen is highlighted or otherwise indicated by a pointer. If several options can be chosen in a value table, these can be marked by pressing the spacebar or a function key. In order to remove this marking, press the marking key once more.

2.   The marked option in a menu, like the marked values in a value table, must also be actually **selected**. This is done by pressing <Return>, and may also often be done using a function key.

Using <Esc> or another key which functions as **Cancel**, you can discontinue the current process to return to the parent menu level or to the previous position in the form.

The selection of the required option and the specification of the appropriate answer is supported by

1.   additional text,
2.   context-oriented questions,
3.   help text which can be requested using function keys,
4.   value tables.

Forms are objects in which values should be specified at certain positions called **fields**. If the answers are lengthy, the field will contain several lines. Multi-line fields are often hidden and only unfold when the cursor is moved to that field.

When a form is opened, the cursor moves to the first field. Forms are filled in as follows:

1. By moving from one field to the other by means of the cursor keys or - often the only possibility - by pressing <Tab> to move forwards and <Shift-Tab> or <Back-Tab> to move backwards.
2. Acceptance of the value in a form, and progressing to the following action by means of a function key.

There is a distinction between the two types of forms: **specification tables** and **templates**. Templates are not enclosed by a strict frame and are often accompanied by explanatory text.

There are various methods of specifying values:

1. Predefined field:
   (a) remove the value and enter a new value and/or
   (b) in the case of a selection field, select another value by means of a function key or the spacebar.
2. Empty field:
   (a) typing the value
   (b) opening a value list using a function key and adopting a value.

Corrections when typing can be done using <Backspace> and the cursor keys. The specification in a field should not be concluded by pressing <Return>; you only need to move to the next field.

14.2   The shell as instrument

You will probably be wondering why there is no separate chapter about the user interface, the shell, in this book. From the first moment that you logged in as a

user you have been working with the shell. Without it
you would be nowhere. However, in order to illustrate
exactly how the shell works, we would have had to deal
extensively with all kinds of fundamental elements of
the operating system.

The shell provides many possibilities:

- The shell generates processes and remains in the
  background so that you can continue immediately
  after specifying a command.
- The shell manages the input and ouput in such a way
  that not only the flow of data to each required device
  takes place, but also the linkage of processes is
  possible.
- The shell manages the variables which are required
  by you, the system and the shell itself.
- The shell enables you to create groups of file names,
  to submit arguments to a command, and also specify
  parameters by means of different substitution mech-
  anisms.
- The shell checks if the syntax of the command is correct and whether the files which are to be processed
  actually exist.
- With the test possibilities and the control structures
  provided by the shell, the user has a powerful instrument available to link multiple programs and execute
  commands without having to develop new programs.

This summary outlines the significance of the shell for
users. The shell is the instrument with which they can
construct the optimal work environment and execute a
wide diversity of both multiple and complex instructions
with minimum effort. This is particularly useful to the
work of the system manager.

APPENDIX A
The ASCII character set

Before showing the list of ASCII codes, we shall explain the column headings.

Bit pattern

A bit pattern represents the actual character. A bit is the elementary unit in which the computer stores data. A bit can assume one of two physical states: on or off. To represent letters or characters, eight bits are combined to form one byte. These eight bytes then form a bit pattern. Each character has its own combination (see table). A total of 256 combinations can be made using these eight bits, thus 256 characters can be produced. In the American standard code for these bit patterns, the ASCII code, only 128 characters were originally defined. This is known as 7-bit ASCII. The rest of the world was apparently forgotten. In a reaction to this, extended character sets have now been defined.

At the moment, however, there is no uniform standard in this area. In Japan, they are working on a 32 bit code since the Japanese language has many more characters than the Western languages.

ASCII values

The ASCII value is the sequence number of the bit pattern. This value can be expressed either in the decimal, octal or hexadecimal system. You will find them arranged in the table in this order of sequence, separated by a space. A binary code is read rather like shorthand:

0000 = 0	0100 = 4	1000 = 8	1100 = 12
0001 = 1	0101 = 5	1001 = 9	1101 = 13
0010 = 2	0110 = 6	1010 = 10	1110 = 14
0011 = 3	0111 = 7	1011 = 11	1111 = 15

Key

In the Key column, you will find the lettering of the key on the keyboard which generates this bit pattern. Many systems support *remapping*. Remapping means that you can assign a different function, thus a different bit pattern to keys. In many cases, it makes no difference to the control characters whether you press the <Ctrl> and <Shift> keys simultaneously or merely the <Ctrl> key. However, this is not always the case: the bit patterns 0, 30 and 31 (decimal) are linked to, respectively, <Ctrl-Shift-'>, <Ctrl-Shift-^> and <Ctrl-Shift-space>.

Name

The name of the bit pattern in the ASCII code.

Function

The function indicates what this character produces as a control character. The function is always ultimately determined by the receiving program or device. Many of these functions date from the days of wireless telegraphy and now sound outdated.

Bit pattern	ASCII value dec-oct-hex	Key	Name	Function
0000 0000	0 000 00	^'	NUL	null
0000 0001	1 001 01	^A	SOH	start of heading
0000 0010	2 002 02	^B	STX	start of text
0000 0011	3 003 03	^C	ETX	end of text
0000 0100	4 004 04	^D	EOT	end of transmission
0000 0101	5 005 05	^E	ENQ	transmit answerback message
0000 0110	6 006 06	^F	ACK	acknowledge
0000 0111	7 007 07	^G	BEL	bell
0000 1000	8 010 08	^H	BS	backspace
0000 1001	9 011 09	^I	HT	horizontal tabulation
0000 1010	10 012 0A	^J	LF	line feed
0000 1011	11 013 0B	^K	VT	
0000 1100	12 014 0C	^L	FF/NP	formfeed/next page
0000 1101	13 015 0D	^M	CR	carriage return

Bit pattern	ASCII value dec-oct-hex	Key	Name	Function
0000 1110	14 016 0E	^N	SO	shift out
0000 1111	15 017 0F	^O	SI	shift in
0001 0000	16 020 10	^P	DLE	data link escape
0001 0001	17 021 11	^Q	DC1	XON - enable transmission
0001 0010	18 022 12	^R	DC2	device control 2
0001 0011	19 023 13	^S	DC3	XOFF - disable transmission
0001 0100	20 024 14	^T	DC4	device control 4
0001 0101	21 025 15	^U	NAK	negative acknowledge
0001 0110	22 026 16	^V	SYN	synchronous idle
0001 0111	23 027 17	^W	ETB	end of transmission block
0001 1000	24 030 18	^X	CAN	cancel control sequence
0001 1001	25 031 19	^Y	EM	end of medium
0001 1010	26 032 1A	^Z	SUB	line feed
0001 1011	27 033 1B	^[	ESC	escape
0001 1100	28 034 1C	^\	FS	file separator
0001 1101	29 035 1D	^]	GS	group separator
0001 1110	30 036 1E	^^	RS	record separator
0001 1111	31 037 1F	^_	US	unit separator
0010 0000	32 040 20	BAR	SPACE	space
0010 0001	33 041 21			!
0010 0010	34 042 22			"(inverted commas)
0010 0011	35 043 23			#
0010 0100	36 044 24			$
0010 0101	37 045 25			%
0010 0110	38 046 26			&
0010 0111	39 047 27			'(apostrophe)
0010 1000	40 050 28			(
0010 1001	41 051 29			)
0010 1010	42 052 2A			*
0010 1011	43 053 2B			+
0010 1100	44 054 2C			,
0010 1101	45 055 2D			-
0010 1110	46 056 2E			.

Bit pattern	ASCII value dec-oct-hex		Key	Name	Function
0010 1111	47 057 2F				/
0011 0000	48 060 30				0
0011 0001	49 061 31				1
0011 0010	50 062 32				2
0011 0011	51 063 33				3
0011 0100	52 064 34				4
0011 0101	53 065 35				5
0011 0110	54 066 36				6
0011 0111	55 067 37				7
0011 1000	56 070 38				8
0011 1001	57 071 39				9
0011 1010	58 072 3A				:
0011 1011	59 073 3B				;
0011 1100	60 074 3C				<
0011 1101	61 075 3D				=
0011 1110	62 076 3E				>
0011 1111	63 077 3F				?
0100 0000	64 100 40				@
0100 0001	65 101 41				A
0100 0010	66 102 42				B
0100 0011	67 103 43				C
0100 0100	68 104 44				D
0100 0101	69 105 45				E
0100 0110	70 106 46				F
0100 0111	71 107 47				G
0100 1000	72 110 48				H
0100 1001	73 111 49				I
0100 1010	74 112 4A				J
0100 1011	75 113 4B				K
0100 1100	76 114 4C				L
0100 1101	77 115 4D				M
0100 1110	78 116 4E				N
0100 1111	79 117 4F				O
0101 0000	80 120 50				P
0101 0001	81 121 51				Q
0101 0010	82 122 52				R

Bit pattern	ASCII value dec-oct-hex	Key	Name	Function
0101 0011	83 123 53			S
0101 0100	84 124 54			T
0101 0101	85 125 55			U
0101 0110	86 126 56			V
0101 0111	87 127 57			W
0101 1000	88 130 58			X
0101 1001	89 131 59			Y
0101 1010	90 132 5A			Z
0101 1011	91 133 5B			[
0101 1100	92 134 5C			\
0101 1101	93 135 5D			]
0101 1110	94 136 5E			^
0101 1111	95 137 5F			_ (underlining)
0110 0000	96 140 60			' (accent grave)
0110 0001	97 141 61			a
0110 0010	98 142 62			b
0110 0011	99 143 63			c
0110 0100	10 144 64			d
0110 0101	101 145 65			e
0110 0110	102 146 66			f
0110 0111	103 147 67			g
0110 1000	104 150 68			h
0110 1001	105 151 69			i
0110 1010	106 152 6A			j
0110 1011	107 153 6B			k
0110 1100	108 154 6C			l
0110 1101	109 155 6D			m
0110 1110	110 156 6E			n
0110 1111	111 157 6F			o
0111 0000	112 160 70			p
0111 0001	113 161 71			q
0111 0010	114 162 72			r
0111 0011	115 163 73			s
0111 0100	116 164 74			t
0111 0101	117 165 75			u
0111 0110	118 166 76			v
0111 0111	119 167 77			w

Bit pattern	ASCII value dec-oct-hex	Key	Name	Function
0111 1000	120 170 78			x
0111 1001	121 171 79			y
0111 1010	122 172 7A			z
0111 1011	123 173 7B			{
0111 1100	124 174 7C			I
0111 1101	125 175 7D			}
0111 1110	126 176 7E			~ (tilde)
0111 1111	127 177 7F			^? (Del)

APPENDIX B
Key functions at the terminal interface

UNIX name	ASCII value	Key	ASCII name	Changeable
ERASE	8	^H	BS	yes
KILL	21	^U	NAK	yes
NL	10	^J	LF	no
EOF	4	^D	EOT	yes
STOP	19	^S	DC3	no
START	17	^Q	DC1	no
INTR	127	Del	Del	yes
QUIT	28	^\	FS	yes
EOL	0	^'	NUL	no
SWTCH	0	^'	NUL	

APPENDIX C
File name extensions

An extension is a part of a file name after a point, allowing you to recognize the program in question. For instance, ADD.BAS is probably a calculation program
which is written in BASIC. Under UNIX, extensions
have no particular significance and they are not restricted to a maximum length. A list of generally accepted extensions is shown below:

Extension	Significance
.bas	basic
.pas	pascal
.c	C
.C	C++
.f	fortran
.r	Ratfor
.asm	assembler
.obj	object files (modules for programs)
.out	temporary files in outputbuffers
.bak	backups
.rc	executable programs (run command)
.doc	documentation, manuals
.txt	text files

APPENDIX D
Manufacturers and products

Name	Trade mark of
AT&T	American Telephone and Telegraph Information Systems
UNIX	AT&T
Microsoft	Microsoft Corporation
MS-DOS	Microsoft Corporation
XENIX	Microsoft Corporation
SCO	The Santa Cruz Operation, Inc
IBM	International Business Machines Corporation
XT	IBM
AT	IBM
Intel	Intel Corporation
POSIX	The Institute of Electrical and Electronics Engineers (U.S.)
X/Open	X/Open Company,Ltd.

APPENDIX E
List of commands

The commands summarized below are those used in the book. Indications of their usage are given in the index at the back of the book. For a detailed description of the commands and corresponding options, we refer you to the User's Reference Guide, or, if available, the online manual for your particular system.

basename *pathname*	Strips the directory path from a file pathname
cal	Shows a calender of the previous, the current and the next month.
cal *year*	Shows a calender of the specified year.
cal *month year*	Shows a calender of the specified month in the specified year.
cancel *command number*	Discontinues a print command with the specified number, even when it has been submitted for printing.
cancel *printer_name*	Discontinues the current print command on the specified printer and deletes the print command.
cat	Links the standard input to the standard output.
cat *file_name*	Sends the file to the standard output device.
cd	Switches to the login directory.
cd *directory*	Switches to the specified directory.
chmod *permissions object*	Changes the user permissions for the file or directory, here indicated by object.
chown *owner object*	Changes the owner of the file or directory, indicated by object.

chgrp *group object*	Changes the group which has permissions on a file or directory, indicated by object.
clear	Clears the screen.
clear >/dev/tty02	Clears the screen at terminal tty02.
cp *old_file new_file*	Copies files.
date	Displays time and date.
disable *printer_name*	Disables specified printer.
echo	Places a blank line on the screen.
echo *string*	Sends string to standard output device.
echo $HOME	Sends the contents of the HOME variable to the standard output device.
enable printer name	Activates specified printer.
env	Shows a list of the user environment variables.
export $NAME	Place the NAME environment variable in the general part of the current process.
head -n *file_name*	Produces the first n lines of the specified file.
help *program_name*	Gives concise outline of the specified program.
kill *process_number*	Sends the TERM signal (process number 15) to the specified process in order to terminate it.
kill -9 *process_number*	Sends the KILL signal to the specified process in order to terminate it peremptorily.
ln *first_name second_name*	Gives the first name file a second name.
logname	Shows the name of the user.
lp	Links the standard input device to the standard printer.
lp *file_name*	Print the specified file on the standard printer.
lp -dlaser *file_name*	Print the specified file on the laser printer.
lpstat -t	Shows a list of the connected printers.

ls	Shows a list of the files in the current directory, excepting hidden (dot) files and subdirectories.
ls -al	Gives a list of all files and subdirectories in the current directory with full information .
ls *directory_name*	Gives a list of the contents of the specified directory.
ls -l *file_name*	Gives extensive information about the specified file, without displaying the node number, the time of previous modification, the time of previous alteration of the node and the sector addresses.
ls -ld *directory_name*	Gives extensive information about the specified directory.
ls -xF	Gives a summary in columns and marks directories with a slash and executable programs with an asterisk.
mail	Shows a summary of delivered mail.
mail *user_name*	Sends a message to the specified user.
man *program_name*	Gives a description of the program.
mesg -n	Suppresses the display of messages from other users on your screen.
mesg -y	Allows messages from other users on your screen.
mkdir *directory_name*	Creates a directory.
more *file_name*	Shows the contents of the file on the screen page by page.
mv *old_name new_name*	Renames a file. If you specify a path in the new name, the file will be placed in that directory.
passwd	Alters the password.
passwd *user_name*	The system manager initializes a new password for the user.
pg *file_name*	Shows the contents of a file on the screen page by page.

printenv	An alternative name for env.
pwd	Specification of the current directory.
ps	Generates a table showing all processes activated by users.
ps -efl	Generates a table with all information (full and long) about all processes (e).
rm *file_name*	Deletes a file irretrievably without confirmation.
rm -i *file_name*	Deletes a file irretrievably after confirmation.
rm -r *directory_name*	Deletes a directory along with all files and subdirectories without confirmation.
rmdir *directory*	Deletes an empty directory.
set	Installs the user environment variables.
sh	Enables a user to specify commands (Bourne shell).
shift	Moves the parameters of an instruction one position to the left. The first parameter is lost. The number of parameters is reduced by one.
stty	Shows the most important settings of one's own terminal.
vi *file_name*	Executes the text editor vi and loads the specified file.
who	Produces a list of the users who are currently logged in.
who am i	Shows your identity in the system.
write *user_name*	Links the standard input device to the terminal of the specified user.

Index